Program Budgeting
for Welfare

James Cutt

The Praeger Special Studies program—
utilizing the most modern and efficient book
production techniques and a selective
worldwide distribution network—makes
available to the academic, government, and
business communities significant, timely
research in U.S. and international economic, social, and political development.

Program Budgeting
for Welfare
A Case Study of Canada

PRAEGER SPECIAL STUDIES IN INTERNATIONAL ECONOMICS AND DEVELOPMENT

734893

Praeger Publishers New York Washington London

PRAEGER PUBLISHERS
111 Fourth Avenue, New York, N.Y. 10003, U.S.A.
5, Cromwell Place, London S.W.7, England

Published in the United States of America in 1973
by Praeger Publishers, Inc.

Library of Congress Catalog Card Number: 72-76448

Printed in the United States of America

CONTENTS

LIST OF TABLES

LIST OF FIGURES

Program Budgeting
for Welfare

1

RESOURCE ALLOCATION IN THE PUBLIC SECTOR: A CONCEPTUAL REVIEW OF THE PROGRAM BUDGETING APPROACH

THE EVOLUTION OF THE CONCEPT OF PROGRAM BUDGETING AND A FIRST DEFINITION

The relevance of examining the principles of resource allocation in the public sector lies in the classic economic dilemma: competition for scarce resources among competing ends in the widening gamut of public sector activities. In the context of re- source scarcity the opportunity costs of poor resource allocation, i.e., the benefits foregone by uninformed choice among policy options or failure to consider all options, either <u>within</u> a broad functional cate- gory, such as education or social security, or <u>be</u>- tween such categories, are increasingly high, and direct attention to the need for more efficient and more effective resource allocation procedures.* The

---

*The efficiency of an organization may be defined in terms of its capacity to achieve results with a given expenditure of resources--in short, the ratio between organizational inputs and outputs. Effective- ness is more broadly defined to refer to the degree of success an organization enjoys in doing whatever it is trying to do--in short, its degree of success in goal achievement. The two are clearly related but need not always coincide; for instance, an orga- nization's attempts to husband its resources in the

object of this book is to examine under the general
rubric of program or output or performance budgeting*
the attempts, sharply increasing in range and depth
of application over the last decade, to introduce a
more systematic, managerial approach to public sector
decision-making.

The fundamental premise of program budgeting is
that policy and budgets are inseparable and that the
relationship between the structure and implementation
of budgets and the determination and achievement of
policy objectives should be made explicit. Program
budgeting is thus a set of procedures designed to improve the basis for public policy decisions and to
secure a more effective and more efficient allocation
of scarce resources in the public sector, the output
of which does not generally command a market price.
Program budgeting is, in effect, a marriage between
overall planning and the translation of planning objectives into programs, on the one hand, and budgeting procedures, on the other--the happy union being
intended to obviate the detachment that budgetary
authorities traditionally have from the content of
plans and programs and planners have from the constraints imposed by scarce resources.

Program budgeting may be seen as the most recent
stage in a continuing process of budgetary evolution.
Alan Schick has described at length the evolution of
the budgetary process in the United States and has
argued that program budgeting accommodates the multiple functions of budgeting--control, management, and
planning--but represents the first approach in which
planning has been accorded primacy.[1] The package

---

interests of efficiency may seriously limit its effectiveness. This important distinction will emerge
clearly in the subsequent discussion of the constraints under which the analysis of public sector
resources allocation generally takes place. (See A.
Etzioni, Modern Organizations [Englewood Cliffs,
N.J.: Prentice-Hall, 1964], pp. 8-10.)

*An attempt is made here to explore the distinc-
tions between these terms and to establish a consistent terminology for the balance of the book.

that constitutes program budgeting developed first
in the United States and represents the third stage
in a process of evolution.[1,2]

The first stage may be referred to as the con-
trol-oriented or input-oriented stage, where budgetary
allocations were made with respect to detailed inputs
or objects of expenditure and the primary emphasis
was on "accountability" for the use of funds in the
detailed manner prescribed. This input-oriented
view of budgeting has been held to dominate U.S.
budgeting procedures until the mid-1930s[1,2,3] and,
if the lamentations of the Glassco Commission are to
be accepted, would seem to have prevailed in federal
budgeting in Canada until the 1950s.[4]

The next stage of reform in the United States
may be called the management-oriented or performance-
oriented phase, in which expenditure inputs were
specifically related to outputs of government programs. This phase, officially advocated by the Hoover
Commissions of 1947-49 and 1953-55, emphasized the
establishment of a budget based on functions or programs, the identification of the outputs of these
programs, the establishment of quantitative indicators
of such output, and the development of work-cost mea-
surements as a means of evaluating the efficiency of
programs.

Between post-Hoover performance-oriented budgeting and program budgeting came several major policy
developments, in particular the development of national economic accounting and macroeconomic analysis
after World War II with the associated emphasis on
the effects of government taxing and spending on objectives; the development of increasingly sophisticated macroeconomic models and the development of
more sophisticated data on all government revenue
and expenditure; the increasing use of macroeconomic
techniques to appraise competing public projects;
and, finally, the development of a series of deci-
sional and informational techniques growing out of
the operations research procedures developed during
World War II and culminating in what has come to be
called "systems analysis"--defined broadly as involving "a continuous cycle of defining . . . objectives, designing alternative systems to achieve
these objectives, evaluating these alternatives in

terms of their effectiveness and cost, questioning
the objectives and other assumptions underlying the
analysis, opening new alternatives and establishing
new . . . objectives, and so on indefinitely."[5]
    These new techniques in the broad systems analy-
sis context were developed and refined in the U.S.
Department of Defense in the 1950s and provided a
conceptual and analytical framework for long-range
planning. A budget framed in program (output) and
financial (cost or input) terms on a multiyear basis
is essentially an instrument for the implementation
of long-range planning. It is this integration of
long-range planning with the budgeting procedure--
with planning as the master and budgeting as the
servant--that is the essence of program budgeting.
In traditional line budgeting outside a planning context the flow of budgetary decisions is upward and
aggregative; in a program budgeting context the budget is a means of implementing a long-term or multiyear plan, and the decision-making and informational
flow is downward and disaggregative. Program budgeting is then essentially a long-term rolling planning
system under which budgeting is an allocative process
between competing claims and the budget itself a
statement of policy for the appropriate planning pe-
riod--for instance, in a five-year planning period the
budget statement in any year would present cost and
output information for the year in question and the
subsequent four years, i.e., from year t to year
t + 4; the budget for year t + 1 would present consistent data until the year t + 5, and so on. The
budget in a program budgeting system is the cost and
output expression of a long-term plan, translating
on the cost or financial side program expenditure
decisions into appropriation requests. It must be
noted, however, that while a program budget gives
primacy to the planning function of budgeting it also
embraces the control and management functions of
budgeting by providing various conversion devices
such as "crosswalk" grids, which convert data from a
planning framework to a management and/or control
framework.
    We may now attempt to distinguish program, out-
put, and performance budgeting in terms of the evolutionary process described above. Output budgeting

is regarded as synonymous with <u>program budgeting</u> as broadly defined above--simply, indeed, as the preferred term in some of the British literature.[6],[7] <u>Performance budgeting</u>, however, we may define as less comprehensive than program budgeting, being addressed only to the management function described above. It is thus viewed as a fundamental stage in the evolution of program budgeting in which government activities are restructured by function and a variety of basic indicators such as work measurement ratios and productivity ratios used to relate inputs to outputs. It is essentially seen as a <u>tool of internal management</u>. Program budgeting, on the other hand, is taken to include the whole panoply of systems analysis defined above, and implies the definition on a continuing basis ("dynamic" definition) of public objectives, the design and analysis of alternative means of achieving these objectives, the measurement not only of efficiency but effectiveness through relating costs to broader, more composite program output indicators defined in terms of program objectives, and the explicit display of the opportunity costs or trade-offs between alternative resource allocations patterns. It is thus seen as a <u>tool of planning or resource allocation</u>. In adopting this convention we adopt what would appear to be the more broadly accepted view in the literature and reverse the definitional order of priority established in the U.N. manual on the subject.[8]

The success of program budgeting* in the U.S. Department of Defense and the able proselytizing of Rand and Defense Department analysts set the stage for the U.S. Presidential Memorandum of October 1965, which provided for the introduction of program budgeting in all government departments and thus by aggregation over the entire executive budget system. The success of this policy has been mixed, reflecting the differential amenability of government agencies

---

*In the United States and Canada the acronym PPBS, meaning Planning-Programming-Budgeting Systems, seems to be the most popular way of referring to the package of procedures that has been defined above as program budgeting.

and departments to the new approach, in particular
its analytical requirements, and has been comprehen-
sively reviewed by the Joint Economic Committee of
Congress.[9]

In Canada the federal government has also adopted
program budgeting, and its initial work in the field
culminated in the publication in July 1968 of a planning-programming-budgeting guide for all government
departments, providing the conceptual base for program budgeting in the form of a classification of
government activities by objectives and programs and
a guide to the analytical procedures required to im-
plement the system. For fiscal year 1969-70 the estimates of all government departments were submitted
to Parliament in both a program budgeting format and
in the traditional line budget format; for fiscal
year 1970-71 only the program budgeting format was
employed. Development of the program budgeting approach in Canada has been recently reviewed.[10]

In the United Kingdom a process of reform and
review, beginning with the first Public Expenditure
White Paper in December 1963,[11] culminated in the
submission of a comprehensive set of proposals in
the form of a Green Paper in April 1969[12] and the
publication in December 1969 of a White Paper on Ex-
penditure--the first of a projected annual series,
with estimates displayed in the new multiyear program
format.[13] The background and development of program
budgeting in the United Kingdom recently has been
reviewed by a senior treasury official.[14]

In France the analytical support system required
for program budgeting has made considerable progress
through the application of management techniques in
the public sector in what is referred to as RCB (Rationalisation des Choix Budgetaires), though these
new procedures are not yet formally integrated with
the national plan and their application in a program
budgeting context has been hindered to date by the
absence of a functional or program-oriented budget
presentation and by what has been referred to as a
"paralysing structure of the control of public expenditure," geared entirely to the old control function of budgeting.[15]

In the developing countries experience to date
has been limited to performance budgeting--defined

above as the first phase in the development of program
budgeting. A U.N. Workshop on Problems of Budget
Reclassification and Management recorded in 1957 that
"within the framework of the traditional budget and
on a selective basis, countries should make efforts
to apply program and performance techniques."[16] In
general the success of the first attempts at performance budgeting in the developing countries appears
to have been limited. Reviewing the problem, B.
Gross concluded:

> In many developing nations the solution to
> internal and external pressures to moder-
> nise budgeting has been a half-hearted com-
> mitment to performance budgeting as an ex-
> planatory supplement to the traditional
> budget with little attempt to integrate it
> with national planning.[17]

Despite initial pessimism, those developing nations that aspire to national or aggregate or macro
planning may offer a fruitful ground for program budgeting inasmuch as a tradition of analysis--albeit
at a macro level in relation to the aggregate plan--
already exists. The application of this analytical
ability at the micro level (in relation to projects,
programs, and sectors), coupled with the structural
changes required in performance budgeting, would make
possible the evolution of performance budgeting into
program budgeting and its integration as a basic
building block with aggregate planning. In this way
the reliability of aggregate plan forecasts, to this
point frequently unrealistic in the sense that they
do not reflect an analysis of the costs and outputs
of the individual projects and programs that make up
the aggregate plan, would seem likely to be greatly
improved. The prospect in India, where the central
government has accepted and is implementing in a
phased manner the recommendation of the Administrative Reforms Commission to introduce performance budgeting in all developmental departments, and where a
rich tradition of analysis has developed around the
aggregate planning system, would seem particularly
favorable.[18]

A COMPREHENSIVE DEFINITION: THE
STRUCTURAL AND ANALYTICAL
COMPONENTS OF PROGRAM BUDGETING

The complete implementation of program budgeting
requires the development of a multiyear financial
plan and a corresponding multiyear program plan, the
former specifying the estimated inputs or costs of
the appropriate government, agency, or institution
in terms of its activities classified and displayed
by a set of objective-oriented programs, the latter
specifying the corresponding outputs or benefits.
The number of years over which inputs and outputs are
estimated will reflect planning practice in the organization in question.

Implicit in the presentation of a program and
financial plan are: first, the articulation of operational institutional objectives and the translation
of these objectives into programs, subprograms, and
program activities or elements;* second, the conceptualization of indicators that may be used to
measure, either in monetary or physical terms, the
output of the various programs; third, the development of an information system that makes possible
the computation of program costs and, where additivity
of benefits applies (i.e., where benefits are defined
in monetary terms), program benefits, by a process
of aggregation from program elements; fourth, a cost
model that operates in conjunction with the information system to estimate costs over the planning period; fifth, and perhaps most difficult, the development of an effectiveness model or, more explicitly,
a production function model for the various programs
that makes possible the translation of a given set
of inputs into indicators of program output or performance over the planning period; sixth, the determination of criteria by which alternative programs
can be appraised in an ex-ante sense (before the

_____

*The terminology used to describe the components
of the hierarchy varies considerably. The term "program element" is used throughout this study to describe the lowest component of the hierarchy.

programs are implemented), in a monitoring sense
(while the programs are in the course of implementation), and in an ex-post sense (after the programs
have been in operation for a specified time); seventh,
the design of an analytical framework in which the
opportunity costs--specified either in real or monetary terms--of alternative resource allocation patterns can be made explicit; eighth, and finally, the
establishment of a general ex-post evaluation procedure in which appraisal criteria are brought to bear
on demonstrated program performance, objectives and
program structures are reconsidered in the light of
program performance, new circumstances, etc.

This continuing, feedback-oriented process is
clearly ambitious and complex, but it would be a
counsel of despair to suggest that nothing can be
done until everything can be done. Program budgeting
can be seen for any particular organizational activity
essentially as a modeling process of that activity.
The submodels, or component parts of the overall program budgeting model, though interrelated and interdependent in the operation of the entire activity,
may be developed and implemented in module form, the
final program budgeting model being the aggregation
and integration of these submodels. For instance,
in designing a program budgeting model of higher
education the various required submodels include a
cost model, a student-flow model, and a set of effectiveness models relating to various definitions of
educational output; each of these may be developed
and implemented independently before its incorporation in a complete program budgeting model.

In reviewing the requirements of a program budgeting system it is convenient to distinguish two
general components: a taxonomical or structural
component that categorizes the activities of the organization by their objectives and corresponding programs, subprograms, and program elements displaying
program outputs and financial inputs on a multiyear
basis; and an analytical component that estimates
the costs (inputs) and benefits (outputs) of alternative means--"systems designs"*--to the attainment

---

*The word "system" has been used in the text in
two distinct senses. The first, more general, sense

of objectives, evaluates these costs and benefits
(in an ex-ante, monitoring, and ex-post sense) by
some predetermined decision-making criterion or set
of criteria, and computes and displays the opportunity
costs--in real or monetary terms--of alternative resource allocation patterns. The two components are
clearly interdependent: the cost model from the analytical component makes possible the multiyear cost
estimates that go to make the final structural presentation of the financial plan; the production function
model relates inputs and outputs and makes possible
the final structural presentation in matrix form of
the program or output plan corresponding to the financial plan, and, reciprocally, the articulation of
objectives and their translation into a program
structure displays information in a form amenable to
analysis--as distinct, say, from the previous budgetary presentation by input objects.

It is with the analytical component of program
budgeting that this chapter is primarily concerned.
Appendix A, however, is provided to demonstrate the
structural component. The appendix shows, first,
the function (program grouping, or, in the sense used
above, major public activity), program, program element classification introduced by the Canadian federal
government and, second, a sample five-year program
and financial plan for the Income Maintenance program
in the Canadian classification.

The balance of the chapter is devoted to an
elaboration of the analytical component of program
budgeting.

----

refers to the broad gamut of structural and analytical techniques brought to bear on problems of resource
allocation--what we referred to initially as "systems
analysis" but preferred to call "program budgeting";
the second sense, and the one used in the term "system design" above, is used to describe the various
program structures that are examined and evaluated
in the pursuit of that particular resource configuration or system design that ranks highest according
to the decision-making criterion in question. Unless
otherwise specified, the term "system" will be used
in this second sense in the balance of this work.

THE ANALYTICAL COMPONENT OF PROGRAM
BUDGETING: AN OVERVIEW

The core of the analytical component of program
budgeting is the conceptualization and computation
of costs and output measures and their juxtaposition
in the form of a decision-making criterion. The
various constituent parts of the analytical component
of program budgeting are examined in turn in the
balance of this section.

Basic Definition

Both cost-benefit and cost-effectiveness analysis require the measurement of inputs to and outputs
from public programs. Although for programs of other
than a purely transfer nature costs involve the use
of real resources, it is assumed that these resources
are purchased or can otherwise have imputed to their
use a monetary value. On the cost side of the function then it is assumed that under both cost-benefit
and cost-effectiveness analysis computation is possible in monetary units. The distinction lies on the
output side.

The term "cost-benefit analysis" is reserved in
this chapter for the situation in which program inputs and outputs are commensurable, i.e., where outputs can, either directly through their sale or indirectly through imputation, be computed in monetary
units. There are several ways of juxtaposing monetary costs and benefits in the form of a decision-
making criterion; discussion of these alternatives
is postponed until the section dealing with alternative decision-making criteria.

The term "cost-effectiveness analysis" is reserved for the situation in which inputs and outputs
are incommensurable, i.e., where outputs, although
quantifiable, cannot be quantified in monetary terms
either directly or indirectly and must be expressed
in physical units appropriate to the program in
question. The criteria relating monetary cost and
physical effectiveness will always be expressed in
terms of a constraint, relating exclusively either

to cost or effectiveness; these are examined in detail, along with cost-benefit criteria, in the appropriate section of the chapter.

The two approaches are generally viewed hierarchically, cost-benefit analysis being seen as the purer form of economic analysis and cost-effectiveness analysis as the alternative where cost-benefit analysis is not feasible. The two approaches may, of course, be used in complementary fashion for different aspects of a given program. In the appraisal of an education program, for instance, it may be appropriate to employ cost-benefit analysis for that portion of output that can be computed in monetary terms--e.g., the income differentials associated with the education program--and cost-effectiveness for other aspects of output that cannot be expressed in monetary terms--e.g., a weighted index of graduates as a measure of the "cultural" output of the program or an index of performance in a standardized test as a measure of teaching effectiveness.

Both cost-benefit analysis and cost-effectiveness analysis are generally viewed as comparative-static partial equilibrium analytical procedures, i.e., they are concerned with the before-and-after comparison of two situations, each of which reflects a full adjustment of the immediately affected parts of the economic system to a stable (or negligibly affected) general environment. If, however, the program being appraised cannot be considered marginal, i.e., it is of such a scale as to have price and related allocative effects elsewhere in the economy that cannot reasonably be excluded by a ceteris paribus clause, then a full analysis of the implications of the program would necessarily have to be of general equilibrium form. The degree of marginality, up to which partial analysis can be considered to offer a reasonable approximation of total effects, must remain a matter of judgment, and the only general conclusion that suggests itself is that the reliability of cost-benefit analysis and cost-effectiveness analysis is inversely related to the relative scale of the program in question. The approach is explicitly partial and, in circumstances such as the building of a massive irrigation and electrification program in a developing country, where the program may be considered to have

an economic impact that is not marginal, must be seen
as of limited usefulness.

It was pointed out previously that the computation and juxtaposition of costs and output measures
required the construction of a cost model, which
would be used to compute costs at a point in time
and to estimate costs over the planning period, and
an effectiveness or production function model, which
would be used to translate costs over the planning
period into output measures.

The general question of system design and model
building is examined next.

Models and System Design

E. S. Quade has argued that the essence of systems analysis is to construct and operate within a
"model" a simplified abstraction of the real situation appropriate to the question.[19] A system model
is thus an analogue of reality--a homomorph rather
than an isomorph--made up of the factors relevant to
a particular situation and the relationships between
them. The model may be seen as a "black box" into
which inputs (costs) are fed and from which emerge
outputs (performance or effectiveness characteristics). The black box may be thought of as containing
one overall system model, or, as is more likely, a
group of submodels, say at the very least a cost
model and a model that deals with the transformation
of inputs into outputs. The nature of a system model
or submodel may vary from a set of mathematical equations to a purely verbal description of the situation
where human judgment and intuition are used to predict the consequences of particular alternative system design choices. By way of introduction to a
rough classification of the range of models used, it
should be emphasized that the primary function of a
system model is explanatory--to account for the operation of the particular system--and its basic nature
therefore systemic, i.e., describing the "mode of
action" or structure and transformation relationships
of the system, rather than the mathematical ones.

In program budgeting all the model forms described below will tend to be probabilistic rather

than deterministic. Exclusive of actual physical
analogues of reality, system models have been classified by R. D. Specht into five categories in diminishing order of mathematical sophistication but not,
of course, explanatory and predictive usefulness--
analytical, computer, people and computer interaction,
people as integral model components, and, finally,
verbal.[20] In this classification the first two categories are described as mathematical models, the
second through fourth categories as simulation models,
and the last as simply a verbal description of the
situation. Since these categories are geared primarily to defense systems analysis, this study adopts
a related but slightly different classification--into
mathematical models, computer simulation models, and
nonquantitative models. These categories are not,
of course, mutually exclusive, but it is felt that
the broad classification into three general categories focuses on the major distinctive features of
alternative model forms. Further, most program budgeting models will involve a combination of model
forms.

Mathematical Models

By a mathematical model is meant one in which
the relationships between the variables and parameters
can be represented by mathematical equations. Mathematical models employ such techniques as linear and
dynamic programming, queueing theory, and network
theory or, where conflict is involved, game theory,
and while a computer may be used in a mathematical
model it is primarily as a computational aid after
the mathematical structure has been completed. The
primary characteristic of mathematical models is
that they do not deal with specificity but with generality, not, as it were, with a single run of a
situation but with all possible runs. A mathematical
model will most probably represent, by omission or
aggregation, a simplification of the real world situation, i.e., will be detailed but homomorphic.
Seldom would one have complete information on system
structure and transformation to permit the construction of a mathematical model isomorphic with reality.
O. Lange has set out with great clarity the general

theory of system structure and operation, defining
systems as sets of coupled elements, the mode of
action of which depends not only on the transformation matrix applicable to each element in the system
but also on the structure of the system itself, i.e.,
the network of couplings of the elements of which
the system is composed.[21] In a program budgeting
model, the part of the model likely to be most amenable to mathematical representation is the cost side,
where general regression relationships are frequently
established.

Computer Simulation Models

The distinction between the use of a computer
in a mathematical model and computer simulation is
blurred. The essence of the difference lies in the
generality of the mathematical model as against the
specific case-by-case approach of computer simulation. The iteration of a range of specific system
designs in a computer simulation defines the method
fundamentally as experimental rather than mathematical.

Simulation as a technique does not demand the
services of a computer, and some of the nonquantitative models to be described below are of this nature.
Simulation may be generally described as the abstract
representation of a particular system design, intended to be examined or played through by computer
or by some verbal technique such as scenario writing
or operational gaming. Simulation has two distinct
uses--in the design of systems and in the analysis
of system performance;[22] both uses are of direct
relevance in program budgeting. Subsequent comments
in this discussion of the second model category refer
only to computer simulation.

The use of computer simulation is generally
called for where the relevant factors in the real system are too numerous or their relationships too complex to be comprehended intuitively or described in
a set of mathematical equations. There are two significant advantages of the technique. First, where
experimentation on the real system is unfeasible or
inordinately costly, the experimental, iterative nature of computer simulation gives the analyst the

opportunity to conduct a whole series of specific excursions, parametric investigations, and sensitivity analyses and thus to investigate system designs under a whole range of assumptions. The technique is thus extremely flexible. Second, and perhaps even more important, simulation does require specific decision rules but does not require a formal apparatus; further, these rules need not be numerical. Simulation thus comes into its own where data are short and where formal mathematical properties are unknown. Simulation relates primarily to the structure of a system rather than to its formal relationships and serves to explore iteratively the consequences of a wide range of assumptions about that system structure. Simulation may thus be seen as the beginning of theory where none previously existed.

Computer simulation has been used successfully in industry and in military and civil government operations.[22,23,24,25] A most interesting and successful recent example is the use of simulation in planning the expansion of the medical faculty at the University of Toronto.[26]

Two developments augur well for the use of computer simulation methods. First, there has been a rapid expansion of the number of simulation languages geared to different types of problems. Many of these languages, such as GPSS and SIMSCRIPT, are entirely nonmathematical. Second, simulation has found fruitful marriage with other modeling techniques, with both mathematical analysis and nonquantitative methods, creating a family of mixed modeling techniques capable of dealing with an increasing range of problems in the civil and military sectors of government operations.

Nonquantitative Models

There are many varieties of nonquantitative models, most relying on some technique of focusing the informed judgment of experts on the problem at issue. Only three methods will be briefly mentioned here: scenario writing, operational gaming, and the Delphi method.

The scenario technique is particularly useful where broad political and social issues are in question. It amounts to asking an expert or group of experts to begin with the present state of affairs and to show, step by step, how the future might evolve in plausible fashion. A collection of scenarios or plausible chains of events is then used to define policy options and the implications of policy choices.[27]

The operational game amounts to a laboratory simulation involving role-playing by human subjects who simulate real world decision-makers. The players, operating within carefully defined constraints and conditions, use their intuition as experts in a variety of fields to simulate the attitudes and decisions of their real world counterparts. The major advantage of the technique lies in providing ideas and insights on policy options and consequences.[28]

In the Delphi method, which may be seen as a variation on the theme of the operational game, direct debate among experts is replaced by the interchange of information and opinion through a carefully designed series of questionnaires. It is an attempt to improve on the panel or committee approach by subjecting the views of individual experts to the criticism of fellow panel members without actual confrontation. Whereas gaming is most appropriate where experts from different disciplines are required, the Delphi method is used where experts are of the same specialty. After each questionnaire is completed, the players are given new refined information in the form of opinion feedback, which is derived from a computed consensus from previous interrogations. The process continues until a consensus is arrived at or until further progress to a consensus appears unlikely, at which point the conflicting views are documented.[29]

The most important points in the foregoing discussion of models in program budgeting are the facts that there is a wide and growing range of model forms available and that model building does not involve only, or even mainly, mathematical forms. In, for instance, a program budgeting approach to alternative system designs for the introduction of an income maintenance scheme into the welfare system, a variety of models might be used. This is, of course, one of the "soft areas" where little information is available

at this point about transformation relationships and
where reasonably precise data on relationships may
have to be obtained ex-post by social experimentation
of the sort recently conducted in New Jersey.[30] This
does not mean, however, that nothing can be done ex-
ante in the evaluation of alternatives. The cost side
of the model may be set up with reasonable preci-
sion--except for the thorny issue of real costs resulting from work disincentives--and informed expert
discussion can almost certainly focus reasonably ac-
curately on the <u>directional</u> if not the magnitudinal
changes in the various factors in the effectiveness
vector. Further, a knowledge of the structural relationships in the overall welfare system and the establishment of a set of decision rules make possible
the initially rather crude construction of computer
simulation models that, over a range of parametric
investigations and sensitivity tests, may serve to
offer important ideas and insights on policy options
and choices. Particularly with the emergence of data
from the New Jersey experiment,[30] such models could
be progressively increased in refinement and usefulness.

Perhaps one final qualification on the use of
models: The purpose of models--of whatever variety--
in systems analysis is not to provide a scientific
or quasi-scientific substitute for judgment but rather
to facilitate informed judgment. Judgment is involved not only in interpreting the results of model
operations but in designing the models, in deciding
which model type to use, which factors are relevant,
and what the relationships between these factors are.

Inputs: The Role of Cost Analysis
in Program Budgeting

The precise annual cost estimates and rougher
multiyear estimates over the planning life of a particular program design reflect detailed cost or resource requirement analysis. There are several significant aspects of program cost analysis.

Output-Orientation

The basic principle of cost analysis is that
all requirements for diverse resources be identified
and associated with system or program outputs, e.g.,
the output, however defined, of an income maintenance
program as one subprogram within an overall welfare
program or of a supersonic transport aircraft as one
subprogram within an air transportation program.
The problems of categorizing the outputs of such programs will be explored below. The point to be made
at this time is that output-oriented cost analysis
is intended to identify the total resource impact of
adopting a particular program design as a means to
attain the specified output.

The Time Horizon

Cost analysis in a planning context must estimate the total program costs involved over the life-
time of the program or, where a program is open-ended,
present cost estimates for a time period sufficiently
long to indicate the resource implications of the
program as part of a long-range plan. The question
of discounting is discussed below in relation to both
inputs and outputs. The more extended the time hori-
zon, of course, the greater the degree of uncertainty.
Sensitivity analysis, one method of dealing with uncertainty of particular usefulness in cost analysis,
is dealt with below. The general problem of uncertainty is also dealt with in a separate section.

Incremental and Life Cycle Costing

The relevant costs in program analysis are the
marginal or incremental costs associated with the
specified program output. The incremental cost of a
program is perhaps best seen as the difference in
cost between two total program aggregates, one with
the additional program and one without it. The appropriate program costs for the extension of the
Canadian welfare system (program aggregate) by the

addition of an income maintenance program would be
the cost of the total welfare system including the
new income maintenance program minus the cost of the
welfare system excluding the new income maintenance
program. Sunk or bygone costs must therefore be excluded from the analysis.

Life cycle costs must be distinguished and included in program costing. This will involve defining fixed costs--related to initial research,
planning and evaluation, and capital costs in land,
buildings, equipment, etc.--and variable or recurring
costs, best seen as operating and maintenance costs
varying directly with the size and duration of the
programs. The actual presentation of total program
costs in the budget format may make distinctions between fixed and operating costs, the translation being made by a crosswalk grid; in the analysis, however, all relevant program costs must be aggregated
to present the total additional resource requirements
of the program. Figure 1.1 indicates roughly the
manner in which the costing of an open-ended income
maintenance program might be displayed.

Complete program costing in the case of public
programs requires the inclusion of negative externalities or external diseconomies attributable to
the program. This question of externalities, in relation to both output measures and costs, is dealt
with on pages 38-40 of this chapter; for the moment
it may suffice to note that the inclusion of such
external diseconomies is one of the major distinctions between private program cost analysis and public program cost analysis. The notion of secondary
or indirect costs is subsumed under the head of external diseconomies.

Quite apart from the question of externalities,
a difficult question of interpretation is posed by
interdependencies between public programs and the
common or joint use of equipment, facilities, and
personnel. The allocation of such joint costs requires the determination of the differential contribution of the costed factors to the various programs
in question. If such determination is not feasible
the most useful approach would seem to be to establish
what is essentially a separate support program category for such joint costs; the alternative is the

FIGURE 1.1

Total Program Costs

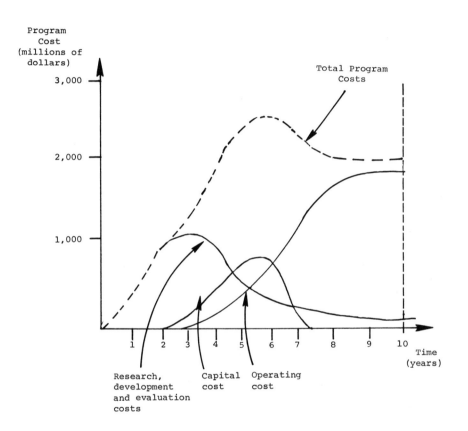

essentially arbitrary distortion of separate program
costs.

It was pointed out on page 13 of this section
that in both cost-benefit and cost-effectiveness
analysis inputs can be aggregated in terms of monetary units. The question does arise, however, as to
the treatment of inflation. If money prices are
used in costing programs over time, those programs
will be favored in which costs occur early in relation to benefits. There would appear to be two ways
of avoiding such distortion. The first and most common is constant monetary unit costing, in which constant prices are used in all estimates and a discount rate is employed that does not take into account
the anticipated rate of inflation. The alternative
is to allow for anticipated inflation in the estimation of costs (and benefits) or in the determination
of the appropriate rate of discount. The two methods
may be considered identical--it would, e.g., give
the same result either to discount costs at 7 percent
and make no further provision for inflation or to
allow for a 3 percent rate of inflation and use a
discount rate of 10 percent--but the former method
is arithmetically simpler and avoids the necessity
of forecasting the rate of inflation. The problem
arises further, however, of allowing for changes in
relative prices. There is no ready solution to this
difficult problem; R. Turvey suggests measuring inputs
at prices the weighted average of which is constant,[31]
but the problem remains of determining the appropriate
weights. Most studies to this point deal with the
problem by ignoring it.

The question of costing in the case of public
programs such as education or redistributive policies
such as income maintenance, where redistribution is
a significant or primary output of the program,
raises some particularly difficult problems. In
these cases redistribution involves strictly transfer
costs; there are no costs in the standard sense of
removing command over real resources from the private
sector to the public; rather command is simply transferred from one group to another in the private sector. Real costs may occur, however, first, if the
recipients of transfers reduce their work effort,
and, second, if the presumably progressive tax mea-

sures used to finance the redistributive scheme
diminish private sector incentives to work, save,
and invest and result in a diminished rate of growth
of national income. Such costs may, of course, result from progressive tax financing of any government
program, but one can assume in the case of public
programs for which redistribution is not a primary
objective that the financing provisions are set up
so as to be distributionally neutral. Complete program costing in the case of redistributive programs
thus requires in other than a simplistic static situation an attempt to indicate "second-stage" real
cost implications.

The establishment of cost estimates over the
life of the program requires the derivation of cost-
estimating relationships. The aggregation of these
cost-estimating relationships constitutes the building of a cost model and provides the time-phased estimates of resource requirements for the program.
By a cost-estimating relationship is simply meant a
functional expression that states that the cost of a
particular component of the program may be expressed
as a function of certain variables. The problem then
becomes one of determining what these variables are,
what the functional form is, and what the numerical
values of the parameters are in that functional form.
The cost model will generally reflect a variety of
ways of arriving at the required cost-estimating relationships, ranging from simple extrapolation of
current data into the future through internal "engineering" estimates, say, for new component configurations, the use of price quotations from vendors of
program components, and regression analysis of varying complexity. In terms of the degree of sophistication attained it is in the building of cost models
that much of the most thorough and meaningful analysis
has been done in program budgeting.[32,33,34,35]

One final point on the derivation of cost estimates remains to be made. A cost model should indicate the sensitivity of program costs to two forms
of uncertainty--uncertainty in specifications, i.e.,
an indication of how total program costs change with
variation in program configuration characteristics,
and uncertainty in estimation, i.e., an indication
of how program costs may vary as a consequence of

uncertainties in cost-estimating relationships, errors in basic data, etc. The former is of much greater significance than the latter. Cost sensitivity analysis provides a range of possible program costs that may be more useful than a single estimate of spurious accuracy. Further, sensitivity analysis serves to draw attention to those system configuration characteristics--variables and parameters--to which total system cost is more or less sensitive. Much of the sophisticated work in cost sensitivity analysis to this point has been done in the U.S. Department of Defense and in relation to the space program.[33,34,36,37] The model to be developed in Chapter 3 examines the sensitivity of income support program costs to the removal of an upper limit on the number of eligible family members, to variation of the payment reduction rate--the rate at which income support payments are reduced as work income rises--and to the definition of income on the basis of which income support eligibility is calculated.

Outputs: The Performance Indicators of Programs

The multiyear financial plan displaying the resource requirements of a program over the prescribed planning period must be accompanied in program budgeting by a corresponding program or output plan displaying in equivalent matrix cells the expected outputs from the program over the same planning period. The specification of outputs is generally more difficult than that of inputs for two major reasons: first, output determination requires an understanding of program performance that may be present in a greater or lesser degree according to the nature of the program; second, feasible output measures may be incommensurable with inputs in monetary units, and, further, are likely, if purporting to offer a full description of program performance, to be multidimensional. These points are dealt with in turn, the former rather briefly, the latter at some length.

The determination of outputs requires the specification of an effectiveness or production function model, which translates input requirements into some specified measure or set of measures of output. If

the functional relationship between inputs and outputs is specified in precise mathematical form, say
in terms of engineering performance indicators of
weapons systems, then output measures can be, at
least in principle, specified ex-ante in precise
terms. For the bulk of public programs, however,
such a precise relationship is not known, and the
relationship must be estimated by other than an exact
mathematical model. A variety of modeling techniques
is of course available, as was suggested in the previous section, but the fact remains that in program
budgeting that requires the ex-ante estimation of
outputs the accuracy of output specification will
clearly be directly related to the state of knowledge
on the program production function. The experiment
on income support in New Jersey[30] is an attempt to
clarify through the ex-post evaluation of the experimental results the complex relationships between
income support dollar inputs and outputs in terms of
work effort, family stability, and a set of related
indicators. An assessment of the nature of this
problem across the range of public programs is offered
in this chapter.

The second major difficulty, the manner in which
the output measure or set of output measures is to
be specified, can be dealt with as a set of four related questions. First, given the quantifiability
of outputs in some form, to what extent is quantification possible in monetary units, thus making possible cost-benefit analysis? Second, if outputs can
be quantified but cannot reasonably be expressed in
monetary units, in what alternative physical unit
forms can outputs be displayed, thus making possible
cost-effectiveness analysis? Third, how are outputs
to be treated that are not amenable to quantification
of any kind, either in monetary or physical terms?
Finally, if output must be realistically conceived in
multidimensional terms how is the question of weighting to be treated? Each of these is examined in
turn, with the question of the monetary conceptualization of outputs dealt with rather more briefly than
the question of the conceptualization of outputs in
physical terms, reflecting the structure of the model
of redistributive programs to be developed in Chapter
3.

Outputs in Monetary Units

If it is economic philistinism to attempt to reduce all outputs to monetary units,[38,39] so it may also be considered economic irresponsibility to fail to impute a monetary value to an output that can be so expressed. In other words, it behooves an economist to push conceptualization in monetary units as far as possible, particularly where failure to provide an explicit monetary valuation simply prepares the way for an ultimate implicit valuation in the actual decision-making process; this injunction applies in the case of both "direct outputs" and externalities. The frontiers of conceptualization of outputs in monetary terms are being continually expanded, in particular in the United Kingdom recently in the area of transport planning[40,41,42] and in North America in water resource development[43] and the broad field of human resource development.[44] Such conceptualization, though fraught with the dangers that, first, the economist may be tempted to expose the analysis to attack by stretching conceptual heroics too far* and, second, and partly in consequence of the first point, those in disagreement with

---

*Some of the unease about the famous Victoria Line study (C. D. Foster and M. Beasley, "Estimating the Social Benefit of Constructing an Underground Railway in London," Journal of the Royal Statistical Society, ser. A, 126, pt. I (1963), 46-92), has focused on the benefit imputed to increased convenience for underground passengers, calculated in terms of the increased probability of getting a seat once the new line was completed. This particular benefit amounted to about 22 percent of the total discounted gross benefits, and its exclusion would not make discounted net benefits negative. In a case where alternatives are being compared, however, choice between alternatives may depend on the credibility given to such a factor, and it seems reasonable to conclude that the probability of rejection of the analysis will be greater, the greater the proportion of benefits computed in such a heroic fashion.

the analytical results may simply fall back on an
ex-post rejection of the concepts employed,* must
nevertheless be the lot of the economist in resource
allocation analysis in the public sector.

A fundamental broad conceptual distinction may
be drawn between two major components of the output
of public programs conceived in monetary terms--what
may be referred to as allocative efficiency benefits
(and costs) and redistributive benefits (and costs).**

Programs are considered to generate streams of
outputs (benefits) over time and require streams of
inputs (costs) over time. These benefit and cost
streams may be real or transfer in nature, and it is
on this basis that we distinguish allocative efficiency costs and benefits from redistributive costs
and benefits.

In the broadest terms allocative efficiency benefits are defined as the market value of the increased
output of real resources consequent on the program,
and the corresponding costs are defined as the market
value of the real resources used up by the program.
If allocative efficiency benefits are given by B_e
and corresponding costs by C_e then net allocative
efficiency benefits are given by $B_e - C_e$ and may be
positive or negative. Net allocative efficiency benefits are thus defined basically as the contribution
of the program over the planning period to national
income, i.e., the difference between national income
generated by program outputs, on the one hand, and

----

*The most recent case here is Professor Buchanan's
dissent on the siting of the third London Airport
(Report of the Commission on the Third London Airport, Final Report [London: H.M.S.O., 1971], pp.
149-60).

**The distinction of outputs into allocative ef-
ficiency benefits and redistributive outputs has a
corresponding input classification. This distinction
was mentioned briefly in the section on inputs and
is discussed here as a symmetrical equivalent of the
output classification. In effect, net benefits are
defined.

national income <u>displaced</u> by program construction
and operation, on the other.*

This definition can be couched in terms of a potential Pareto improvement, i.e., in terms of hypothetical overcompensation. A positive measure of
net allocative efficiency is taken to indicate an
unambiguous increment in welfare, inasmuch as the
gainers from the program would obtain more than sufficient hypothetically to compensate the losers; the
program with a positive measure of net allocative
efficiency is thus capable of producing an excess of
benefits so that everyone in society could, by a
hypothetical costless redistribution of the gains,
be made better off.

Much of the literature on cost-benefit analysis
has been exclusively concerned with allocative efficiency benefits in the sense defined above, in effect
weighting a unit of national income identically regardless of who receives or has to part with it, or,
in other words, regarding as negligible, or as of
no importance relative to the net efficiency change,
the movement of some indicator of income distribution.

It is likely, of course, that allocative efficiency change will be accompanied by redistributive
change, i.e., that there will be transfer costs and
benefits in addition to real costs and benefits, and
a full evaluation of the program must include the
computation of net efficiency benefits and the computation of the change in a defined indicator of income distribution consequent on the program.

The discussion to this point presupposes separate
calculation of efficiency and redistributive benefits,
the former in terms of the change in national income
occasioned by the program, the latter in terms of
the movement in some indicator of income distribution, which measures the change in income distribution either at a constant level of national income

---

*At this point we abstract from the deficiencies
of national income defined in terms of market prices
as a measure of national welfare. The subject is
dealt with below.

or between the (different) before-and-after levels
of national income. Another approach to incorporating redistribution is that used by S. A. Marglin,[45]
where the redistributive implications of a program
are measured not by the computation of a separate indicator but by the explicit incorporation of redistribution in the efficiency benefits objective function. This is done by devising a set of weights for
costs and benefits accruing to different income groups
(or, as required, regions of the country, etc.) and
computing total net benefit as a weighted sum of efficiency benefits. In effect, national income is re-
defined in a new unit of account according to a set
of distributive weights. It must be stressed that
the Marglin method of encompassing the redistributive
implications of a program as a weighted sum of distributed efficiency benefits has the merit of offering commensurability and additivity, but it is a
partial view of redistribution as distinct from the
assessment of the global redistributive implications
obtained from the computation of a separate distributive indicator such as the Lorenz coefficient. A
program may generate a wide range of transfers that,
because they do not represent a net change in national
income, are not properly included in efficiency benefits and are thus excluded from a redistributive
criterion that considers only the distribution of
these efficiency benefits. A program that is acceptable under the Marglin combined criterion might thus
be one which, in a global transfer sense, was counter-
redistributive, i.e., made the rich richer and the
poor poorer.

The importance of the distinction between allocative efficiency costs and benefits and redistributive costs and benefits is limited to the cost side
of the criterion in the case of cost-effectiveness
analysis, where output indicators are expressed in
physical or descriptive terms; but costs may be divided into real resource costs and transfer costs.
In the case of cost-benefit analysis the distinction
is fundamental on both sides of the criterion, i.e.,
both costs and benefits may be real or transfer in
nature.

Outputs in Physical Units

It has been argued that although redistributive
benefits represent monetary transfers and can be described in a purely monetary representation of program outputs by weighting allocative efficiency benefits such redistributive benefits are best represented
by the change in a physical indicator of the state
of income distribution. The case for the use of such
physical indicators is essentially the case for explicitness and completeness, as against conceptual
elegance and commensurability, in the representation
of program outputs. In the absence of a monetary
measure of outputs, or perhaps, as in the general
case discussed above, as a complement to a monetary
measure of output, program outputs may be described
where physical quantification is feasible by one or
a set of physical performance or effectiveness indicators. A variety of types of physical indicators
may be distinguished as follows.

Indicators of Program Magnitude in Terms of Input
Resources. Such measures of program inputs are a
crude surrogate for program output and do not provide
any information on what was accomplished by the use
of these program resources. Examples of such indicators are pupil-teacher ratios in an education program, the number of patrol cars in a crime prevention
program, and the number of caseworkers in a welfare
program. Where staffing standards are reasonably
consistent, such input indicators in the absence of
effectiveness indicators may be the best approximation of program output.

Indicators of Program Volume. These indicators show
the volume of public output provided, e.g., miles of
highway in a highway program or number of housing
units in a housing program, or the number of consumers
or beneficiaries of the program, e.g., number of
families assisted in a welfare program or number of
women patients in a family planning program. Such
indicators would usually cover a specified time period, and may be made more meaningful by framing
them in a comparative context, e.g., by specifying
the percentage of families receiving assistance or

indicating the number of traffic accidents per 1,000
vehicle miles.

Indicators of Program Quality. These indicators
would usually be used in conjunction with quantity
indicators and refer to the nature, characteristics,
and duration of the program, or some measure of the
extent to which the program achieves its objective.
Examples would be the change in the separation and
divorce rates associated with a family counseling
program or a welfare program, or the number of children achieving particular grades in an educational
improvement program.

Appendix A suggests some further general examples of quantity and quality indicators. In practice,
the distinction between quantity and quality indicators is not sharp; the distinction between these
indicators and the final category of physical indicators to be discussed—social indicators—is, however, rather new and important.

Social Indicators. Interest has developed recently
in evolving a set of indicators that would serve to
reflect social progress or retrogression—social welfare and "illfare," respectively—in a broader framework than that offered by standard economic indicators. This aspiration to a system of social accounting to supplement conventional economic accounting
has culminated in the United States in a preliminary
study entitled "Toward a Social Report," in which
the possibility of developing indicators in such areas
as health, social mobility, the condition of the
physical environment, poverty, public order and
safety, and learning, science, and art is examined,[46,47,48,49] and in the United Kingdom in an annual compendium of social statistics.[50] This work
reflects a desire to widen the concepts of costs and
benefits from government programs, and is given ur-
gency by the initial attempts to use program budgeting in such areas as health, welfare, and education.

Many social indicators may be seen as broader
versions of the qualitative economic indicators mentioned above; others cover areas ignored by economic
indicators—personal freedom and security, the participation of minorities in society, status, satis-

faction, social mobility, etc. The negative income tax experiment in New Jersey[30] seeks to determine-- albeit by simple questionnaire--the effects of the various negative income tax experiments not only on work participation but also on a range of wider areas such as family cohesion, political integration, general mobility, and social integration and anomie. Information on this broad range of issues is intended to facilitate the evaluation in a broad benefits or effectiveness context of the various income maintenance program designs.

The grandest and most universal social indicator to which research must presumably aspire is some aggregate measure of welfare, happiness, or gross social product. Although such a measure does not and probably will never exist, some interesting steps in the right direction have been taken using three basic approaches: first, index numbers, e.g., a crime index weighting crimes according to the degree of heinousness; second, proxy variables, e.g., the use of the correlation coefficient between father's occupational status and son's occupational status as an indicator of social mobility; and, finally, threshold or critical-valued social indicators, e.g., the specification of the numbers of houses that fail to meet certain minimum standards as a measure of the quality of housing.[51]

Intangible Outputs

The argument for explicitness in the case of physical indicators applies equally in the case of intangibles, i.e., those program outcomes that are not amenable to quantification either in monetary or physical terms. The simple omission of consideration of outcomes of this nature, or their relegation to a footnote or parenthetical qualification, implicitly attributes a zero or negligible weight to an outcome that might be significant in the final political decision-making process. The relevance and usefulness of the analysis is thus diminished. It follows that an analysis that recognizes multiple objectives and corresponding multiple outcomes ought to deal as explicitly as possible with all outcomes judged to be relevant, if necessary resorting to such simpler

indicator devices as ordinal scales to rank alternatives according to an intangible outcome. It follows,
further, that the toolbox of the economist and the
engineer may not always be adequate for such conceptualization exercises and that the design of indicators for intangible outcomes, in situations where
the capacity of the economist to conceptualize in
monetary terms or the economist-cum-engineer to conceptualize in direct, measurable physical terms has
been exhausted, must inevitably be a multidisciplinary
or interdisciplinary endeavor, relying on the skills
of such related disciplines as psychology, sociology,
and politics to complete the definition of outcomes.
The temptation in the interests of elegance to circumscribe the analysis in terms of those outcomes
directly amenable to quantification would seem likely
to be greater in cases where an attempt is being made
to use cost-benefit analysis exclusively than in
cases where either cost-effectiveness analysis, with
its generally more explicit identification of multiple outcomes, or a combination of cost-effectiveness
and cost-benefit analysis is being employed.

The general case, in sum, is for explicitness
in the conceptualization of outputs. The economist
must push monetary conceptualization as far as it is
meaningful and defensible but must recognize that
the task does not end there--that other outputs
amenable to physical if not monetary quantification
must be so specified and that intangibles must be
explicitly incorporated, if necessary, by simple
ordinal ranking in the final output set.

As in the case of costs, outputs from public
programs must be conceived in social terms and must
include external economies, or what we have preferred
generally to call positive externalities. The value
of such external benefits would be added to output
computed in monetary terms and incorporated as an
additional item in the set of output indicators in
output represented in terms of physical indicators.

The range of indicators surveyed above suggests
that public programs may generally be considered to
be designed for the pursuit of more than one objective and, reflecting this multiplicity of objectives,
to have multiple outputs. If it can be reasonably
argued that such outputs can be seen as a linear

combination of efficiency benefits in monetary terms,
then outputs may be aggregated into one monetary measure and, further, are then commensurable with inputs
in monetary terms. Cost-benefit analysis is thus
feasible. If, on the other hand, only a portion of
outputs can be described in monetary terms the outputs that cannot be so described must be represented
by physical indicators or, in the case of intangibles,
by simple ordinal ranking devices or some such measure. In this case outputs are not commensurable,
either among the various output indicators or with
inputs, and cost-benefit analysis for that portion
of output conceived in monetary terms must be supplemented by cost-effectiveness analysis for each
physical indicator employed. It may also be the
case that no part of output can be conceived in monetary terms, in which case physical indicators or the
corresponding measures for intangibles must be employed for each component of output. Given this
multidimensionality and incommensurability of outputs there will be as many output indicators as
there are objectives; these output indicators may be
presented simply as the components of an output vector or in a hierarchical form, the hierarchy reflecting either time--so that indicators of short-term,
intermediate, and long-term or ultimate impact may
be distinguished--or the degree of aggregation, the
highest indicator or set of indicators representing
the highest order of conceptually viable aggregation.
In the crudest case all outputs would be intangibles,
and all output measures, ordinal ranking scales,
cardinal points scores, etc. Paradoxically, if identical ranking or points score indicators are employed,
commensurability of outputs among each other (though
not in relation to inputs) is restored; an example
of this aggregation is offered below.

<u>Weighting</u>

Multidimensionality of outputs raises the question of weighting the various output components; the
variety of ways of approaching this problem are
briefly examined below.

An <u>implicit weighting</u> approach to the problem
of multidimensional outputs and incommensurability

has been suggested by R. McKean.[52] He suggests that
the decision-makers be provided with a schedule showing the net dollar-valued benefits as well as de-
scriptions of the other benefits (and costs, if appropriate) for each alternative system design. The
decision-maker would then choose that alternative
that conforms best to his subjective evaluations or
his interpretation of society's preferences for or
valuation of dollar-valued benefits as against other
benefits. Weighting is thus implicit and discretionary. This view, which in its general formulation envisages weighting as emerging implicitly as an outcome of the political process in a specific, case-by-
case sense, would appear to be the most widely held
view of the weighting problem and is found in, among
others, the arguments of R. A. Dahl and C. E. Lindblom, A. Maass, and O. Eckstein.[53,54,55]

Most recently, A. M. Freeman suggests an explicit
ex-ante weighting system in which explicit weights
are assigned by decision-makers to benefits, an explicit objective function is determined, and the implications of different weight assignments for ultimate system choice are displayed.[56]

An alternative procedure has been proposed by
Marglin.[45] He suggests that some minimum or threshold
level be set for the (n - 1) incommensurable benefits,
and the nth benefit be maximized subject to these
constraints.

Although explicit ex-ante weighting is attractive
to the analyst (and indeed essential if a meaningful
objective function is to be defined in the case of
outputs defined as a linear combination of efficiency
benefits), inasmuch as the discretionary political
dimension of the resource allocation process would
appear to be diminished, or at least constrained by
the ex-ante weights specified, it is probably most
realistic to expect that weighting will remain an
essentially implicit, discretionary process. The
role of the economist remains that of presenting an
explicit, complete representation of program costs
and output indicators; we must probably be content
with the fact that in the light of a specified output vector the weights assigned by the decision-
makers to that vector will emerge implicitly in the
decision-making process and that these revealed
weights are presumably subject to political sanctions.

The following illustrates the implications of
weighting in the case of the evaluation of welfare
programs with a hypothetical vector of output indicators each conceived as a simple points score. In
this case commensurability of outputs is possible
and a determinate solution to choice between program
designs emerges in the presence of specified ex-ante
weights. Each effectiveness indicator is defined as
an ordinal ternary scale with a points score of 1
assigned if the effect of a particular program design
on a particular indicator is positive, 0 if the effect is neutral, and -1 if the effect is negative.
Table 1.1 illustrates such a scheme for evaluating
three alternative program designs for a welfare program with five incommensurable components in the output vector. In the situation represented in Table
1.1, program design A would be preferred.

Externalities

Externalities are defined in the widest sense,
described by McKean as "spillovers"[52] and in the
classical definition by A. C. Pigou as "external

TABLE 1.1

Program Selection Under a Three-Point Common
Evaluation Procedure and Point Weighting System

Weighting	Effectiveness (vector components)	Weighted Preference		
		Design A	Design B	Design C
4	Income and assets	4	4	4
2	Basic services	2	0	0
2	Social mobility	2	0	2
1	Family cohesion	0	1	0
1	Political acceptability	0	1	1
	Total	8	6	7

economies and diseconomies."[57] They cover those benefits and costs resulting from the operation of the public program in question that are not compensated in the market and thus do not appear in the commercial accounts of that public program. In this case of "market failure," i.e., of uncompensated benefits and costs, consistent provision must be made for the definition and inclusion of externalities. In the case of cost-benefit analysis, monetary values must be imputed to external benefits and costs, and net efficiency benefits computed accordingly. In the case of programs in which only cost-effectiveness analysis is to be employed, i.e., in which outputs are to be measured by physical indicators and/or by other devices such as ordinal scales or points scores, the question of externalities on the output side (the input side being determined, as in cost-benefit analysis, in monetary terms) requires the inclusion in the output vector of all significant direct and indirect performance effects.

The valuation of externalities will frequently fall into the intangible category, but even here E. J. Mishan has pointed out that the economist can at least offer contingency calculations,[58] which, e.g., in the case of negative externalities, would be threshold or critical values of the externalities that would just offset the net benefits from a program calculated without including the externalities. If, e.g., a new highway project is estimated to provide net benefits of $5 million without calculating the negative externalities attributable to the increased number of people killed and injured and if, over the life of the project and as a differential consequence of that project, it is estimated that 200 people will be killed and 1,000 injured, then contingency values of $1,000 for each person injured and $20,000 for each person killed would be sufficient to eliminate the net benefits of the program.

It is important to distinguish technological externalities, which operate through changes in the productivity of factors owned and operated outside the public program in question, provide in consequence for a change in national income, and must be included in the computation of benefits and costs, and pecuniary externalities, which operate through

changes in relative prices, do not result in changes
in national income, and must therefore be excluded
from the computation of benefits and costs--although
they would have to be considered under a redistributive objective, presumably by some overall redistributive indicator method, since they do not manifest
themselves in an increase in national income and are
not therefore amenable to inclusion in the Marglin
method described above.

Time

In the structural presentation of a program budget both costs and program outputs are set out in
time series form, i.e., over the planning period used
in the budget presentation. This similar presentation in the case of programs chosen using either a
cost-benefit or a cost-effectiveness decision criterion conceals an important distinction between the
two forms of analysis with respect to the incorporation of time in the decision-making criterion employed
in choosing among alternative programs. In the case
of cost-benefit analysis a unit of benefit is treated
differently according to the time at which it can be
enjoyed. In general, a unit of benefit expressed in
monetary terms is less desirable the longer the period before it can be enjoyed, and this differential
weighting of benefits over time is reflected in a
rate of discount. Costs accruing over time are
similarly treated, and the particular cost-benefit
decision criterion employed will thus explicitly incorporate the question of the time streams of costs
and benefits into program selection.*
In cost-effectiveness analysis, on the other
hand, the selection criterion generally does not in-

------

*For example, the present value of any future
cost or benefit is given by

$$\frac{P_n}{(1 + r_1) \ (\ 1 + r_2) \ . \ . \ . \ . \ )1 + r_n)}$$

where P_n is the future value in period n, and r_1, r_2,
. . . r_n are the appropriate discount rates in the

clude time, juxtaposing program costs and corresponding effectiveness levels at a point in time.   It
is possible, of course, to incorporate time in various ways into cost-effectiveness analysis, employing,
for instance, discounting on the cost (monetary) side
and comparing this with a time stream of effectiveness indicators for each program option, or by incorporating time as the third dimension in a cost-
effectiveness-time schedule and comparing cost-effectiveness surfaces; but in both ways described, a
unit of effectiveness is not explicitly weighted differently according to its time of realization, the
physical nature and heterogeneity of effectiveness
indicators not being amenable to a formal, univer-
sally applicable structure of discounting.   In a
limited sense, of course, implicit discounting of
effectiveness may enter into program choice in the
case of programs with a common effectiveness indicator.   For instance, as between two alternative
health programs that provide an identical number of
hospital beds over the planning life of the program
but provide these in two distinct time streams, the
choice between the two programs may reflect the
(presumably distinct) present values of program cost,
and also time in the sense of the immediate need for
hospital beds.   In this program-specific manner time
can be considered to enter into the calculations
either as a conventional set of time weightings or
as a constraint on program choice.   Finally, a historical time series of cost-effectiveness indicators
may serve as an interesting record of "program productivity" over time.   M. Woodhall and M. Blaug have
employed this latter technique in the evaluation of
education programs.[59]

The choice of an interest rate to discount the
time streams of net benefits from public sector pro-

---

first, second, and nth periods, respectively.   If the
r's are equal, as is usually assumed, the formula reduces to the standard form where present value equals

$$\frac{P_n}{(1 + r)^n}$$

grams amenable to cost-benefit analysis (or the time streams of cost in cost-effectiveness analysis) is a factor in program analysis on which there is little agreement, even in principle, in the abundant literature.[60,61,62,63,64,65]

Without attempting a review of the tortured debate, one can identify two major schools of thought on the question, reflecting the use of a social time preference rate and a social opportunity cost rate of interest.

The social time preference rate of interest (STP) is taken to reflect the community's marginal rate of substitution of present for future consumption, i.e., the relative value that the community assigns to present as opposed to future consumption at the margin. There would appear to be a consensus in the literature that the prime rate on government bonds is an inadequate measure of the STP, inasmuch as the bond rate is affected by a variety of factors unrelated to the choice at the margin between present and future consumption, but there is little agreement on the precise manner in which the STP should be distinguished from the prime rate.

The social opportunity cost rate of interest (SOC), which may on balance be considered to be preferred among economists, reflects the view that it would be undesirable--inefficient in terms of the definition of net efficiency gains offered above-- to employ scarce capital resources on public sector programs where these resources could have been used to exploit investment opportunities with higher social rates of return in the private sector. The calculation of the SOC therefore requires an assessment of the social costs and benefits from the best alternative private programs, and the result represents the cost to society of undertaking a public program instead of the best alternative private program. This rate typically will differ from the STP as a consequence of corporation tax and externalities. Since the returns from public programs are generally not subject to corporation tax, it is the before-tax rate of return to private investment that measures the social returns foregone, leaving aside for the moment the question of externalities. W. J. Baumol has argued that in a situation where the prime rate

(taken as a surrogate for the STP) is 5 percent, the
corporate tax rate is 50 percent, and the corporate
sector earns a 16 percent rate of return, 6 percent
of which is a risk premium, the appropriate social
rate of discount is that which incorporates both the
allowance for corporate taxation, bringing the rate
from 5 percent to 10 percent, and the risk premium
of 6 percent, bringing the rate to 16 percent.[66]
Quite apart from the use of the bond rate as a surrogate for the STP, no allowance is made in this argument for externalities. The inclusion of externalities reflects the broader notion of social benefits
and costs as distinct from private or accounting
benefits and costs and may operate, depending on the
nature of the relevant externalities, to make the
SOC greater or less than the average private opportunity cost. The externalities argument has been recently articulated by Marglin[67] and debated by G.
Tullock.[68] There is, finally, some debate in the
literature as to the modification of SOC to allow for
the lower riskiness of public program investment,
but the developing consensus would seem to be that a
lowering of the SOC in this way would effectively
undervalue the social returns from private investment.

There is agreement, in sum, neither on the definition of the STP or the SOC nor on the appropriate-
ness of employing either concept, or some hybrid of
the two, as a general social rate of discount. This
lack of agreement has led to a proliferation of rates
in the U.S. government agencies--ranging widely between and within departments from 0 percent to 12
percent[67]--and to a variety of attempts to incorporate both major viewpoints on the choice of a discount
rate into the actual rate used. Following U.S. government procedures on the estimation of the opportunity cost to the government of borrowed funds--in-
volving consideration of revenue foregone by divert-
ing funds from the private sector--the Treasury
Board of the Canadian federal government has recently
suggested incorporating such an opportunity cost factor in cost discounting.*[69]

---

*So that while benefit discounting is carried out
using as the rate of discount the prime rate on gov-

Two concluding comments may be offered on what
is a rather unsatisfactory debate. First, the general use of discount rates on government projects
that are significantly lower than a realistic evaluation of social opportunity costs would suggest may
place in an unduly favorable light public long-term
projects, which have as their major redistributive
effect a redistribution between generations, relative
to government short-term projects directed, say, to
immediate housing and poverty needs, which have their
redistributive effect more or less immediately. The
difficulties of the latter form of program with respect to undervaluation of output, neglect of externalities, etc. are thus compounded.

Second, the lack of agreement among experts on
a consistent policy in the determination of a social
rate of discount suggests that the political component of the specification of a social discount rate
or set of rates is likely to predominate.

Uncertainty

The multiyear planning aspect of program budgeting brings uncertainty into the heart of the analytical procedure. Program appraisal involves in general
an evaluation of how a set of simple events interacts
to produce a final outcome. If the analyst is certain
about the nature and values of the relevant events,
e.g., a set of inputs, a vector of input prices, and
the transformation relationship and corresponding
set of outputs, then the appraisal of a program consists in the identification of these events and the
computation through logical procedures of some single-

---

ernment bonds, the present value of costs in year n
is given by

$$c_0 = \frac{c_n(1.0483)}{(1 + r)^n}$$

where 1.0483 is the opportunity cost factor derived
from the model of foregone revenue and r is the prime
rate on government bonds.

valued measure of the returns from that program. The
importance of explicitly introducing uncertainty into
the analysis is simply that many of the events or
variables affecting the outcome of a particular program design are not controllable by the analyst or
the decision-maker. Thus, program appraisal that
takes account of uncertainty requires, first, judg-
ments about the probability of occurrence of the
variables over which control cannot be exercised;
second, corresponding computation by aggregation procedures of a whole set or probability distribution
of possible outcomes or returns from the program;
and, third, the design of selection criteria for
choosing among program designs on the basis of probability distributions of returns. In essence, then,
the analytical core of program budgeting may be defined as a method of looking at problems of choice
under conditions of uncertainty, where the analysis
must take into account the various contingencies or
states of nature that may occur.

No attempt is made here to survey the literature
on decision-making under uncertainty.[70,71] Only a
small set of uncertainty hypotheses and decision
criteria are explored in this chapter, all of which
are variants on expected value theory, where the
analyst is assumed not to be certain of future events
but to have a subjective or partially objective view
of a probability distribution of these events, and
where selection criteria reflect the assumed maximization of the expected value of the outcome in question.

Strictly, uncertainty should be distinguished
from risk. Situations of risk and uncertainty are
similar in that in each an uncontrollable random
event or set of events is present. In the former
situation, however, previous experimentation or analysis makes possible the assignment to the event or
events of an "objective" probability distribution;
in the latter case, on the other hand, there is no
objective basis for the assignment of a probability
distribution, and the probability distribution employed must be subjective in nature. In practice,
of course, there is a spectrum of increasing subjec-
tivity as one moves from situations of more information to those of less, and the formal distinction

between uncertainty and risk will not be further pur-
sued here. We note simply at this point that what
may be referred to as the "degree of uncertainty" as
one moves along the spectrum of increasing subjec-
tivity may vary a great deal for the different variables and parameters within a given system design.
On the basis of past experience it might, e.g., be
possible to offer with high confidence a probability
distribution of input costs but to provide only a
somewhat vague probability distribution of ultimate
outcomes--perhaps simply best and worst outcome estimates; such a disparity would reflect uncertainty
on the transformation relationship, e.g., in a soft
program such as health or welfare. The term "uncertainty" is used in the balance of this study to cover
situations of both uncertainty and risk as distinguished above.

     The situation of uncertainty is best set out in
decision matrix form, with n strategies or system
designs $(S_1, S_2, \ldots S_i, \ldots S_n)$ defining the rows
and m states of nature or contingencies $(N_1, N_2, \ldots$
$N_j, \ldots N_m)$ defining the columns. To each of the
states of nature an objectively defined probability
$(p_1, p_2, \ldots p_j, \ldots p_m)$ is assigned. At the intersection of each row and column an outcome measure
$(O_{ij}, i = 1, 2, \ldots n; j = 1, 2, \ldots m)$ is found.
Each state of nature indicated may involve several
factors, the probability assigned to a particular
state of nature having been derived on a joint or
conditional basis from a whole series of probability
matrixes.[72,73] Given the probabilities of the various states of nature, the expected value of the outcome of a particular strategy, E_i, is then given by
$\Sigma_j p_j O_{ij}$. Other things being equal, the program design
whose outcome has the highest expected value in the
case of benefits (gross or net) or lowest expected
value in the case of the costs will be selected.
Table 1.2 illustrates the procedure for three program
designs and three states of nature, the latter being
assigned objective probabilities of 1/2, 1/4, and
1/4, respectively. If the outcomes are considered
to be program costs, the least cost program design
in terms of expected value is shown as design 1;
correspondingly, if the outcomes are benefits, design
3 is to be preferred. Given that the probabilities

TABLE 1.2

The Expected Value of Alternative Program Designs
(in dollars)

	Probability			
	1/2	1/4	1/4	
	1*	2*	3*	Expected Value
Program design 1	40	60	90	57.5
Program design 2	60	80	60	65
Program design 3	70	80	50	67.5

*State of nature.

although "objective" remain subject to error, sensitivity tests on the matrix using differing probability assignments can easily be carried out.

Perhaps the more usual situation in program budgeting is that of uncertainty in the strict sense where no objective probability distribution is available. The first alternative would be the assignment of subjective probabilities on the basis of an educated guess or "guesstimate." Where, as is frequently the case, differential subjective probabilities can only be assigned arbitrarily, the "equal likelihood criterion" may be used. According to this criterion, if no basis exists for assigning probabilities objectively or subjectively, then an equal probability should be assigned to each state of nature, i.e., if there are five states of nature, each should be assigned a probability of 1/5. Having assigned such probabilities, expected value calculations can be made as above.

Other methods use the decision matrix as the payoff matrix familiar from game theory. The pessimist criterion uses the maximin principle in the case of a benefit payoff matrix and a corresponding minimax principle in the case of a cost matrix. Viewing Table 1.2 as a benefit payoff matrix, the pessimist criterion suggests the choice of program

design 2, where the decision-maker cannot do worse
than an outcome of 60, as against minimums of 40 and
50 in program designs 1 and 3; correspondingly, the
decision-maker faced with Table 1.2 as a cost matrix
would choose indifferently between program designs
2 and 3, each of which offers a maximum possible loss
of 80.

The optimist criterion would suggest the selection of a program design offering a maximax in the
case of a benefit payoff matrix and a minimin in the
case of a cost payoff matrix. Using Table 1.2 as a
benefit payoff matrix, the optimist would choose program design 1, where he has the possibility of a payoff of 90; the same program design would be chosen
if Table 1.2 is viewed as a cost matrix, 40 being the
lowest cost outcome in the matrix.

A variety of related techniques is available,
in particular the Hurwicz "partial optimist" criterion and the Savage "regret" criterion,[72] and where
decisions are competitive, say, in the choice of
weapons systems, game theory comes into its own with
mixed strategy solutions.

The above approaches assume that a precise outcome can be assigned to each program design/state of
nature intersection. As the previous brief discussion on sensitivity analysis indicated, considerable
uncertainty exists with regard to program configuration and cost estimating parameters and variable relationships. Generally, the situation is even less
precise on the benefit or effectiveness side. Thus,
the rather elegant methods of choice in the face of
uncertainty described above may at best have to be
brought to bear on a matrix of best and worst outcomes for each intersection, or at worst be inappli-
cable in the face of absence of information of any
kind on outcomes; the latter situation is far from
unlikely in the case of the benefit or effectiveness
matrix. In the latter case uncertainty cannot of
course be ignored but has to be faced largely by ad
hoc procedures such as "buying time," "buying more
information," "buying flexibility as a hedge,"[74] and
similar contingency planning methods.

Constraints

Both cost-benefit analysis and cost-effectiveness analysis are procedures designed essentially for dealing with problems of constrained optimization in public sector resource allocation. Using either procedure one seeks to maximize utility subject to whatever constraints are imposed by the socio-political-economic context, optimizing within the feasible region demarcated by these constraints. Eckstein has classified these constraints into categories,[55] and the various categories, though clearly not mutually conclusive, are conceptually illuminating. The following is an adaptation of the Eckstein classification.

In the broadest sense, <u>political</u> constraints circumscribe the freedom of choice, i.e., the number and nature of options in any decision, available to government; although this broad category clearly encompasses what might be referred to as <u>social</u> constraints, it is perhaps worth distinguishing the latter as a significant subset of the former and including under the rubric such factors as the social implications of, say, motorway construction through built-up areas. Related to the broadest category of political constraints are, first, <u>administrative</u> constraints, which preclude the adoption of certain courses of action that involve excessive complication or too drastic a change in existing practice, and, second, <u>legal</u> constraints, which may be considered to define a set of changes that can be introduced without a change in the law. <u>Constitutional</u> constraints may be seen as having both a political and a legal aspect. <u>Technical</u> or <u>physical</u> constraints restrict choices to what is technically feasible <u>and</u> technically efficient,* and <u>financial</u> or <u>budget</u> con-

---

*It is possible to produce in physical terms a particular output by all points on the relevant production isoquant and also by many points lying above that isoquant, i.e., using more of at least one input

straints are seen as setting general or specific
limits to the amount that can be spent by the organization in question over a specified period.*

The problem of multiplicity of objectives can
be couched in constraint terms, and in this sense
constraints serve the positive function of giving
explicit definition to multiple ends. In Marglin's
review chapter on the objectives of water resource
development systems[45] the problem of achieving the
dual objectives of efficiency and redistribution is
presented in terms of constraints, the optional ways
of viewing the problem in cost-benefit terms being,
first, the maximization of efficiency gains subject
to a specified redistribution constraint and, second,
the maximization of a specified redistributive objective subject to the constraint that efficiency
gains attain a specified minimum. Frequently, indeed, the distinction between objectives and constraints may be difficult to define.[75]

A final general point relates to the degree of
flexibility or mutability of constraints. Although
by definition negative, in the sense of limiting the
range of feasible solutions, this very limiting
property can be seen positively as simplifying decisions, and there is a danger that, in the interests
of a simpler life, constraints that keep life relatively simple may be conveniently assumed to be immutable. This point has been stressed by both
Maass[54] and P. D. Henderson.[76] An exploration of
the extent to which constraints are in fact variables
rather than immutable parameters given ex cathedra
should then be a primary consideration in any analytical design.

———————————

without a corresponding reduction in the other input.
All points on or above the isoquant are technically
feasible; only points on the isoquant are technically
efficient.

*Knowledge of the relative prices of inputs and
the budget constraint combine to define the least-
cost technically efficient input combination, i.e.,
the point that is both technically and economically
efficient.

The definition of meaningful criteria in cost-
effectiveness analysis, where inputs and outputs are
incommensurable, requires the specification of a
constraint on either the input or output side. Essentially cost must be minimized in terms of a given
level of effectiveness for the program designs under
consideration, or effectiveness must be maximized for
a given cost. The variations here are developed
later in the text.

Unlike cost-effectiveness analysis, cost-benefit
analysis decision criteria may be defined without
constraints; for instance, limiting the nature of
the criterion to efficiency benefits, the criterion
might specify that all projects with a positive
present value of net benefits should be undertaken.
In practice, cost-benefit analysis will generally be
conducted in the context of a range of constraints,
of the sort classified above. Considering only financial constraints, a fixed budget (cost maximum)
may be allocated to a sector or particular program
within a sector--a procedure we call <u>administrative</u>
<u>or explicit capital rationing</u>; a variation on this
theme by which certain programs with a positive
present value are observed to be excluded on grounds
of financial stringency might be referred to as <u>im-</u>
<u>plicit or behavioral capital rationing</u>. Viewing the
constraint in terms of net benefits, a minimum required benefit level is frequently specified in the
form of a minimum required rate of return on a program, usually a rate reflecting the opportunity cost
of capital.

Criteria for Program Design
Selection and Ranking

<u>Introduction</u>

Having established through cost and production
function models the required information on inputs
and associated outputs for the program or set of alternative programs under consideration, some criterion
is necessary for the selection of a program design--
defining "selection" in the broad sense to include,
first, the decision to proceed or not to proceed with
a specific program and, second, a means of ranking

a set of alternative program designs. The ranking
aspect of criteria definition is the broader aspect
of selection inasmuch as some or all of a set of incompatible programs* under consideration may qualify
positively under the narrower, binary "proceed/do
not proceed" aspect.

All the criteria to be considered will take into
account the two sets of consequences attributable to
programs: program outputs (measures of benefit and/or
effectiveness in relation to program objectives) and
program inputs (measures of the cost of program implementation). Neither consequence alone can serve
as an adequate criterion--the minimization of costs
regardless of gains would in most cases suggest no
action at all, and the maximization of gains regardless of costs is not very helpful in the context of
scarce resources.

Further, the criteria to be considered must not
be overspecified. The most common form of over-
specification occurs in the aspiration to maximum
gain (either monetary benefit or effectiveness) at
minimum cost. The most recent example occurred in
an otherwise unexceptionable article in the Proceedings of the Industrial Relations Research Association,
where J. S. MacDonald defines cost-benefit analysis
as seeking "optimization of resource allocation by
reconciling maximization of benefits with minimization of costs."[77] There is, of course, no such
criterion. Minimum costs will generally mean zero
gain or effectiveness, and maximum gain may corres-
pond to a very large or even infinite cost. There
is clearly no program design that offers both simul-
taneously.

Criteria Relating Monetary Costs and Benefits

Table 1.3 illustrates hypothetical net benefits
(social profit) over a five-year planning period for
six alternative program designs. It is assumed that
capital costs are identical (100 units) for each program design and all are incurred at the inception of

---

*I.e., where the choice of one program design
precludes the choice of other designs.

each program. For each of the five years following,
the figure shown in each matrix cell represents net
benefits or monetary benefits minus operating costs.
Capital costs are distinguished from operating costs,
although in principle program costs include both
capital and operating costs and total costs so computed are deducted from total benefits in each period
to give net benefit in that period. In period 0,
gross benefits are zero, operating costs are zero,
capital costs are 100, and net benefits in period 0,
corresponding to net benefits in periods 1 through
5, are -100 for each program design.

In general the time stream of net benefits for
each program can be seen as $(B_0 - C_0)$, $(B_1 - C_1)$,
$(B_2 - C_2)$, . . . $(B_n - C_n)$, where the subscript indicates the time period and B_i and C_i indicate gross
benefits and costs in period i. If $(B_i - C_i)$ is defined as S_i, i.e., net benefit in period i, the matrix entries represent a stream of net benefits or
social profit, S_0, S_1, S_2, . . . S_n, any of which in
any period can be positive, zero, or negative. In
Table 1.3 net benefits are assumed to be positive or
zero for all program designs in periods 1 through 5.

TABLE 1.3

Program Net Benefits

Pro-gram	Time Period						Net Benefit (periods 1-5)	Net Benefit (periods 0-5)
	0	1	2	3	4	5		
A	-100	100	10	0	0	0	110	10
B	-100	50	50	10	10	0	120	20
C	-100	40	30	30	20	10	130	30
D	-100	28	28	28	28	28	140	40
E	-100	10	20	30	40	50	150	50
F	-100	0	0	0	40	120	160	60

Source: Adapted from figures used by P. D. Henderson, "Notes on Public Investment Criteria in the
United Kingdom," Bulletin of the Oxford University
Institute of Economics and Statistics (1965), pp. 55-
89.

The question of uncertainty is not dealt with
explicitly in Table 1.3. It can be assumed that the
analysis is deterministic, in which case each value
of S is known with certainty or, more realistically,
that the analysis is probabilistic, that a probability
distribution for each S is known, and that each value
of S in the time matrix represents the expected value
of S for that time period.

A variety of crude investment criteria exists;
in this overview attention is confined to criteria
that involve, directly or indirectly, time discounting, i.e., reducing a stream of net benefits to a
single value at a point in time. There are two
broad categories here: first, those that determine
the value of a stream of net benefits at a specified
point in time by reference to an exogenously specified rate of discount--under this head we define,
first, the present value of net benefits method and,
second, the method of computing the ratio of discounted gross benefits to discounted gross costs;
and, second, those that compute a rate of return by
reference to the condition that the value of net
benefits be reduced to zero at the inception of the
program--under this head we define the internal rate
of return.

The net present discounted value (NPV) of a
time stream of net benefits is defined simply as the
sum of the values of all present and future net benefits (benefits minus costs), all such values being
discounted back to the present at a specified rate
of discount. Symbolically,

$$NPV = \sum_{i=0}^{n} \frac{S_i}{(1 = r)^i}$$

where r equals the specified rate of discount, i denotes the time period, and n is the upper limiting
value on i.

In general it is assumed that the discount rate
r is constant across the complete discounting period,
but there is no reason in principle to assume that
this will be so, and, given a basis for assuming a
varying annual rate of decline of time weights, the
formula of NPV may be disaggregated:

$$NPV = S_o + \frac{S_1}{(1 + r_1)^1} + \frac{S_2}{(1 + r_2)^2} + \ldots + \frac{S_n}{(1 + r_n)^n}$$

where $r_1 \neq r_2 \neq \ldots \neq r_n$.

The crucial variable in NPV computation is, clearly, the rate of discount or set of rates of discount employed in discounting net benefits. Table 1.4 illustrates the NPV of the six alternative program designs under consideration for three alternative (constant) rates of discount. All designs have a positive NPV at discount rates of 2.5 percent and 8 percent and a negative NPV at a discount rate of 15 percent.

The admissibility criterion under the NPV approach is unequivocal and is related to the definition of efficiency benefits (and its Paretian hypothetical overcompensation equivalent) set out above. In principle, given a specified social discount rate, all program designs should be undertaken that have at that discount rate an NPV greater than zero. In the case of incompatibility, programs may be ranked according to NPV, and that program with the highest

TABLE 1.4

Program NPV at Different Discount Rates

Program	Rate of Discount (in percent)		
	2.5	8	15
A	7.1	1.2	−5.4
B	14.8	4.5	−6.4
C	22.4	8.0	−6.4
D	30.1	11.8	−6.2
E	37.1	13.6	−8.7
F	42.3	11.1	−17.4

Source: P. D. Henderson, "Notes on Public Investment Criteria in the United Kingdom," Bulletin of the Oxford University Institute of Economics and Statistics (1965), pp. 55-59.

NPV at the specified discount rate adopted. In the
example illustrated in Table 1.4 all programs are
admissible at discount rates of 2.5 percent and 8
percent, while none is admissible at a discount rate
of 15 percent. The significance of the specified
rate of discount emerges in the differential rankings
obtained under each rate: at a rate of 2.5 percent
the ranking is reverse alphabetical; at 8 percent
the ranking, in order of merit, is E, D, F, C, B,
and A, the only change from the first ranking being
the shift of design F from first to third position;
at a rate of 15 percent, where in principle ranking
is irrelevant since no program design is admissible,
the order is almost alphabetical, specifically A, D,
B, C, E, and F.

The NPV approach to program evaluation has several major advantages. First, the procedure specifically reflects the magnitude or volume of net benefit rather than the rate of net benefit reflected in
the internal rate of return criterion to be discussed below. Second, like the internal rate of return, the NPV approach illustrates explicitly the
fundamental intertemporal principle that net benefits differ according to the time at which they accrue. Third, the nature of the computation permits
the variation of the rate of discount between different time periods instead of the implicit averaging
of the internal rate of return.

The major disadvantages of the NPV approach are
its dependence on an exogenously specified rate of
discount and the ranking variability associated with
differential discount rates.

The benefit-cost ratio approach is closely related to the NPV approach. It requires an exogenously
specified social rate of discount, r, which is employed to discount the time streams of gross benefits
and costs. The gross benefit-cost ratio is defined
for any program as the ratio of discounted gross
benefits to discounted gross costs. Symbolically,
the gross benefit-cost ratio (BCR_g) is defined for
a given rate of discount as

$$BCR_g = \sum_{i=0}^{n} \frac{B_i}{(1+r)^i} \Bigg/ \sum_{i=0}^{n} \frac{C_i}{(1+r)^i} = \frac{B}{C}$$

The net benefit-cost ratio disaggregates costs into initial capital costs, C_1, and operating costs, C_2.[78] The rationale of the disaggregation is simply that initial capital outlays (C_1) must be financed independently, whereas operating outlays (C_2) can be met from benefits generated. In the example illustrated in Table 1.3 capital costs are incurred solely at the inception of the program (in time period 0) and operating costs, from periods 1 through 5. In general we may assume that capital costs (and zero benefits) accrue over the first j periods, whereas operating costs accrue over periods $j + 1$ through n. In this case C_1 and C_2 may be formally defined:

$$C_1 = \sum_{i=0}^{j} \frac{c_i}{(1+r)^i}$$

and

$$C_2 = \sum_{i=j+1}^{n} \frac{c_i}{(1+r)^i}$$

The discounted sum of total costs, C, is given by $C_1 + C_2$, and the net benefit-cost ratio (BCR_n) is given by

$$BCR_n = \frac{B - C_2}{C_1} = \sum_{i=j+1}^{n} \frac{B_i}{(1+r)^i} - \sum_{i=j+1}^{n} \frac{c_i}{(1+r)^i} \Big/ \sum_{i=0}^{j} \frac{c_i}{(1+r)^i}$$

as distinct from BCR_g, given by B/C.

The case for the use of BCR_n as distinct from BCR_g is that there is a fundamental distinction between the two categories of costs, capital costs being discretionary in the sense that they might be allocated to other programs, whereas operating costs are committed to the operation of the program and are not available for allocation elsewhere. We have recognized the importance of relating costs and benefits by stressing the concept of net benefits, and the net benefit-cost ratio is, at least in principle, to be preferred. It may, however, be complex to operate where capital costs extend over a considerable portion of the life of the project, or at any rate into time periods in which gross benefits have begun to accrue. This question could perhaps be met by deducting from C_1 gross benefits that accrue over the periods in which capital costs are incurred, so using a concept of net costs in the denominator of BCR_n; but the problem is further complicated by the likelihood that capital costs and operating costs may be, indeed are likely to be, incurred simultaneously-- and perhaps indistinguishably--and in practice the gross ratio may be the less confusing and more useful. In any event, in the simple example set out in Table 1.3 BCR_g and BCR_n are indistinguishable, since we utilize the concept of net benefits and do not distinguish operating costs in periods 1 through 5.

Table 1.5 sets out the BCR_g for the six program designs under consideration for three discount rates. As in the case of NPV, it is clear the BCR_g is directly dependent on the specified r.

The admissibility criterion using the BCR approach (either gross or net) follows from the definition of the admissibility criterion under the NPV approach and specifies that a program design be implemented if the computed BCR is greater than 1. This admissibility criterion will be consistent for either

TABLE 1.5

Program Benefit: Cost Ratios at Different
Discount Rates

Program	Rate of Discount (in percent)		
	2.5	8	15
A	1.07	1.01	0.946
B	1.15	1.04	0.936
C	1.22	1.08	0.936
D	1.30	1.19	0.938
E	1.37	1.37	0.913
F	1.42	1.01	0.866

Source: Computed from data in Table 1.3.

definition of the BCR and, further, will always be consistent with the admissibility criterion defined under the NPV approach.

In the case of incompatibility, in which programs are ranked in order of merit from the highest BCR to the lowest, consistency cannot be guaranteed. Dealing first with the comparison between the NPV approach and the BCR_g approach, the ranking provided in Table 1.5 is identical to that shown in Table 1.4 for all three values of r investigated, although this identical ranking is a consequence of the similar absolute magnitudes of the program designs under consideration. The concept of a ratio is independent of the absolute magnitude of program designs, and in the event that there is considerable disparity in the absolute magnitudes of program designs under consideration, the ranking obtained by using the BCR_g approach need not, indeed generally will not, be the same as that obtained under the NPV approach. The ranking obtained using the BCR_n approach may differ, for the same reasons as in the case of the BCR_g approach, from that obtained under the NPV approach, but may also differ from the ranking obtained using the BCR_g approach. For a given total program cost, the two ratios may give disparate preference rankings for programs in which the ratio of capital to operating outlays differs.

The advantages of the BCR approach to program evaluation lie largely in its roots in the NPV approach. Its major disadvantage is the disadvantage inherent in the concept of a ratio: it disguises disparities in the absolute magnitude of program designs under consideration. The approach shares, of course, the dependence of the NPV approach on an exogenously specified rate of discount and, like the NPV approach, provides differential preference rankings for different values of r (Table 1.5).

The internal rate of return (IR) is defined as that rate of discount that will make the present value of the stream of gross benefits exactly equal to the present value of the gross costs, i.e., the rate of discount that will make the present value of the stream of net benefits equal to zero. Symbolically, the IR is that rate of discount for which

$$\sum_{i = 0}^{n} \frac{S_i}{(1 + IR)^i} = 0$$

Table 1.6 displays the IR for each of the six program designs under consideration.

The admissibility criterion under the IR approach requires the exogenous specification of a cut-off interest rate, r*, the decision criterion requiring that the IR in the program under consideration exceed r*. If r* is defined as equal to the rate of discount, r, employed in the NPV and BCR approaches, then the three criteria provide a consistent decision rule. Comparing Tables 1.4, 1.5, and 1.6, all programs are admissible under the NPV and BCR approaches at r values of 2.5 percent and 8 percent. Correspondingly, where r* = r, all programs in Table 1.6 would be admissible, since all the values of IR exceed 2.5 percent and 8 percent. If, however, r is defined as 15 percent, none of the programs is admissible under the NPV and BCR approaches, and, correspondingly, none is admissible under the IR approach since in every case the computed IR is less than an r* value of 15 percent.

Unfortunately, the same consistency is not obtained in the ranking of incompatible programs unless

TABLE 1.6

Program Internal Rates of Return

Program	IR
A	9.1
B	10.7
C	11.8
D	12.4
E	12.0
F	10.4

Source: P. D. Henderson, "Notes on Public Investment Criteria in the United Kingdom," Bulletin of the Oxford University Institute of Economics and Statistics (1965), pp. 55-89.

a two-stage approach is taken to the definition of
the IR ranking criterion. Limiting the comparison
to the NPV and IR approach, the simplest ranking procedure under the IR approach, ranking programs in
order of merit from the highest IR value to the lowest, ranks programs D, E, C, B, F, and A.[79] It is
possible to reconcile the ranking procedures, however,
provided a unique value for IR exists, by adopting
the procedure suggested by Henderson,[80] which requires that in the event of a disparate ranking of,
say, two programs using the NPV and IR approaches a
second value of IR ought to be recalculated on the
stream of differences between the net benefits of
the two programs. Given r* specified as equal to r,
the previous ranking under the IR criterion ought to
be reversed to a position consistent with that obtained under the NPV approach, if the IR calculated
on the stream of differences in net benefits (sub-
tracting the stream of the program with the lower
NPV from that with the higher NPV) exceeds r. If
this exercise is conducted for the six programs under
consideration, the ranking obtained under both the
IR and NPV approach is consistent. It might be argued, of course, that this elaborate exercise amounts
to calculating NPV in a particularly complex manner
and that there is a measure of redundancy in the
procedure. It does have the merit, however, of reconciling the two sets of preference ranking and provides an answer, albeit a somewhat tortured one, to
the neglect in the simpler IR ranking approach of
the absolute magnitude of alternative programs.

The chief advantage of the IR approach lies in
its similarity to the conventional notion of a return
on capital. It is occasionally claimed that another
significant advantage is that the computation can be
made directly from program data without reference to
the exogenously specified discount rate that is central to the NPV approach. This advantage is illusory
if the IR is to be employed as an admissibility criterion, since as defined above such a criterion requires the comparison of IR and an exogenously specified r* and holds for the ranking of programs only
if the simpler and less satisfactory ranking approach
under IR is followed.

The disadvantages relative to the NPV approach
are several. First, the computation of the IR of a
program is not a simple matter, requiring indeed a
procedure of iteration until the interest rate that
makes the sum of the net benefits equal to zero is
obtained. If the two-stage IR approach is adopted
the tediousness of the computation is doubled. Second, the simple IR approach shares the deficiency of
the BCR approach in neglecting the absolute magnitude
of costs and benefits of alternative programs. This
deficiency is resolved by the two-stage approach, at
the cost, however, of increased computational tedium
and of the possible redundancy referred to above.
Third, the IR approach has the considerable disadvantage that there may be no unique value of IR; this
situation arises where the sign of the values of the
time stream of program net benefits changes more
than once. In the more common case, of course, the
sign may be expected to change only once, from negative to positive, after some initial phase of the
program. Finally, it has been argued that in a situation of capital rationing the NPV approach is superior both formally and on grounds of computational
convenience.[79,81]

The cost-benefit decision-making and ranking
criteria defined and examined above imply the computation of costs and benefits by analysts operating
with a politically determined social discount rate.
S. M. Greenhouse has recently taken issue with these
standard forms and has suggested as an alternative a
"marginal utility" or "customer verdict" approach,
by which the beneficiaries of a particular program
are asked to rank the received outputs from that program against private goods with ascertainable market
prices.[82] If the unit cost of the public program in
question is known, an implicit customer-determined
cost-benefit criterion would be obtained and a guide
provided to reduction or expansion of that public
program. Greenhouse's point that government seldom
concerns itself explicitly with program customers is
well taken, and it would seem clear that behavioral
analysis could reveal important insights, particularly
into the monetary value of the positive and negative
externalities associated with certain public programs
--the externalities attributed to airport construction

are a case in point[83]--but such a role falls far short
of a complete reliance on a customer verdict cost-
benefit calculus. The major deficiency in the Greenhouse proposal is precisely the <u>social</u> nature of
cost-benefit analysis, which requires the computation
on both the benefit and cost side of the complete set
of social benefits and costs. Individuals may be
considered in general equipped to estimate benefits
and costs only in private terms. This is true even
if a large number of individuals is interviewed; the
average of a set of private valuations does not
equal a public or social valuation. The question
also arises, of course, of how the likely variance in
the answers is to be treated, and it would not seem
that the customer verdict approach can be other than
a useful means of obtaining provisional valuations
on particularly intractable externalities.

Criteria Relating Monetary Costs and Physical Outputs

We have defined the analytical approach that relates monetary costs to output indicators defined in
physical terms as cost-effectiveness analysis. Leaving aside the difficulties of defining appropriate
output indicators for public programs (pages 26-38),
the notion of a "cost-effectiveness schedule" is a
very simple one. The schedule simply relates alternative total program costs with the corresponding
performance level in the effectiveness indicator employed. The locus of such points is a cost-effectiveness schedule. Figure 1.2 illustrates such a schedule
relating performance in a broadly specified effectiveness indicator in an income support program to
total program cost.

The assumption implicit in the alternative total
program cost readings shown on the horizontal axis in
Figure 1.2 is that each such value is a least-cost
program package. To illustrate this point, and demonstrate the case in which the program under consideration has two major inputs, we derive below a cost-
effectiveness schedule for a welfare program from its
roots in conventional neoclassical economic theory.

Imagine a welfare program in which, for geometric
simplicity, there are only two inputs, an income
support scheme and a scheme to provide assistance to

FIGURE 1.2

Income Support Program Cost-Effectiveness Schedule

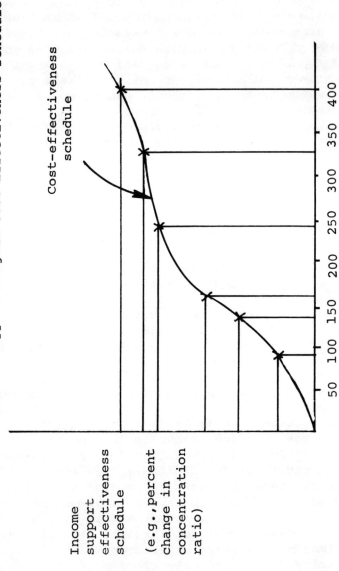

Income
support
effectiveness
schedule

(e.g.,percent
change in
concentration
ratio)

Cost-effectiveness
schedule

Total Program Cost
(millions of dollars)

64

geographic mobility. Further imagine that there is
for the present one effectiveness indicator to which
an index number is attached. One can then imagine
effectiveness isoquants that indicate the various
combinations of the two program inputs that attain a
given level of effectiveness (E), higher isoquants
indicating a higher level of effectiveness. Figure
1.3 illustrates the situation to this point.

The slope of the effectiveness isoquants at any
point gives the marginal rate of substitution between
the two inputs, indicating the trade-off between the
two inputs that is necessary to retain the same level
of effectiveness.

One now superimposes cost information on the
diagram of effectiveness isoquants in the form of
conventional budget constraints that indicate the

FIGURE 1.3

Effectiveness Isoquants

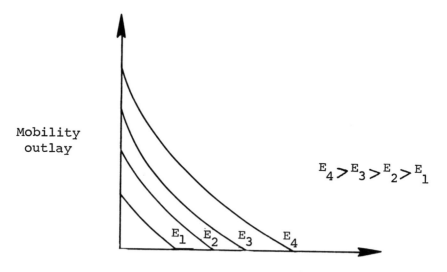

Mobility
outlay

$E_4 > E_3 > E_2 > E_1$

E_1 E_2 E_3 E_4

Income support
outlay

amounts of the two inputs that can be provided for a
fixed budget. If constant input prices are assumed,
the budget constraints are linear and can be added
to the effectiveness isoquants as indicated in Figure
1.4.

For any given budget level the appropriate mix
of inputs is given by the tangency of the budget line
with an effectiveness isoquant; points O_1, O_2, O_3,
and O_4 indicate the optimum input mixes for budget
levels of $20 million, $40 million, $60 million, and
$80 million, respectively. If one then plots total
program effectiveness against total (combined) program cost, one arrives at a series of points equivalent to O_1 through O_4 and the corresponding budget
levels, which, if enough such points are determined,
provides a continuous cost-effectiveness schedule of
the sort shown in Figure 1.5 (a general form of such
a schedule was illustrated in Figure 1.2).

The analysis could, of course, be extended to
three inputs but at the cost of geometrical clarity.
With three inputs one would be working with effectiveness isoquants in the form of a three-dimensional
surface, and the cost-effectiveness schedule would
be derived from the points of tangency of such surfaces with three-dimensional budget surfaces for
various budget levels. It has also been emphasized
on several occasions that no single effectiveness
indicator would suffice to evaluate a welfare program.
With an effectiveness vector one would be required
to generate a family of cost-effectiveness schedules,
one for each component of the vector. The decision-
maker's problem in such a case becomes one of reconciling preference weightings with real trade-off
ratios, an issue to be dealt with in general terms
in the next part of this chapter.

A cost-effectiveness schedule such as that shown
in Figure 1.5 is essentially a schedule of feasible
and efficient alternatives. Points off the schedule
are either unobtainable (U_2) or inefficient (U_1).
The origin (O_o) represents an initial "do nothing"
alternative.

In practice it may not be possible to have enough
data to generate, other than by heroic interpolation,
a continuous cost-effectiveness schedule, and the
analyst may have to deal with the sort of situation

FIGURE 1.4

Least Cost Input Combinations

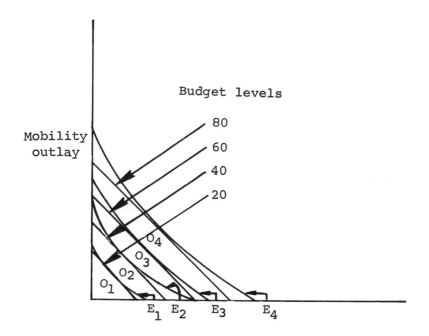

illustrated in Figure 1.6 where information is available on six different input combinations. It is
clear from Figure 1.6 that points U_1 and U_2 are inefficient, i.e., are dominated by superior points
where higher effectiveness can be obtained for similar costs. But the analyst has to fumble toward a
tentative cost-effectiveness schedule running through
0_1, 0_2, 0_3, and 0_4, with the part of the schedule
connecting these points filled in only by intelligent
guesstimates.

Clearly, the more information one has on the
whole curve the more one can say about the effect of
marginal cost changes in a particular program design.
Such information is more useful than knowledge only
of a few average relationships such as those shown

FIGURE 1.5

Income Support Cost-Effectiveness Schedule

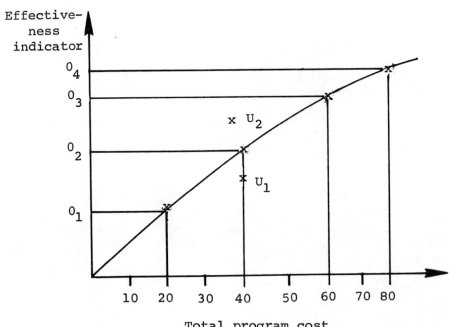

Total program cost
(millions of dollars)

in Figure 1.6. The advantage of operating with a
computer simulation model is that by a process of
iteration one can arrive at a large number of points
on the cost-effectiveness schedule for any particular
program design. This is especially useful when comparing the cost-effectiveness curves of entirely different program designs. Of course, the choice between alternative program designs may be very easy
if, say, one alternative is more effective than
another at every cost. In Figure 1.7a alternative 3
is of this nature and may be considered to dominate
alternatives 1 and 2. The situation may, however,
be much more complex. In Figure 1.7b the alternative
chosen will depend on the level of cost or effectiveness specified. If E_1 is all that is necessary in
terms of effectiveness, then program design 1 is
adequate; if E_2 is required, design 2 is best; and

FIGURE 1.6

Cost-Effectiveness Curves in a Situation
of Limited Information

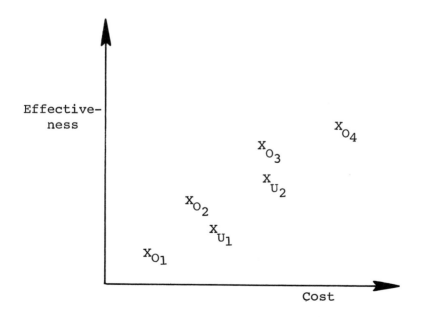

FIGURES 1.7a and 1.7b

Alternative Cost-Effectiveness
Configurations

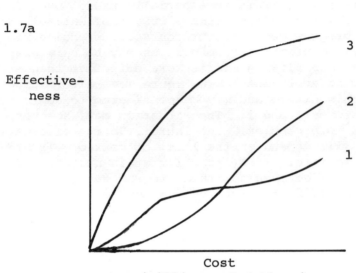

1.7a

Effective-
ness

3

2

1

Cost
(millions of dollars)

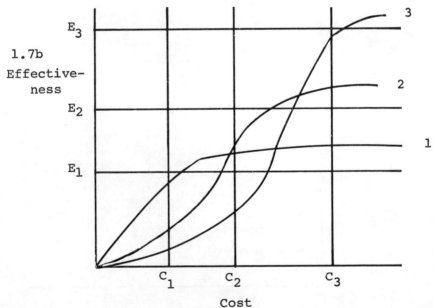

E_3

1.7b

Effective-
ness

E_2

E_1

3

2

1

C_1

C_2

C_3

Cost
(millions of dollars)

if E_3 is required, design 3 is the only alternative
despite its very high initial costs. Similarly, if
the budget constraint is specified as C_1, design 1
is preferable; at C_2 there is little to choose between
designs 1 and 2 (this is where marginal information
is crucial);* and if C_3 is available, design 3 becomes the best alternative.

The situation is, of course, further complicated
by the presence of uncertainty, and it may be necessary to employ some of the techniques discussed previously to arrive at a ranking of alternatives.
L. D. Attaway has approached this problem by representing cost, effectiveness, and contingencies in a
three-dimensional diagram, thus arriving at a surface
relating the three factors. For a specified contingency and, say, cost, one can then read off predicted
effectiveness, etc.[84]

The Opportunity Costs or Trade-Offs
Between Programs

The objective at the highest level of aggregation (not to say aspiration) of a program budgeting
approach to public expenditure is to make explicit
the opportunity costs--in monetary terms, for program
comparison in which cost-benefit analysis has been
employed; in real terms, for program comparison in
which cost-effectiveness has been employed--of alternative packages of resource allocation decisions.

Monetary Opportunity Costs

Monetary opportunity cost may be defined as the
net benefit foregone by undertaking a particular program or part thereof instead of an alternative program
or part thereof. For a package of programs all of
which have costs and outputs expressed in monetary
terms, it is possible, in principle, to define an

---

*Presumably, one would choose design 2 by looking
at the first derivative at cost C_2. It would clearly
be preferable to have a design that offers sharply
increased effectiveness should additional funds become available.

optimal total volume and allocation pattern of public
expenditure. Such an optimum is attained if all programs in which net benefit is positive are undertaken
and if all such programs are extended to the point
at which net benefit is maximized. Consider the
optimal allocation of resources between two programs
displayed in Figures 1.8a and 1.8b. Net benefit is
maximized by extending each program up to volume AD
and EH, respectively, and is given by the sum of the
two rectangles of net benefit, ABCD and EFGH. Sup-
pose now that a decision is taken to reallocate resources from program 2 to program 1 in such a way
that program 1 can now be extended only to AD_1 and
program 2 can be extended to EH_1. The opportunity
cost in monetary terms of such a suboptimal resource
allocation is given by the potential maximum net benefit (ABCD + EFGH) minus the total net benefit attained under the new pattern of resource allocation
$(AB_1C_1D_1 + EF_1G_1H_1)$.

It is, of course, true that it may be considered
very unlikely that sufficient information will be
available on the net benefits attributable to a set
of different program magnitudes to make such opportunity cost computations possible over the range of
public programs amenable to cost-benefit analysis.
But the notion of opportunity costs lies at the heart
of a rational approach to public resource allocation,
and the final stage in resource allocation in the
set of programs amenable to cost-benefit analysis
must be such a general appraisal--albeit an approximate appraisal--of the extent to which maximum net
benefit is attained by the volume and allocation pattern of the scarce public resources so disbursed.
In a political real world where it is not unreasonable
to imagine a suboptimal allocation of resources, the
point of attempting an approximation of the extent
of the default or shortfall from maximum net benefit
is to make explicit the social opportunity costs of
political decisions.

Real Opportunity Costs

Real opportunity cost or trade-off computation
as the final stage in analysis of programs amenable
to cost-effectiveness analysis relates in a specific

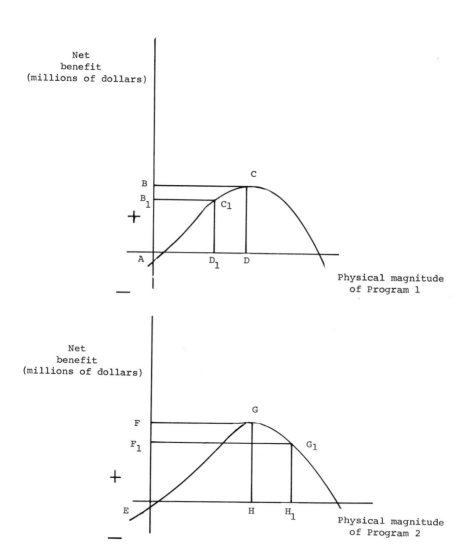

FIGURES 1.8a and 1.8b

Trade-Offs Under Cost-Benefit Analysis,
Programs 1 and 2

manner--quite apart, from the point of view of the
analyst, from any notion of a social optimum--the
decline in the physical effectiveness indicator of
program 1 and the increase in the (different) physical effectiveness indicator of program 2.

Imagine a two-program situation for each of
which a continuous cost-effectiveness schedule has
been generated. Imagine also an initial budgetary
allocation to the two programs and a hypothetical
decision to allocate (as a first control allocation)
the budget as shown by points A and B in Figures 1.9a
and 1.9b. If a small reduction in the budget to program A is now made and these funds transferred to
program B, the diminution in the effectiveness attainment of program A (ΔA) can be demonstrated, as
can the corresponding increase in the effectiveness
attainment of program B (ΔB) that the released budget funds make possible. In other words, the real
trade-off ratios between the two programs at various
levels of effectiveness are made explicit by such
analysis. If such information is then translated
into a production possibility curve for the two programs, showing the real trade-off ratios or marginal
rate of substitution between the programs for a given
budgetary allocation to the two programs, the optimum
choice then emerges from the tangency of the community
preference indifference curve for the two programs
and the production possibility curve, at point P in
Figure 1.10. An alternative way of describing such
an optimum would be to require that each program be
extended to the point where the "value" of marginal
effectiveness--the increment in effectiveness attributable to a unit increment in expenditure on the pro-
gram--is the same for all programs.* The crucial
point from the analyst's point of view is, of course,
the fact that the specification of the community indifference curve--or its equivalent, the specification of the values attributable to marginal effective-

---

*In general if the marginal effectiveness of the
ith program is defined as de_i/de then the optimal
resource allocation condition specifies that the
value of de_1/dc equal the value of $de_2/dc = \ldots =$
the value of de_n/dc.

FIGURES 1.9a and 1.9b

Trade-Offs Under
Cost-Effectiveness Analysis, Programs A and B

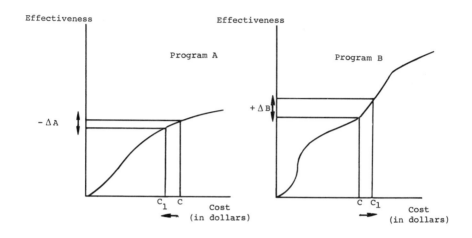

FIGURE 1.10

Trade-Offs Under
Cost-Effectiveness Analysis,
Programs A and B Compared

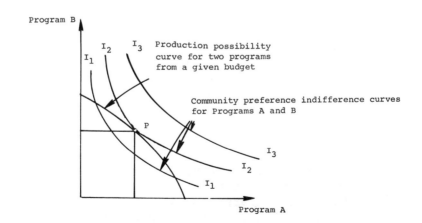

ness--is quite beyond the ken of the analyst and may
be seen as a purely political decision. In cost-
benefit analysis, on the other hand, it was possible
for the analyst to specify, in principle, monetary
opportunity costs for different resource allocation
patterns. Even in this latter case, however, the
analyst is working with terms of reference, such as
the social rate of discount, that are politically
specified.

    Returning to the question of real opportunity
costs, the analysis can clearly be extended to a
wider range of programs; in the case of three programs the final optimum would be at the tangency of
the production possibility surface of the three programs for a given budgetary allocation, with the community indifference surface with respect to the same
three programs. The procedure can be seen as operating first at the interdepartmental level, in the
case where it deals with overall budgetary allocation
between departmental program aggregates; second at
the interprogram level, in the case where it deals
with budgetary allocation to various programs within
a department--an example is the disease control program analyses carried out by the Department of Health,
Education and Welfare in the United States, which
has provided explicit information on the trade-offs
between different disease control programs--and third
at the intraprogram level, in the case where it
deals with allocation between component parts of a
particular program. In general the provision of
real trade-off information may be considered more
likely to be attained first at the intraprogram,
second at the interprogram, and finally at the interdepartmental levels.

    The situation is, of course, complicated by
multidimensional measures of effectiveness and involves in such cases a family of cost-effectiveness
curves for each program. As an example of this problem, consider the case of allocating resources to
alternative means of attaining a program objective
in the field of welfare. By allocating resources in
different ways--i.e., with different design configura-
tions--for a welfare program, a series of effectiveness vectors can be generated that indicate the real
trade-offs between different components of the effec-

tiveness vector. As above, these real trade-offs
can be seen as the marginal rates of substitution
between the different components of the vector. The
theoretical optimum design choice is, then, that
welfare program that is defined as the point of
tangency of the production possibility surface (given
by the marginal rates of substitution) and the community indifference surface for the component parts
of the welfare vector.

2

PROGRAM BUDGETING
IN RELATION TO
INCOME SUPPORT PROGRAMS

INTRODUCTION

The public sector is not homogeneous but typically includes a diverse range of programs across which the analytical methods associated with program budgeting, cost-effectiveness analysis and cost-benefit analysis, are differentially applicable. The balance of this study focuses exclusively on the applicability of these analytical methods to income support programs, where the primary program objectives are conceived in redistributive (transfer) terms and where outputs are defined not in monetary terms but in terms of a set of physical effectiveness indicators. The analytical approach employed is thus cost-effectiveness analysis. In the balance of this chapter the nature of the various income support program designs to be considered is elaborated and a set of alternative approaches to the analysis of income support programs examined. Chapter 3 sets out in detail the particular approach employed in the analysis of income support programs in this study.

THE NATURE OF THE INCOME
SUPPORT OPTIONS CONSIDERED

The likelihood of significant reforms of welfare policy has been increased over the last decade in both Canada and the United States by the happy coin-

cidence of will and means, of both a new concern over
poverty and a comparative affluence to make possible
steps toward its alleviation if not elimination.
Strategy has been directed both to building up the
earning capacity of low income groups and to assuring
every family an adequate standard of living regardless of its earning capacity.[1] On the question of
income support concern is now focused not only on
income interruption but on the whole issue of income
inadequacy or deficiency, and a variety of devices
has been suggested to provide a minimum income floor
either for particular groups in society or on a universal basis. Concern is directed in this work to
three such income support devices: the negative income tax (NIT), the universal demogrant (UD), and
children's allowances (CA). The nature of each of
these programs will be examined in turn.

The Negative Income Tax Approach (NIT)

The negative income tax, or perhaps less ob-
scurely, income subsidy approach, operates through
the existing personal income tax mechanism and takes
two general forms. In the first an official minimum
income level would be established and payments to an
individual or family used to make up all or part of
the deficiency between actual income and the official
minimum. The second, more modest, approach emphasizes the inability of the poor to take advantage of
personal deductions and exemptions in the present
income tax structure. In the Canadian income tax
system, for instance, a married couple with three
children has personal and children's exemptions to-
taling $2,900 and a standard medical deduction of
$100, giving a total exempt income of $3,000. If
the family has no income, then of course its exemptions are of no use under the present system.
Equally the tax payable by a family with three children and an income of $3,000 would be the same--
zero--as that payable by a family with eight children
also receiving a total income of $3,000. To correct
this lack of symmetry and equity in the tax structure,
the second approach suggests the payment to individuals or families of all or a portion of unused exemp-

tions. Both approaches incorporate incentives to recipients to seek further earnings from work.

Both approaches to the NIT have three basic
variables. Each has a guaranteed minimum level of
income, a "tax" rate at which government payments or
allowances are reduced for each dollar of increase in
before-allowance income, and a break-even level of
earned income at which the allowance payment from the
government is reduced to zero. The magnitude of two
of the variables will determine the magnitude of the
third, and NIT plans differ to the extent that the
three magnitudes differ. In effect there is a basic
allowance or income guarantee that the eligible individual or family unit may claim from the government
if there is zero income from other sources. There
is also an offsetting tax, which every recipient of
the allowance must pay on his other income. The net
benefit to the recipient is the basic allowance less
the offsetting tax. While the regular or positive
income tax allows the government to share in a family's earnings when those earnings exceed a minimum
that depends on the number and magnitude of allow-
able deductions, the NIT obliges the government to
provide benefits and thus to share in any shortfalls
of family income similarly, if not necessarily identically, calculated.

All NIT schemes are income-tested and are thus
defined as selective as distinct from universal
schemes, which are not income-tested. NIT schemes
may, however, be limited to particular sections of
the population, e.g., the aged and/or children, and
are defined in this limited sense as partial as distinct from general schemes, for which all families,
subject to an income test, are eligible.

Figure 2.1 illustrates the operation of a general NIT scheme that provides a basic allowance of
$2,000 and an offsetting tax rate (NIT rate) of 50
percent. These two variables determine break-even
income at $4,000. Positive tax liability is assumed
to begin above break-even-point income.

Some examples of proposed general NIT schemes
are set out below. J. Tobin[2] suggests payment by
the income tax administration of $400 per family mem-
ber to a recipient if his family has no income from
any other source; a couple with three children would

therefore receive $2,000. The subsidy would be re-
duced by 33 1/3 cents on every dollar the family
earns, the work incentive being that the family improves its position by two-thirds of every earned
dollar. At an income of $1,200 per person the sub-
sidy would become zero, and above that level the
family would pay taxes in the conventional manner.

The E. E. Schwartz[3] proposal is similar but incorporates an ex-ante feature: any family or individual whose anticipated income falls below a predetermined minimum would receive a subsidy--to be
called a "family security benefit"--for the amount
of the difference. The official minimum would be
related to price and productivity indexes. As a
work incentive feature Schwartz would permit the
partial retention of earnings but would reduce the
family security benefit by a percentage that increased
as earned income rose.

R. J. Lampman suggests several alternatives.[4]
His first option applies a flat NIT rate of 50 percent to the difference between a family's total income and a predetermined poverty-line income. Partial retention of earnings from work would be per-

FIGURE 2.1

The Operation of a General Negative Income Tax

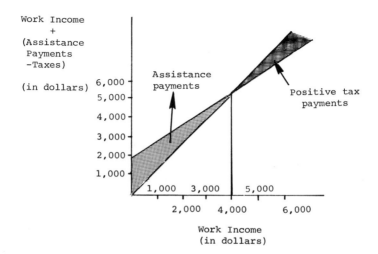

mitted as a work incentive. The payment of 100 percent of the difference between actual income and
poverty-line income is rejected by Lampman on grounds
of cost and adverse work incentives. Lampman's second and third options operate via tax exemptions.
In the first, families and individuals with incomes
below the level at which income tax is payable would
be permitted to claim a flat 14 percent of their unused exemptions and deductions. In the second, a
scale of progressive negative tax rates from 14 percent to 40 percent is suggested, the rate increasing
with the amount of unused exemptions.

M. Friedman[5] suggests either a proportional
negative tax rate, say of 50 percent of unused exemptions, or a progressive set of rates similar to that
proposed by Lampman.

An interesting recent example of a partial NIT
proposal is the Family Assistance Program (FAP) proposed in the United States in the fall of 1969.[6]
The program is limited to families with at least one
child and has the following specifications. The
basic allowance is specified under the scheme as
follows: $500 for each of the first two family mem-
bers and $300 for each subsequent family member.
The basic allowance--guaranteed minimum income, in
effect--for a family of four with no other income
would thus be $1,600. Reflecting the Department of
Labor's concern over work incentives, assistance payments would remain constant for the first $720 of
annual work income (in effect, a NIT rate of zero)
and would be reduced by 50 cents for each dollar of
work income beyond $720 (a NIT rate of 50 percent).
A family of four would thus be eligible for assistance payments up to an annual income of $3,920.
Table 2.1 and Figure 2.2 illustrate this situation.
Positive tax liability is not shown.

There have been several proposals for a general
NIT scheme in Canada. One such proposal[7] suggests
the use of the unused exemptions approach. Exemptions would be defined more generously at $1,500 for
an individual, $2,500 for a couple, and $500 for
each child. A progressive scale of negative tax
rates based on unused exemptions would then be introduced, ranging from 50 percent on exemptions of
$4,000 and over down to 15 percent for unused exemp-

TABLE 2.1

Benefit Schedule for a Family of Four
(in dollars)

Earned Income	Assistance Payment	Total Income
0	1,600	1,600
720	1,600	2,320
1,000	1,460	2,400
1,500	1,210	2,710
2,000	960	2,960
2,500	710	3,210
3,000	460	3,460
3,500	210	3,710
3,920	0	3,920

FIGURE 2.2

Benefit Schedule for a Family of Four

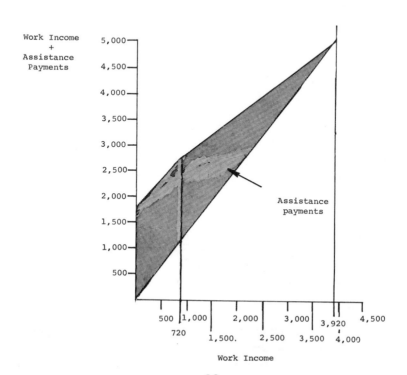

83

tions below $1,000. Special supplementary payments
were proposed for the elderly and others unable to
work.

The most recent proposal is that of the Special
Senate Committee on Poverty,[8] in which basic allowance levels, i.e., basic payment levels in the event
of zero income from other sources, are determined as
70 percent of computed "poverty lines"* for various
family sizes and are specified as $1,500 for a family
of one member, $2,500 for a family of two, $3,000
for a family of three, and so on by $500 increments
to an upper limit of $6,500 for a family of ten.
The NIT rate is specified at 70 percent, and the
break-even point for each family size--the point at
which NIT payments fall to zero as other income
rises--correspondingly determined as the quotient
of the basic allowance and the NIT rate. The specification of the basic allowance levels as 70 percent
of the prescribed poverty lines and the selection of
a NIT rate of 70 percent result in break-even points
that approximate the poverty lines for each family
size. The committee also recommended that no positive tax ought to be payable for a family below the
break-even point at which payments under the general
NIT scheme fall to zero.

The implications of the Senate Committee proposal for a family of four are set out in Figure
2.3 and Table 2.2. The present positive tax liability for a family of four is shown in the shaded
area in the diagram and the proposed new liability
by the dotted area. The logic of this recommendation
is clear. Under the present tax liability the family
of four would reach an effective break-even point at
an income of roughly $4,000, where NIT scheme pay-
ments (ab) are exactly matched by positive tax liability (bc).

A broad range of NIT schemes will be examined
in the model, including examples that, like the FAP
proposal in the United States, are limited to families with children, and the actual scheme proposed
in the Senate Committee report for Canada. The com-

---

*The nature of this and other approaches to pov-
erty measurement is dealt with in Chapter 3.

FIGURE 2.3

Senate Committee Proposal for
a Family of Four

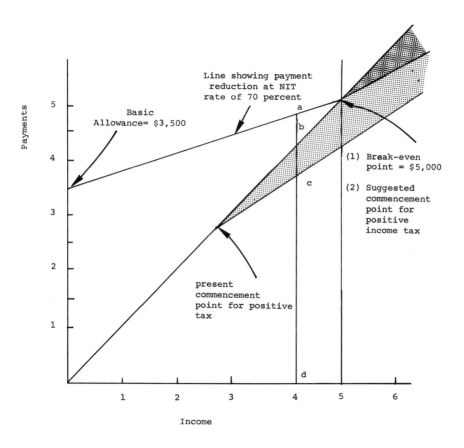

TABLE 2.2

Senate Committee Proposal for a Family of Four
(in dollars)

1 Other Income	2 Basic Allowance (adjusted at a NIT rate of 70 percent*)	3 Final Income Position (1 + 2)
0	3,500	3,500
250	3,325	3,575
500	3,150	3,650
1,000	2,800	3,800
1,500	2,450	3,950
2,000	2,100	4,100
2,500	1,750	4,250
3,000	1,400	4,400
3,500	1,050	4,550
4,000	700	4,700
4,500	350	4,850
5,000	0	5,000

*I.e., reduced by 70 percent of the increment in
other income, so that for the income increment from
$0 to $250, the zero income basic allowance of
$3,500 would be reduced by 70 percent of $250, or
$175, leaving a final income position of $250 +
($3,500 - $175) = $250 + $3,325 = $3,575.

plete list of NIT program designs examined is set
out in Chapter 3.

The Universal Demogrant
Approach (UD)

The UD approach operates on a much broader
scale than the NIT, providing not merely income supplements to those whose incomes fall below an established minimum but a uniform payment to all regardless of means. The UD might or might not be included
in income for tax purposes. If it were so included,

the UD would be partially or wholly recouped from those paying tax. Indeed the description of the NIT as involving a basic allowance, an offsetting tax on earnings, and a corresponding net benefit would equally fit a taxable UD system. The actual administrative details would be slightly more complicated, since everyone would have to receive the basic allowance; those whose total income including the demogrant fell into the taxable bracket as a result, or whose incomes were taxable before receipt of the demogrant, would of course pay taxes for the first time or more taxes, respectively.

The general UD approach, for which the entire population is eligible, is to be distinguished from the widely accepted partial UD approach in which payments are limited to particular groups, such as the elderly, children, and the handicapped. The children's allowances approach, considered in the next part of this section, is, in its form unrelated to family income, an example of a partial UD. The balance of discussion in this part is confined to the general UD approach.

Figure 2.4 illustrates the operation of a flat-rate general UD program, providing a flat rate of $2,000 to all families regardless of means. The break-even point where the UD is exactly offset by positive tax payments is shown at $5,800.

Formal proposals for a UD system have not been as fashionable in recent years as for a NIT. Most of the formal schemes were set out in the 1940s and 1950s following Lady Rhys-Williams' initial suggestions in 1943.[9] The basic principle of the initial scheme was the payment to each man, woman, and child of a "social dividend" that would replace all other welfare payments; it would be payable weekly and would be untaxed. The scheme was to be financed by a proportional income tax. As a work incentive the scheme required employable persons to be willing to accept suitable work as an additional eligibility condition. J. E. Meade's scheme[10] is a variant on the initial proposal, suggesting weekly allowances for adults of 25 shillings ($5) and 10 shillings ($2) for children; the whole again to be financed by an increase in the standard (proportional) rate of income tax. A further variant was suggested by the

British Liberal Party in 1950.[11] This scheme would
provide a uniform allowance of 12 shillings ($2.40)
per week to each adult and child and supplementary
benefits to the sick, unemployed, aged, and widowed.
In effect the scheme would combine a low universal
demogrant with supplementary partial demogrants to
selected groups. The scheme would be financed by a
moderate increase in income tax.

A formal proposal was made in 1965 by D. B.
Smith[12] to replace the entire structure of social
welfare payments in Canada by a UD system. Under the
proposal each adult would receive a demogrant of
$1,000 and each child, $200, the whole to be financed
by a 40 percent income tax; the demogrant would be
included in income for tax purposes. More recently
R. W. Crowley and D. A. Dodge[13] have advocated and
costed several possible taxable UD schemes for Canada.

FIGURE 2.4

The Operation of
a General Universal Demogrant System

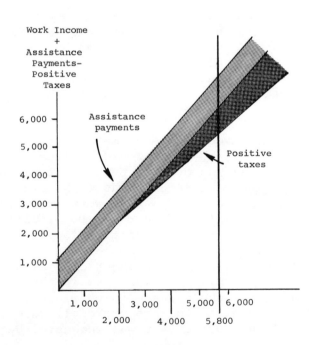

There have been no formal governmental proposals for
a UD scheme in Canada, almost certainly because of
the generally high cost of the approach and the associated implications for major reform of the personal
income tax structure, as in the proposals referred
to above. In the model, however, a set of possible
UD alternatives for Canada are designed and examined,
the object of their inclusion being to demonstrate
the implications of the absence of income-testing
as an eligibility criterion in income support schemes
designed for the population at large rather than for
specific groups in that population.

The Children's Allowances
Approach (CA)

While the NIT is a relatively new idea, that of
CA is an old one and in many nations, including Canada, quite an old practice as well. CA has been defined as "systematic payments made to families with
dependent children, either by employers or by the
government, for the primary purpose of promoting
the welfare of such children. . . . In essence, they
constitute a means of redistributing income in such
a way as to benefit the child-rearing portion of a
nation's population."[14]
In the usual form in which payments are unrelated
to family income, CA amounts to a partial universal
demogrant and, for the specified group of recipients,
may be illustrated diagrammatically in exactly the
same manner as the general UD option. In many cases,
of course, the current Canadian situation being an
example, CA payments are not taxable and therefore
make no difference to positive tax liability. (See
Figure 2.4.)
More than sixty nations currently have a program
of CA. The programs presently in operation are of
two main types, universal or employment-related. A
universal system covers all families in the country
in question, regardless of employment status and income.* Canada is one of the countries that employ a

---

*Specifically in relation to CA, the term "uni-
versal" is broadened in this descriptive section to

universal system. In the majority of countries, however, the programs are employment-related, i.e.,
eligibility is dependent upon the existence of an employment relationship, and unemployed persons or
those working in an industry or occupation not covered
are ineligible for benefits. Some schemes (e.g., in
France and the Netherlands), although employment-related, do make some provision for the unemployed, and
a few of the programs extend to the self-employed.

Most countries pay benefits beginning with the
first child. Some, e.g., the United Kingdom, pay
only with respect to the second child and subsequent
children, and there are instances where benefits com-
mence with the third or fourth child. A few countries limit eligibility to a specified--usually gen-
erous--number of children, but, by contrast, some
programs provide special supplemental payments for
large families.

There are many variations on the rate and form
of allowance, the most usual form being one in which
payments increase for second and subsequent children
--the additional expenses argument prevailing over
the economies of scale argument! There is, however,
at least one example (Yugoslavia) of what might be
called a regressive scale of payments, whereby payments are actually reduced for additional children.

There are many and varied solutions to the problems of regional disparities and cost of living increases, but there do not seem to be at present any
schemes in which an automatic "productivity escalator"
clause is included. Most countries provide for payment on a monthly basis.

There are many different financing patterns,
but two general basic procedures emerge: where a
universal program is used, benefits are generally
financed from general tax revenues; in employment-
related schemes, employers are generally required to
pay uniform percentages of payrolls to a compensation

---

cover both employment status and income. Since employment-related schemes are not considered as policy
options for Canada, the term "universal" is used in
the balance of the study exclusively to mean schemes
not subject to an income test.

fund that disburses allowances or to pay employees directly. In a number of programs governmental revenues supplement employer contributions--in a few
cases self-employed persons are required to contribute; occasionally the schemes are partially financed
by employee contributions.

The redistributive effects of the various types
of CA programs differ considerably. Leaving aside
for the moment the employment-related schemes, in
considering CA as part of an anti-poverty program the
question arises of what effect such a scheme would
have on vertical redistribution, i.e., would the
scheme significantly diminish inequality of income
distribution?

Consider three schemes: the first selective or
income-tested, the second universal with allowance
payments taxable, the third universal with allowance
payments nontaxable; all three schemes are assumed to
be financed by an identical budgetary allocation
from general tax revenue, say $100 million. Any CA
scheme financed from general revenues may be assumed
to be vertically redistributive by definition, since
the incidence (distribution of burden) of the tax
system is progressive[15] and the lower income groups
have larger families and constitute the major recipients under the scheme. Of the three possible
frameworks set out above, however, the least redistributive would be a universal scheme in which allowances are not included in taxable income, since benefits would be paid to families in all income groups
and none of the total payments would be recouped
through income taxation. Slightly more redistributive would be a universal scheme in which allowance
payments were included in taxable income; in this
case larger allowances would be possible (given the
fixed budgetary commitment), since a portion of the
allowances going to those groups paying income tax
would be recouped--for instance, a family receiving
a $10 payment monthly for one child and subject to a
marginal tax rate of 50 percent would receive net
over the year only $60, i.e., the $120 universal payment minus $60 increased income tax liability. Were
it estimated that, say, $20 million would be recov-
erable through increased tax liability, a correspondingly larger initial allocation could be made, so

increasing the universal allowance and the redistributive effect, with the understanding that the
net costs would still come to $100 million. Most
effective in terms of redistributing income vertically
would be an income-tested scheme in which allowances
were paid only to those families with an annual income below a specified qualifying level. If the $100
million were to be allocated solely to those families,
say in the lowest one-fifth income group, the level
of payment per child could clearly be much higher
than in the case of a universal payment.*

Unlike universal CA programs financed from general tax revenues, employment-related programs have
a redistributive effect that is largely horizontal.
The rather high benefits paid under the French programs are financed by a 11.5 percent payroll tax on

---

*The question of tax exemptions or credits for
children is neglected in the discussion. For any of
the above schemes the abolition of income tax exemptions and the deployment of the consequent increase
in income tax revenue as a means of increasing payment
levels under the CA scheme would markedly increase
the redistributive impact of the scheme, since income
tax exemptions presently operate as a regressive CA
scheme, being of greater economic significance the
higher one's income and, consequently, marginal tax
rate. For a taxpayer subject to a highest marginal
tax rate of 20 percent, a $300 child exemption--as
in Canada--is worth $60. For a taxpayer subject to
a highest marginal rate of, say, 60 percent, that
same exemption is worth $180! Income tax exemptions
therefore operate as supplementary CA, but as a regressive supplement that diminishes the redistributive impact of the overall scheme.

Were tax exemptions to be replaced by tax credits, whereby each taxpayer would be given a specified
tax credit for each child--usually an amount derived
by taking the lowest income tax rate as a percentage
of the previous exemption; at a lowest tax rate of,
say, 10 percent and an exemption of $300 as in Can-
ada, this would imply tax credits of $30 per child--
the effect of the credits would be that of a distributionally neutral supplement to a CA scheme.

employers. This tax is apparently treated as an addition to corporate taxation that can be passed forward to consumers in the form of higher prices. The ultimate incidence of the payroll tax is therefore likely to be very similar to that of a general sales tax, thus effectively offsetting in whole or in part the benefits to families who have to pay higher prices for goods and services purchased. A general sales tax without food and similar exemptions will certainly have a regressive incidence, the larger burden of the tax falling upon low income families, and the best that can be said about the French method is that it redistributes income from lower income groups without children (who finance the scheme through the passing forward of the payroll tax) to those with children (whose net benefits under the scheme equal the gross benefits received minus increased indirect tax liability). Only universal CA schemes, financed from general revenue, are considered as interesting options in the balance of this study.

The existing CA scheme (covering family allowances and youth allowances) in Canada takes the classic untaxable partial universal demogrant form. Payments under the family allowances scheme are at a monthly rate of $6 for each child unter ten years and $8 for each child over ten years and under sixteen years. Under the youth allowances component, payments are made at a monthly rate of $10 for each child aged sixteen and seventeen years. Payments under both components are excluded from income for computation of positive income tax liability, and payments are unrelated to family income, varying only with the number and age of children.

Under the reform proposed in a White Paper[16] the new system, to be called the Family Income Security Plan (FISP 1), covers only the family allowances component of the existing system and retains the CA format. Payments are, however, proposed to be a function not only of the number and age of children but also of family income; further, such payments are to be included in income for computation of positive income tax liability. The result is a somewhat curious hybrid scheme, which, despite its CA format, has aspects of a partial NIT scheme limited to families with children.

The details of the proposal are set out in Table
2.3 and illustrated in Figures 2.5a and 2.5b.

A monthly payment of $16 for each child under
sixteen years is to be made to families whose income
is below $4,500. This payment is reduced by $1 each
month for each $500 annual increment in family in-
come, reaching a minimum of $5 each month for each
child for a family income level between $9,501 and
$10,000. No payments are to be made to families
whose income exceeds $10,000. Figure 2.5a illustrates
the stepped diminution in rate of payment, for a
family with one child and a family with two children
respectively, as a function of family income.

Although the basic form remains that of CA, the
system of diminished payments according to income introduces some similarity to a partial NIT scheme
limited to families with children. Specifically the
proposal implies--if one considers a family with one
child that moves discretely across the full specified
ranges, i.e., from $4,500 to $5,000, etc.--the NIT

TABLE 2.3

Benefits Payable Under the Family Income
Security Plan (FISP 1)
(in dollars)

Income	Monthly Benefit (1 child)	Annual Benefit (1 child)	Annual Benefit (2 children)
Up to 4,500	16	192	284
4,501 - 5,000	15	180	360
5,001 - 5,500	14	168	336
5,501 - 6,000	13	156	312
6,001 - 6,500	12	144	288
6,501 - 7,000	11	132	264
7,001 - 7,500	10	120	240
7,501 - 8,000	9	108	216
8,001 - 8,500	8	96	192
8,501 - 9,000	7	84	168
9,001 - 9,500	6	72	144
9,501 - 10,000	5	60	120
10,001 and over	0	0	0

FIGURES 2.5a and 2.5b

Schedule of Declining Payments Under FISP 1

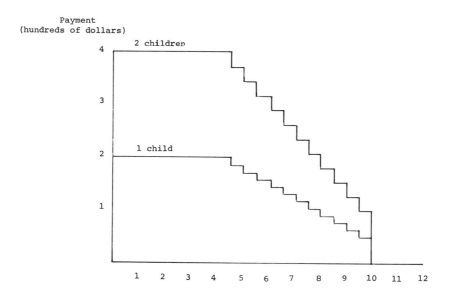

Negative Income Tax Aspect of FISP 1

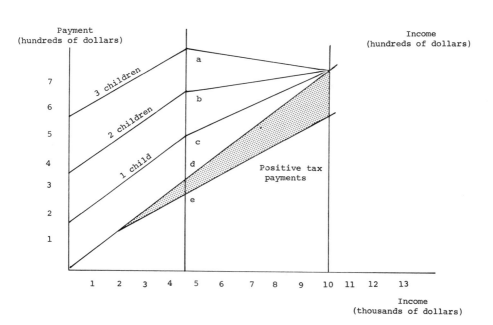

rate is effectively 2.4 percent for each $500 income
increase up to $10,000; the last relevant increment,
from $10,001 to $10,500, implies a NIT rate of 12
percent. These rates increase by the full amount of
the first set of rates for each additional child, so
that, e.g., for a family with two children the NIT
rate is constant at 4.8 percent up to an income of
$10,000 and increases to 24 percent for the last in-
crement to $10,500. For a family with three children
the corresponding rates are 6.2 percent and 36 percent. The problem, of course, is that family incomes
do not always move conveniently in $500 jumps, and
increments of less than $500 imply correspondingly
higher NIT rates. If, e.g., a family with one child
moves from an income of $4,500 to one of $4,600 the
effective NIT rate is 12 percent, etc.

Figure 2.5b illustrates the NIT aspect of the
scheme for families with up to three children. The
final net income position of a family will be the
aggregate of original gross work income and FISP payments minus income tax assessed on that aggregate.
The shaded portion of Figure 2.5b covering positive
tax payments is simply illustrative and demonstrates
that, e.g., for a family with two children and an
income of $4,500 the final net income position is
work income (df) + FISP payments (bd) - positive income tax (de).

The original FISP 1 proposal will be examined
as one possible mode of income support reform in
Canada. The proposals that finally reached Parliament in the form of Bill C-264[17] will also be examined
and will be referred to as FISP 2. The features of
FISP 2 are described below and set out in Figures
2.6a and 2.6b and Tables 2.4a and 2.4b.

The revised program incorporates the present
youth allowances category, but abandons the present
age categories for family and youth allowances, and
creates two new beneficiary categories--children below twelve years and children from twelve up to and
including children of seventeen years.

For the first category the maximum payment is
established at $15 up to an income (for a one-child
family) of $4,500. Payments are reduced by 33 cents
monthly, or $3.96 annually, for each $100 annual income increment, providing an income break-even point

at $7,500. The stepped function showing the rela-
tion of payments to income is much smoother than in
FISP 1 (and is shown in Figure 2.6a, for scale reasons, as a continuous function). The implicit NIT
rate for a family with one child is 3.96 percent for
income increments across the full $100 intervals,
except at the cut-off point where the implicit rate
for a further $100 income increment is 61.20 percent.

Where there is more than one child, the payments
are derived as multiples of the previously listed
payments to one child, but according to altered income eligibility levels. In effect the income level
at which payments become a diminishing function of
income is raised one $500 notch for each additional
child, so that payments are not reduced until family
income reaches $5,000 in the case of two children,
$5,500 in the case of three children, etc., and the
cut-off points are correspondingly increased to
$8,000, $8,500, etc. The payment for each child for

FIGURE 2.6a

Benefits Payable Under FISP 2

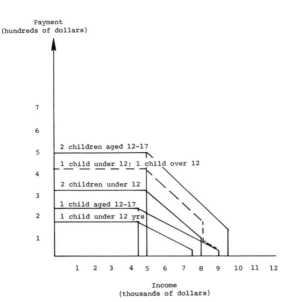

a family in the nth income category is derived by
taking the payment for one child in the n - 1th income category in the one-child case.

The implicit NIT rate for income increments
across the full $100 interval is constant at 7.92
percent for a family with two children, except at
the cut-off point where the rate rises to a devas-
tating 122.4 percent. So for families with three
children the implicit rate is constant at 11.88 percent up to the cut-off point; for families with four
children the rate is 15.84 percent, etc.

For children aged twelve to seventeen years the
maximum payment is $20, again payable up to an annual
family income of $4,500. The reduction rate is the
same as in the previous case, providing a break-even
income of $9,000. The procedure for dealing with
more than one child is also the same, the eligibility
level for maximum payment, and the break-even point,
rising by $500 for each child beyond the first. The
implicit NIT rates are also the same as in the first
case.*

Payments under both categories are not to be
taxed, and authority is provided for adjustments in
benefit levels by Order in Council according to consumer price index changes.

───────────

*It is not absolutely clear in the text of the
bill how a mixed family would be treated. The most
reasonable interpretation for a family with, say,
one child below twelve years and one child above
twelve years would seem to be that the aggregate payment be determined up to cut-off income for the
child below twelve by adding the contributions payable to one child in each category according to the
income eligibility level applicable to two children,
i.e., up to an income level of $8,000, beyond which
point payments would be determined according to the
payment schedule for one child above twelve, i.e.,
up to a final cut-off point of $9,000. The family
would thus start by receiving $420 ($180 + $240) as
basic payment, an additional $178.44 ($61.20 +
$117.24) at an income level of $8,000, $97.44 for the
next increment in income to $8,100, and so on to a
break-even income of $9,000.

FIGURE 2.6b

Benefits Payable Under FISP 2

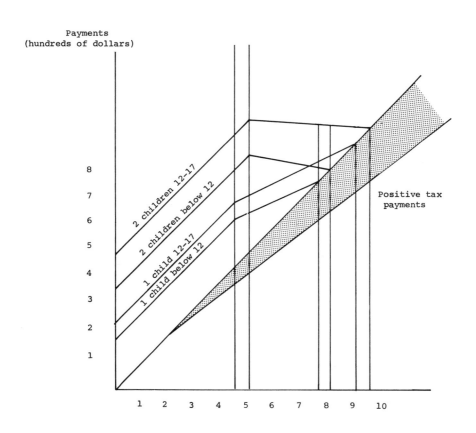

Payments
(hundreds of dollars)

8
7
6
5
4
3
2
1

2 children 12-17
2 children below 12
1 child 12-17
1 child below 12

Positive tax
payments

1 2 3 4 5 6 7 8 9 10

Income
(thousands of dollars)

TABLE 2.4a

Benefits Payable Under FISP 2 (Children Under Twelve Years)
(in dollars)

Income	Monthly Benefit (1 child)	Annual Benefit (1 child)	Income	Annual Benefit (2 children)
Up to 4,500	15.00	180.00	Up to 5,000	360.00
4,501 - 4,600	14.67	176.04	5,001 - 5,100	352.08
4,601 - 4,700	14.34	172.08	5,101 - 5,200	344.16
4,701 - 4,800	14.01	168.12	5,201 - 5,300	336.24
4,801 - 4,900	13.68	164.16	5,301 - 5,400	328.22
4,901 - 5,000	13.35	160.20	5,401 - 5,500	320.40
5,001 - 5,100	13.02	156.24	5,501 - 5,600	312.48
5,101 - 5,200	12.69	152.28	5,601 - 5,700	304.56
5,201 - 5,300	12.36	148.32	5,701 - 5,800	296.64
5,301 - 5,400	12.03	144.36	5,801 - 5,900	288.72
5,401 - 5,500	11.70	140.40	5,901 - 6,000	280.80
5,501 - 5,600	11.37	136.44	6,001 - 6,100	272.88
5,601 - 5,700	11.04	132.48	6,101 - 6,200	264.96
5,701 - 5,800	10.71	128.52	6,201 - 6,300	257.64
5,801 - 5,900	10.38	124.56	6,301 - 6,400	249.12
5,901 - 6,000	10.05	120.60	6,401 - 6,500	241.20
6,001 - 6,100	9.72	116.64	6,501 - 6,600	233.28
6,101 - 6,200	9.39	112.68	6,601 - 6,700	225.36
6,201 - 6,300	9.06	108.72	6,701 - 6,800	217.44
6,301 - 6,400	8.73	104.76	6,801 - 6,900	209.52
6,401 - 6,500	8.40	100.80	6,901 - 7,000	201.60
6,501 - 6,600	8.07	96.84	7,001 - 7,100	193.68
6,601 - 6,700	7.74	92.88	7,101 - 7,200	185.76
6,701 - 6,800	7.41	88.92	7,201 - 7,300	177.84
6,801 - 6,900	7.08	84.96	7,301 - 7,400	169.92
6,901 - 7,000	6.75	81.00	7,401 - 7,500	162.00
7,001 - 7,100	6.42	77.04	7,501 - 7,600	154.08
7,101 - 7,200	6.09	73.08	7,601 - 7,700	146.16
7,201 - 7,300	5.76	69.12	7,701 - 7,800	138.24
7,301 - 7,400	5.43	65.16	7,801 - 7,900	130.32
7,401 - 7,500	5.10	61.20	7,901 - 8,000	122.40
Over 7,500	0	0	Over 8,000	0

TABLE 2.4b

Benefits Payable Under FISP 2 (Children from Twelve to Seventeen
Years)
(in dollars)

Income	Monthly Benefit (1 child)	Annual Benefit (1 child)	Income	Annual Benefit (2 children)
Up to 4,500	20.00	240.00	Up to 5,000	480.00
4,501 - 4,600	19.67	236.04	5,001 - 5,100	472.08
4,601 - 4,700	19.34	232.08	5,101 - 5,200	464.16
4,701 - 4,800	19.01	228.12	5,201 - 5,300	456.24
4,801 - 4,900	18.68	224.16	5,301 - 5,400	448.32
4,901 - 5,000	18.35	220.20	5,401 - 5,500	440.40
5,001 - 5,100	18.02	216.24	5,501 - 5,600	432.48
5,101 - 5,200	17.69	212.28	5,601 - 5,700	424.56
5,201 - 5,300	17.36	208.32	5,701 - 5,800	416.64
5,301 - 5,400	17.03	204.36	5,801 - 5,900	408.72
5,401 - 5,500	16.70	200.40	5,901 - 6,000	400.80
5,501 - 5,600	16.37	196.44	6,001 - 6,100	392.88
5,601 - 5,700	16.04	192.48	6,101 - 6,200	384.96
5,701 - 5,800	15.71	188.52	6,201 - 6,300	377.04
5,801 - 5,900	15.38	184.56	6,301 - 6,400	369.12
5,901 - 6,000	15.05	180.60	6,401 - 6,500	361.20
6,001 - 6,100	14.72	176.64	6,501 - 6,600	353.28
6,101 - 6,200	14.39	172.68	6,601 - 6,700	345.36
6,201 - 6,300	14.06	168.72	6,701 - 6,800	337.44
6,301 - 6,400	13.73	164.76	6,801 - 6,900	329.52
6,401 - 6,500	13.40	160.80	6,901 - 7,000	321.60
6,501 - 6,600	13.07	156.84	7,001 - 7,100	313.68
6,601 - 6,700	12.74	152.88	7,101 - 7,200	305.76
6,701 - 6,800	12.41	148.92	7,201 - 7,300	297.84
6,801 - 6,900	12.08	144.96	7,301 - 7,400	289.92
6,901 - 7,000	11.75	141.00	7,401 - 7,500	282.00
7,001 - 7,100	11.42	137.04	7,501 - 7,600	274.08
7,101 - 7,200	11.09	133.08	7,601 - 7,700	266.16
7,201 - 7,300	10.76	129.12	7,701 - 7,800	258.24
7,301 - 7,400	10.43	125.16	7,801 - 7,900	250.32
7,401 - 7,500	10.10	121.20	7,901 - 8,000	242.40
7,501 - 7,600	9.77	117.24	8,001 - 8,100	234.48
7,601 - 7,700	9.44	113.28	8,101 - 8,200	226.56
7,701 - 7,800	9.11	109.32	8,201 - 8,300	218.64
7,801 - 7,900	8.78	105.36	8,301 - 8,400	210.72
7,901 - 8,000	8.45	101.40	8,401 - 8,500	202.80
8,001 - 8,100	8.12	97.44	8,501 - 8,600	194.88
8,101 - 8,200	7.79	93.48	8,601 - 8,700	186.96
8,201 - 8,300	7.46	89.52	8,701 - 8,800	179.04
8,301 - 8,400	7.13	85.56	8,801 - 8,900	171.12
8,401 - 8,500	6.80	81.60	8,901 - 9,000	163.20
8,501 - 8,600	6.47	77.64	9,001 - 9,100	155.28
8,601 - 8,700	6.14	73.68	9,101 - 9,200	147.36
8,701 - 8,800	5.81	69.72	9,201 - 9,300	139.44
8,801 - 8,900	5.48	65.76	9,301 - 9,400	131.52
8,901 - 9,000	5.15	61.80	9,401 - 9,500	123.60

In sum, the income support alternatives examined
in the model are grouped into three major categories,
NIT, UD, and CA, with the FISP options straddling
both the NIT and CA approaches. All the options under the three heads can be further classified as
either partial or general, and each partial or general option further classified as universal or selective. Four groups of options thus emerge: first,
the partial universal options--a set of CA schemes
similar to the existing family and youth allowances
system; second, the partial selective options--a set
of NIT schemes limited to families with at least one
child after the fashion of the Family Assistance
Program in the United States, designated the CNIT
options, and the two FISP options; third, the general
universal options--a set of UD schemes; and, finally,
the general selective options--a set of NIT schemes,
designated the GNIT options.

INCOME SUPPORT ALTERNATIVES IN A PROGRAM
BUDGETING FRAMEWORK: THE SOCIAL
TECHNOLOGY OF THE REDISTRIBUTIVE PROCESS

Public policy in the "soft" areas of health,
education, and welfare is frequently formulated under
conditions of incomplete information, failure to consider important economic and social implications,
and failure to consider feasible alternatives. Scant
attempt is made ex-ante to explore policy implications
and alternatives, and there has been little effective
ex-post evaluation of program performance. With
specific regard to income support programs financed
from the progressive income tax, we are concerned
in a program budgeting framework with the attempt to
shed light on the contents of the "black box" into
which are poured inputs in the form of cash transfers,
and out of which comes a set of outputs, defined as
the specified characteristics of transfer recipients
changed in some way through transfer payments. The
set of relationships between inputs and outputs in
cash transfer programs we can refer to as the social
technology of the redistributive process.[18]
The requirements for information on the contents
of the black box in the redistributive process make

the case for modeling clear. The first major section
of this work on the nature of program budgeting offers a discussion and classification of models. We
now direct our attention to the specific problems
of modeling in the redistributive area. Any model
of the redistributive process, whether verbal or
mathematical, implicit or explicit, may be seen as
composed of components, variables, and relations.[19]
The components of redistributive systems may be seen
as major sectors, such as the government and household sectors, and as micro-units, such as individual
households or groups of households. The variables
in a model relate to components of the model, and
may be classified as state or status variables, which
describe the state of particular components at a
particular point in time (in a redistributive model
such variables would describe the pattern of income
distribution among households, work and spending behavior, etc.); input variables, which, along with
state variables, generate the behavior of components
(whereas state variables are intrinsic to the components, input variables are exogenous and refer to
the external influences brought to bear on the components in order to modify behavior; in the redistributive process, such input variables might include
a new income support program and set of positive tax
rates); and, finally, output variables, which refers
to what issues from or is generated by the model
components (in a redistributive model such output
variables would describe a modified pattern of income
distribution, changed work and spending habits, etc.).
If it is to generate behavior, a model of the redistributive process must also contain relationships,
which specify how the values of different variables
in the model are related to each other. Relationships are seen as identities or operating characteristics. The former are simply accounting or tauto-
logical statements used for convenience; an example
of such an identity in a NIT program would be the
identity that defines the transfer payment as the
basic allowance divided by the negative tax rate.
Operating characteristics are much more difficult
and interesting, and may be seen as relationships
specific to particular components that specify either
hypotheses or assumptions about how output variables

of the components are related to their state and input variables. An example of such an operating characteristic of a NIT model might be a work supply
function that postulates relationship among work effort as an output, the income and work effort of a
household or set of households as state variables,
and different NIT schemes as input variables. The
development of the social technology of the redistributive process basically involves the development
and verification of hypotheses about operating characteristics such as the work supply function.

In the redistributive process we are dealing
with one of the more inexact parts of a very inexact
science and with "quasi-laws"[20] as against exact physical laws. The justification for our postulating
operating characteristics of a redistributive model
will be that only those hypotheses will be offered
that appear more credible than any comparable alternative and that recommendations based on such hypotheses have a higher probability of proving more appropriate than actions carried out without any explicit model relationships. The operating characteristics of redistributive models may also be held
to be better than mere guesstimates. We explore in
the following pages four approaches to describing
and/or determining the operating characteristics of
redistributive models: qualitative examination, social experimentation, ex-post evaluation, and, finally, the method we shall endeavor to pursue in the
remainder of the study, simulation.

Qualitative Examination

By qualitative examination is understood what
might be called the traditional approach by which,
on the basis of such historical evidence as is available and the body of economic and social theory, an
analyst attempts a qualitative assessment of the implications of a particular redistributive policy.
The example chosen is from an attempt by the author
to assess rather quickly for policy purposes the
choice in Canada between extending the traditional
children's allowances program and introducing a Family
Assistance Program similar to that proposed by the
U.S. President for the United States in the fall of

1969 (and described in detail in the previous section).

Example

The Family Assistance Program (FAP) and Children's Allowances (CA); Relevance for Canada[21]

What is attempted is a brief comparative evaluation of two alternatives for Canada: first, a scheme such as FAP which would offer a negative income tax oriented guaranteed annual income of the order specified in the U.S. proposal to families with children, the gross cost of the scheme being of the order of $1 billion, the net cost working out to roughly $400 million—assuming that the scheme would replace present family and youth allowances (costing $600 in 1967-68); and, second, an improved children's and youth allowances program with allowances taxable costing gross $1.25 billion, an increase of $650 million which would permit increases in rates to $12 per month for each child aged 0-10 years, $14 per month for each child aged 10-16 years, and $16 per month as the Youth Allowance rate. The net cost could be as in the FAP scheme $400 million, given present Children's Allowances and Youth Allowances costs of $600 million, and assuming an average income tax rate on allowances of 20% which would recoup $250 million of the gross cost of $1.25 billion. It should be emphasized that these cost figures are extremely crude, and are intended to offer a rough basis for the comparison of two program alternatives—one selective, the other universal, costing the same amount.

The option of an income-tested children's scheme is not explored for two reasons: first, an income-tested children's allowance scheme using the same budgetary allotment as the two options above would

really amount to a variation on the theme
of FAP, with the available resources allocated simply according to the number of
children, ignoring the adult or adults in
the family; and, two, the issue of greatest
interest is the choice between universality (in the CA scheme) and selectivity (in
FAP).

Criteria for Evaluation

1. Economic Efficiency. This criterion
combines the two criteria of adequacy and
economy, and may be referred to as the
"cost-effectiveness" of the program. The
cost level has been specified at a net
figure of $400 million, and the problem be-
comes one of defining an index of effectiveness. Herein lies a problem. The usual
procedure here is to define as the index of
effectiveness the extent to which a dollar
of resources raised to finance the scheme
goes to diminish statistically defined poverty. For instance, the Economic Council
defined particular income levels as constituting minimum acceptable levels--these
levels being $1,500 for single persons,
and $2,500, $3,000, $3,500 and $4,000 for
families of two, three, four, and five,
respectively. Having specified minimum
subsistence income levels for various family sizes, below which families are defined
as living in poverty, the "poverty gap" or
income deficit in an aggregate sense is
then the difference between the sum of the
income of poor families if these families
in fact received the minimum specified subsistence income levels and the sum of the
actual incomes received by these families.
In the simplest sense, economic efficiency
or cost-effectiveness could then be defined
as 100 percent if each dollar raised to
finance the program in question found its
way directly to reducing the poverty gap
by one dollar.

How then do the two schemes measure up under this definition? FAP, which provides guaranteed minima well below specified minimum subsistence levels, and thus break-even incomes close to poverty levels, may be considered virtually 100 percent efficient or cost-effective.* Clearly, a universal children's allowance scheme compares poorly in this sense. Although low-income families, where, on average, the number of children is larger than in higher-income families, would tend to receive higher payments than higher-income families, the percentage of the total allotment in the program going to those defined as statistically poor would be well below 50 percent. . . .

. . . It is worth noting, as a further clarification of the disparity in economic efficiency between the NIT and CA approaches, specifically the FAP scheme and revised CA scheme outlined previously, the degree to which the two schemes fill the poverty gap in any particular case. For a family of, say, two adults and four children, two of the children aged from 0-10 years, two from 10-16 years, the FAP scheme, using U.S. proposed rates, would provide an annual family income of $2,100 (below the Economic Council poverty level of over $4,000), whereas the CA scheme proposed would provide only a total of $624 per annum. Supplementary provisions would thus have to continue at a much more generous rate under a CA scheme than under a scheme such as FAP.

As one extends payments under a NIT scheme up to the "near-poor" through more

---

*Note that the more comprehensive and generous NIT schemes are less than 100 percent efficient, many as low as 40 percent or 50 percent, in fact, because of the nature of a NIT scheme, which, in the attempt to preserve work incentives, provides payments up to break-even points well in excess of specified poverty levels.

generous NIT schemes with higher break-even
points (making, for purposes of comparison,
appropriate adjustments in CA payments),
the efficiency gap between the two schemes
diminishes--but almost entirely because of
the decline in efficiency of the NIT approach at higher break-even points; the
slight increase in efficiency of a (taxable)
CA scheme as payments increase and are
taxed at higher rates is not of great significance. The conclusion remains that for
any feasible program alternatives in the
NIT or CA framework, the economic efficiency
of the NIT alternative will be considerably
higher in every case.

The question is whether the definition
of economic efficiency is adequate. If one
chooses to define the objective of children-
oriented programs as improving the lot of
children in all income groups (on the defensible principle that families in virtually all income groups, certainly up to
the top 10 percent, could use payments under
a universal CA scheme to improve the welfare
of their children) then the criterion of
efficiency has to be defined quite differently, and the selective approach of FAP may
be seen as less efficient than the universal approach of CA. Clearly we are approaching a fundamental distinction between
the two schemes--a distinction which will
emerge more clearly after the discussion
of broader social and political factors--
that a NIT type of scheme is more efficient
in a specific, "war on poverty," vertically
redistributive sense, whereas a CA approach
is more efficient in a broader, horizon-
tally redistributive sense, redistributing
income essentially from the childless to
those with children. The CA approach, it
emerged however, can only be one part of
a poverty program, since it barely scratches
the surface of statistically defined poverty.

2. Other Economic Effects. (a) Effect on
work incentives: A NIT scheme of the modest
scale suggested in FAP would seem unlikely
to cause serious effects on work incentives.
The provisional evidence from New Jersey[22]
suggests no significant labor withdrawal
as a consequence of the various models in
the experiment. Nevertheless, a selective
scheme does have--according to the static
theory--a double disincentive effect on
work, one through the very fact of payment
in a zero work:zero income situation, the
second through the effect of a high tax
rate on first earnings. A universal scheme
has only the first of these effects, and
in this static sense the CA approach is
superior to FAP. There is now some support
for the view that welfare schemes of any
nature other than the traditional means-
tested hand-outs may in fact exercise a
positive effect on work effort, and the
whole issue of work incentives is now receiving less emphasis than in the initial
discussions on welfare programs.

(b) Effect on expenditure patterns:
In this case there seems little to choose
between the schemes. The first evidence
on the effect of NIT payments on expenditure patterns in New Jersey suggests
that the increases in income of the lower
income groups as a consequence of the
scheme is spent in much the same fashion
as increases in income among other income
groups. The available evidence on the
expenditure of children's allowances in
Canada suggests a wholly respectable expenditure pattern, and both proposals
would appear free from attack on the
grounds that the payments would be idly
dissipated.

How the Options are Perceived

3. Stigma Effects. The first evidence
from the New Jersey experiment suggests no

stigma effect in payments made automatically
through the NIT structure. There is, of
course, an eligibility criterion in the form
of a simple statement of income and family
composition, and it may be argued that something as simple as the income test preserves
the distinction between the poor and the
nonpoor, and will come to define a particular social class who are recipients under
the scheme. The case then follows for a
universal scheme which does not use any
test or declaration of any kind as a criterion of eligibility. In this sense the CA
approach may be held to be superior since
there is no possibility of any stigma effects under a universal scheme--but two
caveats are necessary: first, there is the
provisional evidence from New Jersey, cited
above, and, second and more important, there
is the point that a CA program has a much
smaller effect on the poverty gap than an
FAP approach and therefore will require
the maintenance of a substantial amount of
other assistance programs. If these other
programs are of the traditional means-tested
assistance nature, the aggregate amount of
testing under a scheme which contains a CA
system may actually be larger than under a
scheme which relies substantially on a NIT
(income-tested) approach, and the stigma
effects of the two total schemes may well
emerge as worse under the scheme containing,
paradoxically, the completely untested universal CA system.

4. Administrative Complexity. There can
be little doubt that a selective NIT scheme
such as FAP would be administratively more
complex and more expensive (take a greater
share of available resources for administrative purposes) than a universal CA
scheme. Both for administrator and recipient, a universal scheme is clearly simpler than a selective scheme. In 1967, the
total cost of administering the present

Canadian CA program came to well below 1
percent of total benefits paid. It is, however, likely that administrative costs under
FAP or a broadly based NIT scheme would be
sharply reduced over time as the initial
problems, such as integration with the positive income tax, were overcome, and, with
computer assistance, it would seem inap-
propriate to overstress the administrative
difficulties of a NIT approach.

5. <u>Social and Political Effects</u>. A scheme
such as FAP is by definition aimed only at
those defined as statistically poor, say,
the lowest one-fifth of the population.
Particularly in the U.S. at present, the
principal and rising source of opposition
to new programs which benefit solely and
specifically the poor comes not from high
income groups but from the great range of
families in perhaps the next two-fifths in
terms of income, who find themselves in a
position of financial stringency despite
full and probably rather uninteresting employment, who feel caught by a variety of
forces over which they have no control,
such as inflation and rising taxes, and
have come to resent program proposals in
which they are represented as donors and
not as recipients. FAP is just such a
scheme.

The opposition of this large group
can scarcely be overlooked. There is
clearly the question of basic political acceptability, but the more important question
relates to the social implications of the
scheme. In the U.S. a scheme such as FAP
could be described as follows: one group
will receive it, another group will pay
for it, and such groups are more than
likely to be defined rather sharply by race
and region. Such a scheme may then be considered to exacerbate social tensions and
to emphasize division rather than the uni-
ties of the problem. As Scott Briar recently

observed, "A broad program [such as CA, and
as distinct from FAP] might help to create
the conditions for greater harmony between
the poor and the nonpoor by blurring the
arbitrarily and therefore erroneously sharp
line dividing them and by focusing attention on the needs and discontents they hold
in common."[23]

It is an interesting thought that most
European welfare programs are viewed as a
comprehensive package aimed at redistribution toward a socially tolerable and acceptable degree of inequality, and are not, and
have never been, specifically directed to
a particular income stratum defined arbitrarily as the statistically poor. As a
consequence these European schemes have
generally been multifaceted, containing
aspects which dealt with particular and
specific privation, but in general emphasiz-
ing a broadly based approach to income redistribution rather than poverty, however
defined.

The racial issue is clearly not of as
great consequence for Canada as for the
U.S., but the broad argument holds. The
unease which the middle two-fifths of the
population will feel toward a program for
which they are paying but which does not
provide them with any benefits cannot and
should not be neglected, and it should be
recorded that in terms of social consequences, and political acceptability, the
universal approach of a CA scheme has much
to commend it, certainly as one part of a
comprehensive welfare program.

Conclusion

The separate components of the set of
criteria which have been used to evaluate
the FAP and CA alternatives clearly cannot
be boiled down neatly into one simple decision criterion, and the choice of an

alternative depends on the weighting assigned
each component part. . . .

    . . . What has really emerged from the
comparison is the rather interesting fact
that FAP and CA are really different policy
instruments, and may most effectively be
seen as complements rather than as substi-
tutes. While in this writer's view the
long run orientation of a welfare program
must be as part of an overall policy of redistribution to which many government programs contribute, there can clearly be no
countenancing of absolute privation even in
the short run. There is need therefore on
economic, political, and social grounds for
a package or mix of programs which, on the
one hand, mitigate insofar as is possible
absolute privation or poverty--this might
be along the lines of a broadly based NIT
scheme, or in the short run a categorical
NIT scheme such as FAP--and, on the other
hand, would offer the broadly based partici-
patory sort of scheme of which a CA program
is an excellent example. For a specified
budgetary constraint, such a bifaceted approach obviously involves diluting both programs to make possible the existence of the
broader approach, but it is submitted here
that such an explicit trade-off may be
necessary on grounds of the set of comparative criteria set out above.

    In any event, what is vital is that
program alternatives of the sort examined
above be subject to appraisal in terms of
a broad set of evaluation criteria--in
short, be subject to a general as distinct
from partial analysis. The choice of a
particular program depends on the weighting
assigned each constituent evaluation criterion, and the least that can be expected
from a general analysis is that the weighting assigned each criterion emerge implicitly in the ultimate choice of program design.

Commentary

A traditional analysis of the sort illustrated
above may be seen as an essential first step to the
construction of a model of the redistributive pro-
cess--but no more than a first step. Such an analysis is a descriptive or qualitative assessment of the
operating characteristics of the model. In the case
of certain variables such a broad, qualitative assessment may be as far as we can realistically go,
but in other cases we can go much further in specifying operating characteristics. The actual, quantitative change in the distribution of income after a
particular tax/transfer program may, for instance,
be computed--given, of course, the rather large
ceteris paribus assumption that the tax/transfer program is the only input variable affecting the state
of income distribution over the period of analysis.
Further, a more thorough analysis of the important
variables in the work supply function should enable
us to offer a more effective framework for at least
ranking various income support schemes in terms of
their effect on work.

Social Experimentation

Considerable interest has been generated recently
in the technique of social experimentation, by which
a selected subset of the population is subjected to
alternative programs of one sort or another, the object of the exercise being to observe over time in
an experimental framework the outputs of program alternatives and thus to be able to specify with more
rigor the relationships of a redistributive model.
The example chosen is the New Jersey NIT experiment.
This experiment is described in some detail in the
literature (H. W. Watts, "Graduated Work Incentives:
An Experiment in Negative Taxation," American Economic Review, May 1969); the description below was
prepared by the author for a committee of the Canadian
Senate in the summer of 1969 and is based on a review
of papers on the experiment and consultations with
the field staff who operate the experiment in New
Jersey and with the staff of the Institute for Research on Poverty at the University of Wisconsin.

Example

The Structure of the Experiment

There are many problems under the general heading of guaranteed annual income that the New Jersey study does not attempt to answer. The whole question of selectivity versus universality is not explored, no examination is made of the variety of ways of establishing eligibility, alternative forms of guaranteed annual income are omitted, and only a specified segment of the poor is considered. Though interesting, the experiment is limited, focusing essentially on the effect of various forms of negative income tax payments upon the work effort (incentives) of a group of families in the "working poor" category.

These payments provide a floor in the event of the complete cessation of other income, but they generally act to supplement work income. The negative income tax form of a guaranteed annual income is selective in the sense that an eligibility test is used. It consists of a simple income declaration similar to that presently found in income tax forms.

The Institute for Research on Poverty at the University of Wisconsin and MATHE-MATICA in Princeton, New Jersey, jointly administer the ongoing negative income tax experiment in four urban areas--Trenton, Paterson, and Passaic in New Jersey, and Scranton, Pennsylvania. Scranton was introduced in order to include an appropriate number of non-Puerto Rican whites in the poverty sample.

It is proposed here to describe the structure and objectives of the experiment and to mention briefly proposed complementary schemes.

The Eligible Unit

The basic unit is the family rather than
the individual, as now used in the positive
income tax procedures of both the United
States and Canada. The definition of the
family includes children and stepchildren
and others either living with or deriving
more than half their support from the family
head. Eligible families must consist of
at least two members with a male head between twenty and fifty-eight years of age.
This limited sample of the poor is designed
to focus on work effort responses to income
supplements.

The Definition of Income

The definition of income used in the
experiment is much wider than in the positive income tax systems in the United States
and Canada. It includes such items as gifts
and inheritances, pensions or annuities,
prizes and awards, damages and workmen's
compensation, capital gains, strike pay,
unemployment compensation, and imputed rent
in the case of owner-occupied housing and
rent subsidies if in public housing, plus
a related group of items that combine to
constitute a broad economic definition more
useful in a program aimed at identifying
need than the usual tax-exempt status of
income. Having defined income in this way,
the eligible population is further limited
to those whose normal income places them
in the poor or near-poor categories, i.e.,
less than 1.5 times the official poverty
line shown in Table 1. In Table 1 the
basic schedule assumes that the first two
persons are adults (usually male head and
spouse). The supplementary schedule comes
into play when, for instance, one spouse
deserts. He or she remains eligible for
support under the basic schedule as a one-
person unit; the remaining family with

TABLE 1

Poverty Thresholds
(in dollars)

Number of Persons	Basic Schedule	Supplementary Schedule
1	1,000	--
2	2,000	1,750
3	2,750	2,300
4	3,300	2,700
5	3,700	3,050
6	4,050	3,350
7	4,350	3,600
8 or more	4,600	3,600

only one adult receives benefits according
to the supplementary schedule.

Eligibility in Summary

The basic criteria for eligibility are
(1) the family must be headed by an employ-
able--but not necessarily employed--male
between the ages of twenty and fifty-eight
and (2) family income, broadly defined,
must not exceed 1.5 times the poverty
threshold.

Once a family is determined eligible,
is selected for inclusion, and enrolled in
the experiment, it is involved (if feasible)
for the duration of the experimental period, regardless of where it goes or what the
head does. After an extensive set of screen-
ing interviews, approximately 1,200 families in the four urban areas indicated
above were selected from a total sample of
14,000.

The Experimental Groups

        Except for the control group, which
does not receive income supplements but
does receive a small interview fee, families selected for the experiment are assigned to one of eight different negative
tax plans. In each plan there are two
variables that are manipulated and a third
that is determined by the first two. The
two variables that are manipulated are (1)
the basic guarantee for a family, i.e.,
the percentage of the poverty line (Table
1) that a family will receive if income
from other sources is zero; this variable
is set at 50 percent, 75 percent, 100 percent, or 125 percent; and (2) the negative
tax rate proper specifies the reduction in
payments to families in relation to income
from other sources; this is expressed as a
percentage, and is set at 30 percent, 50
percent, or 70 percent of income in the
various treatment groups.
        The eight different combinations of
these two variables are shown in Table 2
in matrix form, the entry in the eight
relevant boxes indicating the third varia-

TABLE 2

Negative Tax Plans in the New Jersey
Experiment for Family of Four
(poverty threshold = $3,300)

Guaranteed Rate (percent)	Negative Tax Rate (in dollars)		
	30 Percent	50 Percent	70 Percent
50	5,500	3,300	--
75	8,250	4,950	3,393
100	--	6,600	4,714
125	--	8,250	--

ble determined by the first two, the break-
even income at which payments under the
particular scheme drop to zero. An interesting aspect of this sample table is the
relatively high break-even points under the
schemes that use either a high guarantee
rate or a low negative tax rate.

Table 3 illustrates the position of a
family of four under the 75 percent/50 percent scheme.

Participating families receive payments
every two weeks over the three-year duration
of the experiment. They are free to do
whatever they wish with the payments and
are only obliged to provide the investigators with income and family composition
every four weeks. To determine the benefits payable in any particular instance,
income is averaged over the preceding three
months. At the end of each year of participation, the total benefits paid will be

TABLE 3

Income Position of a Family of Four on the
75 Percent Guarantee Rate/50 Percent
Negative Tax Rate Scheme
(in dollars)

Work Earnings	Income Supplement	Total Income
0	2,475	2,475
500	2,225	2,725
1,000	1,975	2,975
1,500	1,725	3,225
2,000	1,475	3,475
2,500	1,225	3,725
3,000	975	3,975
3,500	725	4,225
4,000	475	4,475
4,500	225	4,725
4,950 (break-even point)	0	4,950

compared with the benefits properly claim-
able on the basis of actual income experience and the difference corrected. Families receive in addition to their regular
benefits a payment of $5 as a reward for
answering each quarterly interview, and
members of the control group receive an
extra bonus at the end of each year of co-
operation. As it has turned out, there has
been considerable attrition in the control
group--amounting to almost one-half the
group--and consideration is presently being
given to paying all participants, including
the control group, a demogrant of 6 percent
of the poverty threshold.

The U.S. Internal Revenue Service has
ruled that the benefit payments--excluding
bonus payments or payments for interviews--
are not taxable under the positive income
tax provisions. This rather convenient
ruling allows the investigators to retain
immediate control over the marginal tax
rate to which each family is subject.

Objectives of the Experiment

The primary objective of the negative
income tax experiment is to determine the
response of family labor supply to payments
of the sort described above. The labor
supply question is crucial from two points
of view:

1. Cost. Any reduction in work effort and
therefore work earnings produces a corresponding increase in the amount that must be
paid out through the supplement scheme.

2. Benefit. Any reduction in work effort
and earnings dilutes the impact of the
scheme on final income, and therefore on
living standards, i.e., the reduction of
poverty is not as successful. Particularly
crucial is the problem intrinsic in any
negative income tax scheme--the rather high

tax rate on earnings from work up to the
break-even point. A rate of 30 percent on
first earnings is the most generous in the
experiment and this far exceeds the beginning rates on earnings in the positive income tax. Rates as high as 50 percent and
70 percent may be expected, prima facie,
to have rather serious effects on work effort.

The quarterly interviews also seek information on attitudes toward work and job
satisfaction, by trying to establish whether
reductions in work effort can be attributed
to low attachment to work or to the nature
of a particular job and what the general effect of the transfers is on how recipients
value work.

A second objective is to ascertain the
effect of the various schemes on family consumption and expenditure patterns. What
goods will families purchase with added income? Do the kinds of things they buy change
over time if they have added income? Do
these payments affect savings or credit buying decisions?

Poverty is not definable simply in economic terms but is, in fact, multidimensional. The questionnaires seek to determine the effects of the various negative
tax mixes on a range of what can loosely be
called noneconomic factors:

(a) The family: What difference will
payments make on family attitudes toward
education for the children? Toward family
participation in various activities? Will
support payments, which are not seriously
affected if a parent remains in the home
or leaves, have a noticeable impact on the
stability of the family?

(b) Political integration: What
methods of political action are selected
by recipients and how do these change over
time? Is there any significant change in

the respondent with respect to his identification with the political system and his
willingness to participate?

(c) General mobility: What sort of
occupational aspirations do respondents
have? Are they upwardly mobile? Are they
geographically mobile?

(d) Dependence on government: To what
extent do respondents take advantage of
various government-operated services available to them? To what extent do they depend on them? Are income maintenance payments separated from other governmental
services?

(e) Social integration and anomie:
How do the payments affect people's ties
with society? To what extent does alienation exist among the poor and what impact
do transfer payments have on these attitudes?

Further Negative Income Tax Experiments

The Department of Health, Education
and Welfare in Washington has just financed
a second negative income tax experiment in
Seattle, Washington, and is about to finance
a third in Gary, Indiana. The former dupli-
cates the design pattern of the New Jersey
experiment, with a series of experimental
groups and a control group, but differs from
the New Jersey experiment in that, first,
coverage under the experiment is to be extended to female-headed families and, second, a manpower training program is to be
included with a negative income tax as part
of the experiment. The Gary experiment
does not include a manpower aspect and is
aimed primarily at black, female-headed
families. In both cases funds will be
granted to the state in question, with the
requirement that the experiment be con-

tracted out to a university or research
agency.

The Proposed Rural Scheme

Of considerable interest to Canada is
the proposed rural negative income tax experiment to be conducted by the University
of Wisconsin Institute for Research on Poverty in Iowa and North Carolina. The experiment will be similar in design to that
in New Jersey--a sample of poor and near-
poor families selected from specified areas
and enrolled in several alternative negative income tax schemes. Unlike the New
Jersey scheme, eligibility would be extended
to families with heads over fifty-eight
years of age and to families headed by a
female aged between eighteen and fifty-
eight years. The relevant definition of income would include for any year the working
assets of the family divided by ten, and
the experiment would add to the objectives
of the New Jersey scheme an interest in
rural-urban migration flows.

Commentary

Provisional and intermediate results have been
published on the New Jersey experiment.[24] The first
findings suggest some family labor withdrawal as a
consequence of NIT payments, a diminished degree of
borrowing among recipients, and lower administrative
costs per capita than under the existing welfare system. The findings will be set out in detail in the
section of this work where we attempt to construct
a provisional redistributive model. For the moment
it may be noted that social experimentation of the
sort carried out in New Jersey promises to yield important information on the relationships in socioeconomic models, but that such experiments are costly
and time-consuming in terms of scarce funds and research personnel. In many cases, therefore, where
such large scale experimentation is not possible,
for cost or other reasons, information may have to

be obtained from "pseudo-experimentation" (simulation
of one sort or another) on a model of the system under examination.

Ex-Post Evaluation

No attempt is made here to explore in detail
the growing literature on evaluation methodology[25]
but simply to deal with ex-post evaluation as one
means of determining the outcome of public programs
in relation to inputs of various kinds, and thus as
one means of adding to our store of knowledge and
understanding about the operational characteristics
of these programs. Concern is thus with outcome
evaluation in the broad performance criteria sense
rather than in the narrower administrative monitoring sense, and, in effect, with ex-post use of cost
benefit analysis and cost effectiveness analysis.

There are no published examples as yet of the
application of ex-post evaluation to cash transfer
programs, but there are some outstanding examples
in the general field of human resource development[26]
and one particularly interesting and detailed implicit
cost effectiveness analysis of the U.S. Office of
Economic Opportunity Head Start program;[27] we will
look briefly at the nature of the Head Start evaluation and, finally, comment on the usefulness to this
point of the whole method of evaluation.

Head Start is one of the more interesting programs initiated in the Office of Economic Opportunity,
and deals with preschool education for poor children.
The major evaluation had its origins in the view
that while Head Start children experienced gains in
cognitive and affective behavior during their expo-
sure to Head Start, these gains were not sustained
once the Head Start children entered the public
school system. The study addressed itself to one
basic question: to what extent were the children
now in the first, second, and third grades who had
attended Head Start different in their intellectual
and social-personal development, as measured by a
specified set of indicators, from comparable children
who had not attended? The study did not address itself to other measurable outputs, such as the nu-
tritional and medical impact of Head Start, nor to

broader and less readily measurable indicators such
as the impact of Head Start on the total community,
on the schools, on parental participation, etc. This
very multidimensionality of virtually all human resource development programs is one of the major problems in applying ex-post evaluation usefully, since,
as we shall indicate below for the Head Start evaluation, those who disagree with the results of an
evaluation that for practical purposes cannot cover
every output may simply select as the basis of attack one of these neglected output variables.

To answer the basic question posed by the Head
Start evaluation a sample of 104 Head Start centers
across the United States was selected. A sample of
children from these centers who had gone on to the
first, second, and third grades in local area schools
and a matched sample of control children from the
same grades and schools who had not attended Head
Start were administered a series of tests covering
various indicators of cognitive and affective development (listed below). The parents of both the former Head Start enrollees and the control children
were interviewed and a broad range of attitudinal,
social, and economic data were collected. Directors
or other officials of all the centers were interviewed
and information was collected on various characteristics of the current local Head Start programs. The
primary grade teachers rated both groups of children
on achievement motivation and supplied a description
of the intellectual and emotional environment of
their elementary schools.

Analyses of comparative performances on the assessment measures of all children in the study were
conducted for each selected center area. Findings
were then combined into the total national sample
and into three major subgroupings of centers formerly
attended by the Head Start children, the latter being classified by geographic region, city size, and
racial/ethnic composition. All the findings were
also related to the type of program attended--summer
or full-year program.

The major findings of the study, related to a
set of indicators, were in the broadest summary form
for the national sample:

1. In the overall analysis for the
Metropolitan Readiness Tests (MRT), a generalized measure of learning readiness containing subtests on word meaning, listening,
matching, alphabet, numbers, and copying,
the Head Start children who had attended
full-year programs and who were beginning
grade one were superior to the controls by
a small but statistically significant margin on both "Total Readiness" and the "Listening" subscore. The Head Start children
who had attended summer programs, however,
did not score significantly higher than
the controls.

2. In the overall analysis for the
Stanford Achievement Test (SAT), a general
measure of children's academic achievement
containing subtests on word reading, para-
graph meaning, spelling, arithmetic, etc.
and used to measure achievement at grades
two and three, the Head Start children
from both the summer and the full-year programs did not score significantly higher
than the controls at the grade two level.

3. In the overall analysis for the
Illinois Test of Psycholinguistic Abilities
(ITPA), a measure of language development
containing separate tests on auditory and
vocal reception, auditory and visual mem-
ory, auditory-vocal association, visual-
motor association, etc., the Head Start
children did not score significantly higher
than the controls at any of the three
grade levels for the summer programs.

4. In the overall analysis for the
Children's Self-Concept Index (CSCI), a
projective measure of the degree to which
the child has a positive self-concept,
the Head Start children from both the
summer and the full-year programs did not
score significantly higher than the controls at any of the three grade levels.

5. In the overall analysis for the
Classroom Behavior Inventory (CBI), a
teacher rating assessment of the children's

desire for achievement in school, the Head
Start children from both the summer and the
full-year programs did not score significantly higher than the controls at any of
the three grade levels.

6. In the overall analysis for the
Children's Attitudinal Range Indicator
(CARI), a picture-story projective measure
of the child's attitudes toward school,
home, peers, and society, the Head Start
children from the full-year programs did
not score significantly higher than the
controls at any of the three grade levels.

Apart from the national sample, additional analyses were made for three subgroups of the national
sample: geographic regions, city-size groups, and
racial/ethnic composition categories. Analysis of
the summer programs by subgroups revealed few areas
where Head Start children scored higher than their
controls. Analysis of the full-year programs by the
same subgroupings revealed a number of statistically
significant differences in which, on some measures
(mostly subtests of cognitive measures) and at one
or another grade level, the Head Start children
scored higher than their controls. There were consistent favorable patterns for certain subgroups--
where centers were in the Southeastern geographic region, in core cities, or of mainly Negro composition.

The broad conclusions on the performance comparisons made in the study were, first, that Head
Start summer programs appeared to have been ineffective in producing any gains in cognitive and affective development that persisted into the early elementary grades and, second, that full-year programs
appeared to have been ineffective as measured by the
tests of affective development used in the study,
but were marginally effective in producing gains in
cognitive development that could be detected in the
first three elementary grades; programs were of
greater effectiveness for certain subgroups of centers, particularly in Negro centers, in a few programs in the central cities, and in Southeastern
centers. In sum, with marginal exceptions, Head
Start children did not appear to be appreciably different from their peers in the elementary grades.

It seems self-evident that ex-post evaluation
ought to be an integral part of the management of
public programs and, as such, can add over time to
the understanding of the operational characteristics
of such programs. There are, however, certain present limitations with respect to evaluation that
emerge rather clearly from the Head Start experience.

First, there is the question of the political
climate in which evaluation occurs. The multidimensionality of the output of public programs makes any
evaluation that does not take every output into account subject to attack. Predictably, the Head
Start evaluation was attacked on, among others, the
grounds that it did not deal adequately or at all
with the broader, social effects of the program.
This problem is aggravated by the conflict that must
occur almost by definition between evaluators and
program administrators.[28]

Second, the very ex-post nature of the process
implies that while the information generated can be
useful in modifying existing programs or introducing
new but similar programs only incidental assistance
is provided in defining ex-ante the operational characteristics of new and unprecedented programs.

Finally, with specific respect to the Head Start
evaluation, the very detailed study provides virtuall'
no firm guidance as to what changes should be made
in the program to improve its performance, and a
study that might provide such guidance would require
a substantially more elaborate design, a larger sample size, and hence would place much greater demands
on scarce research resources of all kinds. Much
work remains to be done on evaluation methodology
before the technique may be considered a major input
to public programs, and even a well-developed evaluation methodology would seem likely to be one of the
more costly ways of arriving at information on the
operating characteristics of public programs.

Simulation

The use of simulation to provide ex-ante information on the operating characteristics of alternative program designs was discussed in the section
of this work dealing in detail with the nature of

program budgeting. We confine our attention here to
simulation using a digital computer. The case for
employing computer simulation in the evaluation of
income support programs is particularly strong: the
approach provides an experimental environment for
testing hypotheses, decision rules, and alternative
systems of operation under a variety of assumed conditions. The approach is flexible, experimental--
providing, as it were, experimental data rather than
solutions--and requires only decision rules rather
than a formal mathematical apparatus.

There is a rich and growing literature on simulation.[29] Here we will simply define several basic
distinctions in simulation models--macro and micro
models, static and dynamic models, and deterministic
and probabilistic models--and will illustrate several
recent uses of simulation models relevant to model
building in the area of distribution.

Microsimulation differs from macrosimulation in
that computations are performed on individual records and the results aggregated rather than aggre-
gating first and then doing computations. Microsimulation will generally be addressed to individual
economic units, such as the individual household or
consumer or the individual firm, whereas macrosimulation will generally be addressed to aggregate
variables such as total personal consumption or saving. In income distribution models there are some
clear advantages of using microsimulation. To make
computations of the effect of an income support program or a new set of income tax rates on the basis
of the aggregative published data on income distribution is not only laborious but approximate. To make
such computations, it is generally assumed that returns are distributed evenly within any given cell
or income group. Cell midpoints are then computed
for individuals with different marital and dependency
statuses, and it is assumed that the average income
at the midpoints can be used to represent the incomes of all the individuals in each cell. The wider
the income limits of each cell, the larger the error;
on the other hand, the narrower the income limits,
the more unwieldy the computation. This problem can
only be avoided by dealing directly with individual
observations in the frequency distribution. G. H.

Orcutt has further demonstrated that errors in initial aggregates are greatly compounded when simulation projections are carried out and that the margin of error is much smaller in a microsimulation.[30] The case for microsimulation in evaluating income support programs of the sort that interest us in this study is therefore convincing. There is, unfortunately, always the constraint of data availability. The only available data for use in the model that forms the larger part of this study were aggregative income distribution data, displaying income groups (in $500 intervals) by various family sizes, and further disaggregating income into several different components. The model constructed is thus strictly a macrosimulation as defined above, and we deal essentially with averages rather than with individual circumstances.

A static simulation model in, say, an income support evaluation would simply recompute the income distribution of the families or groups of families being examined according to a set of rules specified in the tax/transfer program design. Time is therefore involved, but the recomputation is only over one time period—say, a year—over which the specified redistribution is assumed to take place. A more accurate term for such a simulation might thus be comparative static simulation; we continue to use the term "static" simply as a clear distinction from dynamic models that take time explicitly into account. A dynamic model of income support programs would follow a sample of families through time, moving these families either deterministically or probabilistically from one state to another throughout the process. The question of feedback becomes integral in dynamic models. In income support models, for instance, a work disincentive effect postulated in period 1 of the analysis would be taken into account explicitly in the higher costs of the income support scheme, as a consequence of diminished labor supply, in period 2; stigmatization and political acceptability effects would be treated in the same way.

The model we shall attempt to construct below is static in nature. It is difficult and costly to use Markov processes (processes that postulate probabilities of transition from one state to another) with data in complex aggregative form. Our main reason, however, for moving to a static model as a first step is simply that the social technology in this area is very primitive and that the highest returns in the short run would seem to come from directing scarce resources toward shedding some light on this technology. A dynamic model based on individual records, given the availability of data, is envisaged as a logical development of the model.

The final distinction to be explored is that between deterministic and probabilistic models. Almost all dynamic models are probabilistic in nature, i.e., the occurrence of events in the model is controlled by finding or estimating a probability that an event will occur, comparing this probability with a random number, and, depending on the results of the comparison, causing the event to occur or not to occur. A deterministic model, on the other hand, postulates the certainty of events, i.e., implicitly assumes the postulated events will occur with a probability of 1.0. We have chosen to begin with a deterministic model in an attempt to define a working, basic social technology of redistribution. The next stage lies in making the model both dynamic and probabilistic, i.e., aging our sample through time and doing so according to a specified set of transition probabilities.

The most interesting macrosimulation models are all dynamic in nature. Complex econometric simulation models have been developed in both the United States[31] and Canada[32] with the objective of analyzing economic conditions and exploring the consequences of policy alternatives. Jay Forrester has developed a dynamic model-building approach to examining the behavior of industrial and urban systems over time.[33] E. P. Holland and R. W. Gillespie have used the simulation language developed by Forrester to explore the impact of planning, policy, and parameter variations on an underdeveloped economy.[34]

There is an interesting series of static microsimulation models directly relevant to redistribution. J. A. Pechman[35] and J. Bossons[36] have developed microsimulation models of the personal income tax that use a sample of tax returns to generate very quickly the revenue and distributive consequences

of tax base and rate schedule changes. The Unemployment Insurance Commission in Ottawa[37] has developed
a simulation model that uses a sample of the popula-
tion--determined in the first run for 1965-66 by taking 5 percent of all Social Insurance numbers--to
determine the costs and distributive consequences of
changes in Unemployment Insurance provisions. Directly relevant to the consideration of income support alternatives are the recent studies by M. David
and J. Leuthold[38] and by N. McClung.[39] The David
study used a rather small sample compiled by the
Survey Research Center at the University of Michigan
to compare the distributive effects of alternative
income support plans. The larger McClung study explored a detailed census file on low income families
and developed a static microsimulation procedure to
determine the distributive effects of various NIT
schemes.

Some interesting dynamic microsimulation models
have also been recently developed. James Schulz
used a dynamic microsimulation model to project the
characteristics of the retired population of the
United States to 1980[40] and, further, to examine the
effect on that retired population of introducing the
more generous West German pension system in the
United States.[41] At the Institute for Social Research
at the Florida State University R. L. Michielutte
and J. T. Sprehe have conducted a dynamic, probabilistic simulation of demographic processes in the United
States from 1970-80.[42] Finally, and most ambitious
of all, the Urban Institute in Washington, D.C.,
currently has under way a project that seeks to de-
velop a microsimulation model of the entire household sector in the United States.[43] The data base
for the microanalytic model is the Survey of Economic
Opportunity (SEO) conducted by the Bureau of the Census for the Office of Economic Opportunity in 1966
and 1967. The basic data file is being expanded to
large sample size by appropriate replication techniques to simulate the entire U.S. population, and
the resulting population base, dated at a point in
time, is being subjected to two kinds of statistical
treatments: first, the population is changed from a
static state to a dynamic state by introducing
various change parameters (age, births and deaths,

human capital accretion, labor force participation
and unemployment, income growth, earnings from assets and asset accumulation, and capital gains); second, the dynamic population is treated by policy
parameters to determine the effects of given policies
on the socioeconomic characteristics of the popula-
tion--the policy parameters include various income
support schemes and changes in the personal income
tax base and rates. The model extends substantially
the previous demographic work published by G. Orcutt,
et al., in 1961.[44]

Conclusion

The four approaches to the determination of the
social technology of the redistributive process
should be seen as essentially complementary. Qualitative examination will generally be the first stage
in program appraisal, to be supplemented over the
process of policy formulation by simulation of various
kinds and, over the longer run, by social experimentation, again of various kinds. The results of previous ex-post evaluations of similar or related programs may also be employed to provide ex-ante information on the nature of the relationships in question,
and ex-post evaluation of the actual program itself
will serve after the initial phase of the program,
either in total or in some pilot project form, as a
basis for modifying initial views. In the nature of
income support programs, however, the importance of
providing ex-ante information fairly quickly in the
formulation of essentially novel programs suggests
the peculiar importance of simulation as a validatory
process for detailed qualitative examination, and
the usefulness of simulation in the context of
Canadian data limitations is explored in the balance
of this work.
The model to be described below is a somewhat
modest one. It employs aggregative data and, although
focusing on the effects of various redistributive
policies on households, must be described as a macrosimulation. Further, it is static, in the sense
that it simply recomputes income distribution and
associated output variables after the introduction
of various redistributive schemes, and is determinis-

tic in the sense that the postulated operating characteristics of the model are assigned a probability
of 1.0. Much work therefore remains to be done; the
point of the exercise is to make a first essay into
a comparatively uncharted area the social technology
of which is of increasing relevance in public policy.

3

A STATIC
MACROSIMULATION MODEL
OF INCOME SUPPORT
PROGRAMS IN CANADA

INTRODUCTION

The purpose of the model is to examine the consequences of the introduction of a set of alternative
income support programs in Canada. It is initially
postulated that the consequences of income support
programs must be viewed in multidimensional terms
and that the output definition from the model must
therefore be multidimensional, encompassing a set of
economic, social, and political variables. This
raises the issues of commensurability and weighting.
If all the elements of the vector of outputs were
commensurable, some overall aggregative utility index for each income support program alternative
might be determined. In the manifest absence of
such a perfect world (how would one add, e.g., two
output components such as the change in income distribution and the political acceptability of a particular program?) what is done is the presentation
of a vector of distinct, incommensurable outputs as
the basis for evaluating ex-ante the various program
alternatives. Even crude ordinal (directional) indicators of certain outputs for which no precise
measures are available are clearly superior to ignoring such outputs (which implicitly gives them a
zero weight). In the case of several of the output
variables examined, the transformation relationship
between inputs into the model, in the form of income

135

support payments and increased tax rates to finance
these income support payments, and outputs, in the
form, say, of family stability or stigma, is known
only in the crudest terms, and one of the primary
tasks of the model is to attempt to shed more light
on such relationships, which we have aggregatively
described as the social technology of the redistributive process. As to weighting of the output vector,
explicit numerical weights may be assigned, or
weights may be left to emerge implicitly in decision-
makers' choice of program alternative. The latter
procedure is followed in this model. We do not employ the linear programming formulation of a multidimensional output problem, in which one would seek
to optimize one output component subject to minimum
threshold attainments of the other components.

The model is a static macrosimulation of income
support programs, i.e., the computations are performed on aggregative data rather than on individual
records, and the model merely recomputes the income
and other output variables for a given period--one
year in the model--according to a set of rules (transformation relationships) specified in the design of
the income support model, rather than following a
distribution of families probabilistically through
time. The model employs real data--derived from a
sample of the Canadian population--as distinct from
artificial or hypothetical data.

An important aspect of the model is its emphasis on the tax/transfer view of redistribution. One
of the disturbing aspects of the program budgeting
approach to redistribution has been the tendency to
begin the analysis with a given budget sum to re-
distribute and to ignore the implications of raising
that budget sum in a variety of different ways through
taxation. In this model an attempt is made to keep
the analysis general at least in the sense that both
the tax and transfer implications of each policy
choice are examined. The primary emphasis of the
model remains, however, the evaluation of various
transfer or income support alternatives.

The redistributive programs considered are limited to alternative income support programs, i.e.,
to various cash transfer programs. This may be
legitimately considered a partial approach, since

redistribution may be approached in many ways--through
in-kind programs such as food stamps or free school
meals or, in the broader sense, through the whole
range of manpower and education programs. The justification for our approach is basically our conten-
tion that an adequate income support program is a
prerequisite for the success of in-kind programs of
all sorts and that redistribution is a more tractable
problem if the target is viewed in compact rather
than diffuse terms. Molly Orshansky sums up the
situation:

> If money alone will not solve the problem
> of poverty it is still true that without
> money nothing else will avail much either.
> Mathematically it falls in the category of
> necessary but not sufficient conditions.
> Pragmatically it is undoubtedly true that
> the persons who declaim loudest that "money
> is not everything" are those who already
> have some.[1]

Finally, it should be noted that the consideration of redistributive programs in the manner followed in this model implies a given stabilization
policy. The model deals with 1967 income distribution data and defines a poverty problem or aggregate
income deficiency in terms of the rate of unemployment in that year--4.1 percent of the labor force.
Any projection of the costs of the income support
alternatives over time would employ a rate of unemployment that remained constant at the 1967 level.
Although we have no precise information on the relationship between the rate of unemployment and the
pattern of income distribution in Canada and do not
attempt to derive any in this model, it seems reasonable to assume that the size of the poverty problem would increase as the rate of unemployment increased.
Finally, income support programs in Canada are
administered by all three levels of government--
federal, provincial, and municipal--and the question
arose how the model might be adapted to reflect the
complex constitutional reality.

In the absence of income distribution data disaggregated by level of government, we decided to
examine the implications of multilevel jurisdiction
by dividing the available federal data according to
a predetermined set of rules into two hypothetical
provinces and each province in turn into two components, one of which would represent a hypothetical
municipality and the other the "rural" balance of
the province. The procedure followed was to allocate
two-thirds of all families (and corresponding incomes) for those with incomes of less than $4,500
per annum to hypothetical province 1--the "poor"
province--and the remaining one-third of families
in the same income categories to hypothetical province 2--the "rich" province. For those with incomes
of $4,500 and over the allocation procedure was
simply reversed, two-thirds of all families in each
category being allocated to province 2 and the balance
to province 1. By exactly the same allocation rule,
province 1 and province 2 were each divided into a
rich component, which we envisaged as a hypothetical
municipality, and a poor component, which we envisaged, perhaps with more convenience than subtlety,
as the rural balance of the province. In sum, the
aggregate data were divided into four components.
The first component, defined as the rural component
of the poor province, contained 1,427,200 families
with an average annual income of $4,325. The second
component, the municipality in the poor province,
contained 1,343,400 families with an average annual
income of $6,570. The third component, the rural
part of the rich province, contained 1,353,800 families with an average annual income of $6,526. The
final component, the municipality in the rich province, contained 1,946,500 families with an average
annual income of $8,177.

To illustrate the implications of multilevel
jurisdiction we first explored the implications for
each of the four components, and for the aggregate
of these components, of two major federal schemes,
a general NIT scheme and a FISP 2 scheme (nontaxable),
then repeated the procedure using a provincial supplement to the federal scheme in the two components
of the rich province, the poor province being assumed
to rest content with the federal largesse. Under

both federal options examined we used a provincial
NIT scheme (taxable) as a supplement. We then,
finally, repeated the procedure using the provincial
supplement used in stage 2, further supplementing
the aggregate of federal payment and provincial supplement in the municipality component of the rich
province with a municipal NIT scheme (taxable). The
final multilevel run thus provided us with a set of
output indicators that illustrated, first, the implications of "pyramiding" schemes, i.e., the cost
and output implications of a federal scheme, a provincial supplement, and, finally, a municipal supplement, in one of the four components; second, the implications of a federal scheme and a provincial supplement in a second component; third, the straight
implications of a federal scheme in the remaining
two components; and, finally, the aggregative implications of the complete set of federal, provincial,
and municipal schemes.

THE DEFINITION OF POVERTY
USED IN THE MODEL

Introduction

Two broad approaches to the definition of poverty may be distinguished: the absolute or budget-
oriented approach and the relative or inequality-
oriented approach. The absolute approach is that
developed by Molly Orshansky in the Social Security
Administration in the United States, focusing on
"poverty lines" for different family sizes based upon
estimated food requirements; basically, an income
less than three times the cost of an adequate diet
priced at minimum costs for a particular type of
family is defined as below the poverty line.[2]
The Dominion Bureau of Statistics (D.B.S.)--
now Statistics Canada--has developed similar poverty
lines for Canada, defining families or individuals
in poverty as those using 70 percent or more of their
incomes for food, clothing, and shelter.[3] By this
standard, the poverty lines were drawn at $1,500
for single persons, $2,500 for families with two
persons, and $3,000, $3,500, and $4,000 for families

with three, four, and five persons, respectively.
Taking a family of four as reference poverty income,
the basic payment and increments for additional members are arrived at by assigning to the first member
three-sevenths of $3,500, two-sevenths to the second
member, and one-seventh to the third and fourth.
Further members would also receive one-seventh. The
poverty lines illustrated are on the basis of 1961
data and are updated below.

The relative approach stresses the problems of
the absolute, subsistence minimum approach, particularly the fact that such absolute levels are difficult to change and may fall increasingly behind other
incomes in a relative sense. Poverty should therefore be seen as a subset of inequality, and the poverty line framed in a relative sense. Alternatives
here include specifying the poverty line as some percentage of median income, or in terms of the share
of income going to the bottom 10 percent, 15 percent,
etc., or perhaps according to some index of inequality such as the Lorenz ratio or Gini ratio,[4] or
finally, as a more direct indicator of the impact of
programs on the lowest income groups, as the ratio of
the share of income going to the top quintile in the
income distribution to that going to the bottom
quintile.

The difficulty with such relative definitions
in the particular problem we have here is that two
of the major expenditure alternatives to be appraised
--NIT and CA--gear payments to particular family
composition as a rough approximation of need, and
poverty lines are therefore required for a range of
different family sizes. The relative approach provides, say, only one Gini ratio or one median family
income, unless we were to calculate such indexes for
subgroups, say, the median income for families with
four persons. The latter technique is not particularly useful, since, for instance, it seems likely
that the median income would diminish with larger
family units, thus specifying, for a given percentage of the median, payments that would be inequitable
in relation to those going to other family unit sizes.
We therefore begin with the absolute poverty lines
set out above for Canada but eschew the conventional
method of updating such lines by simply escalating

according to the cost of living index; such an approach leaves unchanged the initial absolute nature
of the lines. Instead we use an escalator based on
the growth in per capita personal expenditure on consumer goods and services (current dollars) over the
period 1961-67. In this manner the change in the
poverty lines over time will be related to a measure
of average well-being, and the updated poverty lines
may be considered to be relative in this sense.
Further, we shall define explicitly the change in
the relative distribution of income effected by the
various income support programs to be investigated.

To examine the changes in poverty defined in
both absolute and relative terms we shall need then
as essential model specifications a definition of,
first, absolute poverty lines, and the associated
"poverty gap"--the extent to which the sum of the
incomes of those defined as living below the poverty
lines falls short of the sum of their incomes had
all the units in question been receiving the prescribed poverty line incomes--which the various
schemes are intended to fill in whole or in part;
and, second, a measure of the relative distribution
of incomes--viewed as the degree of inequality--
changes in which will be effected in varying degrees
by the alternative income support programs. These
two measures are dealt with in the following sections.

The Absolute Measure of Poverty--The Poverty Gap

The derivation of the poverty gap is set out in
several steps, the first of which is the appropriate
first broad definition of income in terms of which
poverty may be defined.

The available Statistics Canada data from the
1967 family income survey define income in a categorical manner to include wages and salaries, military pay and allowances, business income, income
from professional practice, farming income, other
self-employment income, gross income from roomers
and boarders, interest and dividends, other investment income, family allowances, old age pensions,

other government income, retirement pensions and annuities, and a residual other money income category.

The question that arises is whether or not the
above definition of income is sufficiently comprehensive. In the NIT experiment in New Jersey the definition of income used to define eligibility under
the schemes is considerably wider than that used for
positive income tax purposes and includes an allowance
for imputed rent and assets (the latter are generally included either in the form of an annuity or in
a simple percentage fashion, say, 10 percent of
specified assets included in the definition of income). C. W. Meyer calculates the U.S. poverty gap
according to various definitions of income, defining
progressively smaller poverty gaps the larger the
number of imputed factors included.[5] Meyer also
specifies several ways of allowing for the inclusion
of assets. With regard to assets, data are not
available for 1967; further, the usefulness of wait-
ing to get the data is perhaps not great in view of
Gail Oja's confirmation that, apart from elderly individuals and couples, asset holdings are very small
among those defined as poor.[6]

For consistency and symmetry with tax data,
therefore, and on grounds of immediate data availability, the definition of income used in all cases
will be that specified in the Statistics Canada
sample.

The second stage in the derivation of the poverty gap is the specification of absolute poverty
lines. We used the Statistics Canada poverty lines
for 1961 as a starting point but updated the lines
by using an escalator based on the growth in per
capita personal expenditure on consumer goods and
services over the period 1961-67. This method
treats poverty in both its absolute and relative
senses by relating changes in poverty over time to
a proxy for changes in general living standards.

Table 3.1 gives the poverty line escalator, i.e.,
the growth in per capita personal expenditure on
consumer goods and services (current dollars), for
1965 through 1969. The poverty line in the respec-
tive years is shown in Table 3.2. The updated poverty lines are rounded to the nearest $100.

TABLE 3.1

Poverty Line Escalator

	Personal Expenditure[a] (hundred-thousand dollars)	Population[b] (hundred-thousands)	Personal Expenditure per Capita Index	
			(dollars)	(1961 = 100)
1961	25,120	18.238	1,377	100.0
1965	33,134	19.644	1,687	122.5
1967	37,714	20.405	1,848	134.2
1968	42,360	20.744	2,042	148.3
1969	46,359	21.061	2,201	159.8

[a]Annual average.
[b]In the month of June.

The two final stages in the definition of the poverty gap relate, first, to whether income should be defined before or after positive income tax liability and, second, to whether existing transfer payments should be included in income.

With regard to taxes, there are two related points to consider. First, since families become subject to positive income tax before their income passes the poverty lines, and certainly well before their income reaches the break-even points of the various NIT schemes, it is clearly essential to specify eligibility for transfers in terms of income net of positive taxes. Second, since the receipt of income support payments will bring new families into the tax net, or increase the tax liability of those already so entrapped, it is also essential, if one wishes to determine the final distributive picture at the lower end of the income scale (quite apart from the final distributive picture on the balance of the income scale, which will be determined by the higher tax rates necessary to finance the income support scheme in question; we postpone the question of the distribution of these higher tax rates until

the section in the model dealing with financing the
various schemes--the issue to be immediately resolved
is the final distributive pattern at the lower end
of the income scale, given a set of income support
options and the existing set of tax rates and deductions), to apply standard rates and deductions to
after-transfer income. The issue basically is that
an income support recipient may be subject to positive tax payments before receiving any income support payments in a particular time period, say, a
month. On the basis of after-tax income such a family
may then be considered eligible for income support
payments designed to bring their income up to a certain level. Unless such income support payments are
specifically declared nontaxable, however, the family's tax liability in the following month will be
higher as a consequence of the income support payments, and the final year-end position of the family
will include earned income plus income support payments, minus tax liability on the sum of earned income plus income support payments, i.e.,

$$Y_d = (Y_e + Y_s) - t(Y_e + Y_s)$$

where

Y_d = disposable income
Y_e = earned income
Y_s = income support payments
t = average tax rate on $(Y_e + Y_s)$

TABLE 3.2

Poverty Lines for Different Family Sizes

Size of Family	1961	1965	1967	1968	1969
1	1,500	1,800	2,000	2,200	2,400
2	2,500	3,100	3,400	3,700	4,000
3	3,000	3,700	4,000	4,400	4,800
4	3,500	4,300	4,700	5,200	5,600
5	4,000	4,900	5,400	5,900	6,400
6	4,500	5,500	6,000	6,700	7,200
.		.	.	.	.
.		.	.	.	.
10	6,500	8,000	8,700	9,600	10,400

The two points referred to above may each be elaborated slightly. Figure 3.1 illustrates the situation of a family of four subject to a NIT scheme with a basic allowance of $2,000, a NIT rate of 50 percent, and, consequently, a break-even point of $4,000. While the family receives NIT payments up to $4,000, they start paying positive taxes at an income (exclusive of NIT payments) of $2,700 under the Canadian Income Tax Act. From $2,700, therefore, the NIT payments serve to compensate at a diminishing rate for positive taxes paid. At around $3,200 there is a break-even point at which the NIT payment equals positive taxes paid, and at $4,000 there is a second break-even point at which NIT payments drop to zero but at which the family pays several hundred dollars' tax.

Between the two break-even points indicated in Figure 3.1 the role of the NIT payment is simply to play a diminishing role in offsetting positive tax paid, and, more important for experimental purposes, the unit is subject to an effective tax on earnings greater than the specified NIT rate of 50 percent. This is confirmed by the short excerpt from the unit's income situation table shown in Table 3.3.

If one were concerned with a social experiment of the sort carried out in New Jersey on the work incentive effects of various NIT rates, it would be necessary to devise some method of positive tax reimbursement if the effective tax rate on earnings were to remain the same for all families. Without such reimbursement, the effective tax rate for a particular family would be the NIT rate plus marginal rate or rates of positive tax on earnings up to the break-even point. This may be done, as in Table 3.3, by simply adding positive tax paid back on to the allowance payment or by allowing positive tax due as a "double deduction" (tax due multiplied by two as a deduction) from income for the calculation of allowance payment due. (This double deduction operates in the case of a 50 percent NIT rate only.) No such compensation payments are made in the present model.[7]

Turning to the second point of concern with respect to taxes--the increased tax liability on income after receipt of income support payments--it

FIGURE 3.1

Combined Effect of Negative Income Tax and Positive Tax Payments

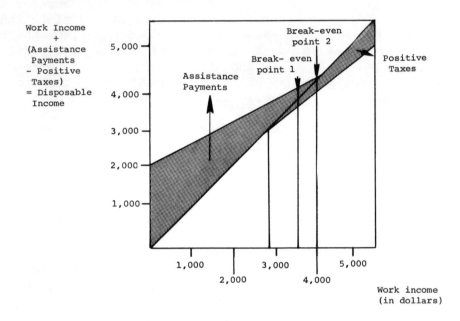

TABLE 3.3

Section of Disposable Income Situation Under NIT Plan with Basic Allowance of $2,000[a]

Earnings (dollars)	NIT Rate (percent)	Positive Income Tax Rate (percent)	NIT Subsidy (dollars)	Positive Tax Payment (dollars)	Effective Marginal Tax on Earnings (percent)		Disposable Income (dollars)	
					Without Reimbursement	With Reimbursement	Without Reimbursement	With Reimbursement
1,000	50	0	500	0	50	50	1,500	1,500
1,100	50	10	460	10	60	50	1,540	1,550
1,200	50	10	400	10	60	50	1,580	1,600
1,300	50	10	350	10	60	50	1,620	1,650

[a]NIT rate of 50 percent (and marginal positive tax rate on each increment of income of $100 over basic exemption of $1,000).

may be observed that the establishment of the pattern
of income distribution in the lower income groups
without provision for additional tax due as a consequence of the income support payments would imply a
situation where either all income support recipients
received compensation for positive tax paid or tax
rates and deductions were so modified as to eliminate
all income support recipients from the income tax
net.

In sum, in defining the poverty gap and the effectiveness of various income support schemes in
filling that gap, it is important to define income
as disposable income after all positive income tax
liability, both that liability that was incurred before income support payments were added to recipients' income and liability incurred as a consequence
of the income support payments in taxable income.
In calculating the initial poverty gap, therefore,
we apply standard Canadian exemptions and deductions
to all individuals and families to define the gap
in terms of disposable income; in evaluating the
effectiveness of the various income support programs
in filling the poverty gap, we apply standard rates
and deductions to after-transfer income.

With regard to transfers, the question arises
whether disposable income should be defined gross or
net of positive government transfer payments. Clearly, the gap will vary greatly in size according to
the inclusion or exclusion of the various forms of
transfer payments. The available Statistics Canada
data provide information on children's allowances,
old age pensions--this term includes Old Age Security
payments, the Guaranteed Income Supplement, Old Age
Assistance payments, and Canada/Quebec Pension Plan
payments--and, in catch-all form as one item, other
income received from government--mainly Unemployment
Insurance, but including Workmen's Compensation,
disability and veterans' pensions, and sundry small
items such as mothers' allowances. Given the limitations of the data, we take the sum of children's
allowances and old age pensions as noninsurance
transfers and the catch-all item as a first approximation of insurance transfers.

Taking into account the problems relating to
the definition of income and the specified poverty

lines for various family sizes, four poverty gaps
are defined in the model:

  1. PG1 = poverty gap in terms of gross
income minus taxes, i.e., income net of
taxes but including all current insurance
and noninsurance transfers. The poverty
gap is thus defined in terms of supplementing all existing transfers.

  2. PG2 = poverty gap in terms of
gross income minus taxes and children's and
youth allowances. The gap is defined here
in terms of replacing children's and youth
allowances but supplementing existing old
age pensions and all insurance transfers.

  3. PG3 = poverty gap in terms of gross
income minus tax and all noninsurance transfers. The gap is here defined in terms of
replacing existing noninsurance transfers
but supplementing all insurance transfers.

  4. PG4 = poverty gap in terms of gross
income minus taxes and all transfers. Here
the gap is defined in terms of replacing
all existing transfers.

  $PG1 < PG2 < PG3 < PG4$

  $PG4 - PG3 = T_i$ (sum of all insurance
transfers)

  $PG3 - PG2 = T_{nio}$ (sum of old age pension payments)

  $PG2 - PG1 = T_{nic}$ (sum of family and
youth allowances)

  $PG3 - PG1 = T_{ni}$ (sum of all noninsurance transfers)

The Relative Measure of Poverty--
The Degree of Inequality

  An index of the degree of inequality is required
to enable us to examine the redistributive implications in a relative sense of the various income support programs in question. The index must refer to
disposable income and must be defined in the four
senses indicated above in defining the poverty gap--
i.e., including all transfers, excluding children's
and youth allowances, excluding all noninsurance
transfers, and excluding all transfers.

A traditional way of displaying inequality is by
the Lorenz diagram, where the measure of inequality
is the proportion of the triangular area that falls
above a Lorenz curve. A Lorenz curve--illustrated
in Figure 3.2--is a plotting of the cumulative proportion of family units (on the horizontal axis) ar-
rayed in order from the smallest income to the
largest, against the cumulative proportion of total
income accounted for by these units.

We will not illustrate inequality by the method
of drawing Lorenz curves, since the scale of repro-
duction appropriate to this book would not indicate
small changes in inequality and since intersecting
curves present difficulties of interpretation. We
use instead the income concentration ratio (often
referred to as the Lorenz ratio or Gini ratio) derived by dividing the difference between the area
subtended by a Lorenz curve describing perfect
equality (the 45° line indicated in Figure 3.2) and
the area subtended by the Lorenz curve of actual income distribution by the total area under the Lorenz
curve of perfect equality. The concentration ratio
must, therefore, for all distributions of positive
incomes, have a value between zero and unity. A
zero value denotes no area of inequality, and thus
perfect equality; the closer the ratio approaches
unity, the greater the degree of inequality.[8]

We define the concentration ratio, C, as follows:

$$C = 1 - \sum (F_j - F_{j-1}) (Y_j + Y_{j-1}),$$

where

F_j = cumulative jth percentage of family
        units (60 percent in Figure 3.2)

F_{j-1} = cumulative j-1th percentage of fam-
        ily units (50 percent in Figure 3.2,
        the interval being thus defined as
        10 percent)

Y_j = cumulative jth percentage of total
        income (approximately 35 percent in
        Figure 3.2)

Y_{j-1} = cumulative j-1th percentage of total
        income (approximately 25 percent in
        Figure 3.2, again defining the inter-
        val as 10 percent)

FIGURE 3.2

Lorenz Curve for Canada, 1963

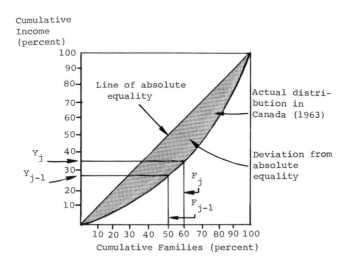

	Proportion of Income	
Proportion of Families	Absolute equality	Actual distribution 1963
0	0	0
20	20	4
40	40	17
60	60	35
80	80	56
95	95	81
100	100	100

and these terms are all expressed as decimal fractions.

$$C \text{ is defined: } 0 \leq C \leq 1$$

There are some disadvantages to the concentration ratio as a measure of income inequality. H. T. Oshima has pointed out that besides being laborious to compute "the concentration ratio is a misleading term because a highly concentrated income distribution (in the sense of a high, single peak in a frequency distribution of families according to size of income) will mean a more equal distribution (in the sense of dispersion) of income than a low, plateau distribution, with arithmetic means equal for the two distributions."[9] More important for the particular focus of this study, the concentration ratio is not sensitive to the question of which points in the overall distribution suffer most from inequality. To cope with this difficulty we resort to a measure that, although not yielding an overall measure, emphasizes the redistributive effects on the lowest income groups. The measure is the ratio of the highest quintile of incomes to the lowest quintile, which we call the high/low ratio and calculate as a basic model specification in terms of the four definitions of disposable income.

THE OUTPUT INDICATORS DEFINED FOR
THE INCOME SUPPORT SCHEMES

Introduction

For each income support alternative the model generates a set of output indicators. In this section these indicators are defined in the light of the input criteria specified in the previous section. Two basic distinctions are made. First, outputs are classified as direct or indirect, the former measuring those changes in income due solely to reassignment under the program in question of income from certain families or groups of families to others, the latter measuring changes in income and

other characteristics of families that are the result
of modifications in behavior induced by the income
support program. Second, a distinction may be made
between the partial effects of the program--the effects of either the income support payments unrelated to the increase in taxation required, ceteris
paribus, to finance the various schemes or the effects of the tax changes necessary to finance the
program unrelated to the corresponding income support
payments--and the general effects of the program,
which include the combined effects of both tax changes
and income support payments. We define, first, the
partial direct indicators attributable solely to income support payments, second, the partial indirect
indicators attributable solely to income support payments, and, third, in a section on the financing of
the various income support schemes, the partial direct
indicators attributable solely to tax financing, the
general direct indicators and the general indirect
indicators attributable to both income support payments and tax financing.

Partial Direct Indicators Attributable
to Income Support Payments

The indicators defined in this section are program cost, aggregative adequacy, weighted adequacy,
vertical efficiency, the number of families crossing
the poverty line, the change in the concentration
ratio, and the change in the high/low ratio. The
first four of these indicators may be clarified,
specifically in relation to NIT programs in terms of
Figure 3.3, and for UD and CA programs in Figure 3.4.
As in Figure 3.3, OA = P, the basic guaranteed income
support payment, and OB is defined as poverty income
in weighted average terms. In the case of the universal programs illustrated in Figure 3.4, however,
the net income support payment, which is the same
at all work income levels, is shown by the constant
vertical distance between the income support payment
line AD and the work income line OE. Further, there
is no break-even income (ignoring the effects of
positive tax payments), and OI = W indicates the
highest income category in the complete income distribution.

FIGURE 3.3

Cost and Output Indicators
for Negative Income Tax Programs

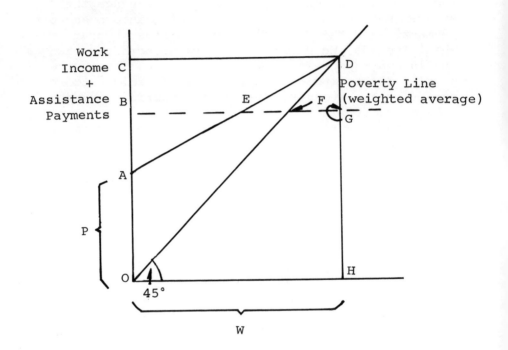

Program Cost

Program cost is generated simply as the direct
transfer cost in dollars attributable to the scheme
in question. The concept is essentially static, it
being assumed that the earnings levels that are supplemented under the various schemes are not altered
as a consequence of scheme payments. We thus ignore
the possibility of "real" economic costs attributable
to diminished work effort as a consequence of the
schemes; it is further assumed that there are zero
economic costs attributable to changes in saving and

investment behavior attributable to financing the
income support schemes. Program cost is defined before and after existing taxation for all four definitions of disposable income and is greater the wider
the definition of the poverty gap.

For the selective schemes illustrated in Figure
3.3, the area OAD reflects total income support payments and, weighting each work income level by the
appropriate number of families, represents the total
cost of the program in question. Correspondingly,
the total cost of a universal program is illustrated
in Figure 3.4 by the area OADE.

Formally, in the case of selective programs,
where the NIT rate is given by t = P/W, the total

FIGURE 3.4

Cost and Output Indicators for
Universal Payment Programs

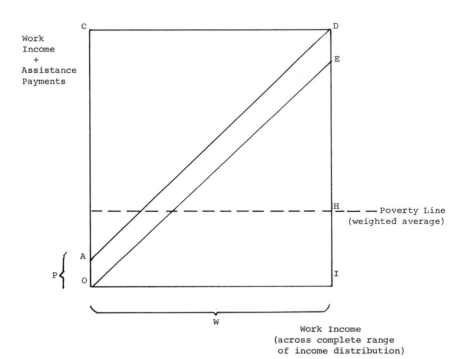

program cost, C, is defined as

$$C = \sum_{i=o}^{H} n_i (P - it)$$

where i's = the work income levels from 0 to H and
n_i = number of families at work income level i.[10]
     Similarly, in the case of universal programs
where the NIT rate is zero, total program cost is
defined as

$$C = \sum_{i=o}^{H} n_i P$$

Aggregative Adequacy.

     Discussion of the adequacy of the payments under
an income support scheme implies some prior specification of the standard against which adequacy is to
be measured. Such a standard may be considered to
exist in a micro sense in the specification of the
poverty line for a particular family and in a macro
or aggregative sense in terms of an aggregative poverty measure, defined above as the poverty gap.
"Aggregative adequacy" is defined as the percentage
of the poverty gap, defined for each of the four
definitions of disposable income, closed by each
scheme. In effect the poverty gap after each scheme
is deducted from the poverty gap before the scheme
and the difference taken as a percentage of the latter. Aggregative adequacy will be inversely related
to the size of the poverty gap—reflecting the progressively narrower definition of disposable over
PG1 through PG4—for any scheme. In Figure 3.3 the
poverty gap may be defined as the area OBF, i.e.,
aggregative income deficiency in relation to poverty
line BG and aggregative adequacy as the ratio of the
area AEFO to the area OBF. Similarly, in Figure 3.4
the poverty gap is given by the area OBG and aggregative adequacy by the ratio of the area AFGO to the
area OBG.

Weighted Adequacy.

     In the broad definition of aggregative adequacy
a dollar of income support payment is weighted identically regardless of the extent to which the before-
payment income of the recipient family falls below
the appropriate poverty line. The concept of
"weighted adequacy" introduces differential weighting
to family incomes below the poverty line. Weights
were assigned as follows: 4 to family incomes less
than 25 percent of poverty income, 3 to family incomes above 25 percent but less than 50 percent of
poverty income, 2 to family incomes above 50 percent
but less than 75 percent of poverty income, and 1 to
all other incomes below the poverty line. The
weighted poverty gap was calculated before and after
each scheme, and the difference taken as a percentage
of the former to give weighted adequacy. A variety
of alternative weighting approaches are, of course,
possible,[11] including differential weighting of payments rather than initial incomes, but the simple
approach chosen seemed the most logical extension of
the concept of aggregative adequacy. Weighted adequacy will be positively related to the extent to
which payments under the various schemes are directed
to the lowest income groups and, like aggregative
adequacy, will be inversely related to the size of
the poverty gap. In the nature of a weighting scheme
the computation is not quite as simple as in the case
of aggregative adequacy, the complication arising
from the fact that the weighted gap after payments
is not given simply as the difference between the
poverty gap before payments and the sum of income
support payments but must be calculated after payments under each scheme as the sum of all incomes
below the poverty line weighted in similar fashion
to incomes in the before-payment computation of the
poverty gap. If the poverty gap before scheme payments is given by PG_b, the poverty gap after scheme
payments by PG_a, and the weighting procedure by w,
then weighted adequacy is given by

$$\frac{wPG_b - wPG_a}{wPG_b}$$

or, in terms of Figure 3.3, the ratio of the area
OBF, calculated according to the specified weights
minus the area ABE recomputed according to the same
set of weights as an after-payment weighted poverty
gap, to the original weighted area OBF.

Vertical Efficiency

B. A. Weisbrod has defined an interesting variant
on the distributive adequacy theme[12]--"target efficiency" or "the degree to which the actual redistribution achieved by the scheme coincides with the desired redistribution." There are two aspects to
this definition: the first, defined as "horizontal
efficiency," measures the extent to which a program
intended to benefit a particular group, in fact benefits all the members of that group, and may be seen
in two senses--as the ratio of benefits going to the
target group to the total benefits needed by that
group and as the ratio of the number of beneficiaries
in the target group to the total number of persons
in the target group. The first sense amounts to the
definition of aggregative adequacy set out above,
and the second is really only of interest in the
case of in-kind programs where members of an intended
beneficiary group for one reason or another do not
in fact receive benefits. In schemes of cash transfer in a static sense, payments are made, by definition, to all those in the intended target group--
there may, of course, be specific exclusions, such
as undergraduate students, from the category of needy
individuals, but the defined target group would
still be treated in toto--though not necessarily up
to the point of individual poverty gap elimination
and thus not adequately in the broad sense defined
above.*

---

*The second aspect of horizontal efficiency may,
of course, be interesting in an administrative sense
in schemes where recipients are required to register
or apply for payment, as a measure of the proportion
of intended beneficiaries failing to apply for payment. In this sense the concept is related to questions of stigmatization and alienation, to be discussed below.

More directly interesting as a measure of distributive adequacy is Weisbrod's second aspect of
target efficiency, defined as "vertical efficiency,"
or the ratio of benefits received by intended beneficiaries to total benefits distributed. In this
sense vertical efficiency measures the percentage of
the total cost of each scheme that goes to close the
poverty gap, and shortfall of vertical efficiency
below 100 percent is a measure of the spillover or
leakage of payments under the scheme to those not
defined as statistically poor.

Under NIT schemes one of the features of the
procedure is that the setting of a NIT rate below
100 percent implies a break-even income point well
above the poverty line in many cases and, by definition, payments to families above that line. In
Figure 3.3 the area EDF represents the spillover of
payments under the scheme to families whose initial
earnings are above poverty income OB, and the ratio
of the area OAEF to the area OAD is defined as the
vertical efficiency of the scheme. Under universal
schemes payments are made, by definition, unrelated
to initial income; and in Figure 3.4 the area FDEG
represents spillover, and the ratio of the area FDEG
to the area ADEO defines the vertical efficiency of
the scheme. Clearly, in the very nature of universal schemes, vertical efficiency will be much lower
than in the case of selective schemes.

Vertical efficiency may be seen as a surrogate
for the cost-effectiveness of the scheme in question,
in the sense that the greater the vertical efficiency
ratio the smaller the per unit cost of benefits to
the target group. Thus, between two programs that
bring equal benefits to a given target group, the
program having the higher vertical efficiency ratio,
ceteris paribus, would be the least costly. Vertical
efficiency is defined in the model for each definition of disposable income, tending to be greater the
wider the poverty gap.

The definition of vertical efficiency implicitly
introduces another concept of weighting to the measurement of distributive adequacy. In effect, payments to those not defined as statistically poor are
given a zero weight. Even if payments to families
outside the target group may be regarded as value-
less in terms of eliminating the poverty gap, such

payments may be considered useful in a more broadly
defined redistributive objective that might aim at
increasing the disposable income of families in the
lower-middle or near-poor income groups as well as
that of families in poverty, and might be particularly important if one considers a wider set of
evaluation criteria including political acceptability
and stigmatization. These additional output criteria
are defined below.

The Number of Families Crossing the Poverty Line

A final measure of the distributional impact of
programs geared to the definition of poverty lines
is the number of families whose incomes cross the
poverty line as a consequence of income support payments. This indicator has the serious deficiency of
weighting a movement across the poverty line, even
by one dollar, at 1 and weighting at 0 a $1,000 in-
crease in income that does not result in a poverty
line crossing. In effect, this criterion focuses
only on improvements in income of families that were
fairly close to the poverty line in the first instance, rather than on the lowest income groups whose
income improvements, our previous weighting scheme
implied, should be regarded as more important; the
weighting implied by this criterion is thus distributionally perverse. It is, however, a politically
popular statistic and is included in the output description of each income support program. The indicator will generally be directly related to the cost
of the income support program.

The Percentage Change in the Concentration Ratio

The concentration ratio was measured before and
after each scheme, and the difference expressed as a
percentage of the before-scheme measure. This indicator will be directly related both to the cost of
the scheme and its selectivity, and was calculated
for each definition of disposable income.

The Percentage Change in the High/Low Ratio

As in the case of the concentration ratio, the
high/low ratio was calculated before and after each

scheme for the four definitions of disposable income,
and the difference expressed as a percentage of the
before-scheme measure. Like weighted adequacy this
statistic may be expected to be directly related to
both cost and the emphasis of the scheme on the lowest
income groups.

Partial Indirect Indicators Attributable to Income Support Payments

The indicators formally defined in this section
are the work incentive indicator, the family stability
indicator, the stigmatization-alienation indicator,
the political acceptability indicator, and the administrative efficiency indicator.

The Work Incentive Indicator

The question of work incentives is a part of the
grander question of the allocative effects of redistributive programs--the effect on the incentives to
work, save, and invest of those who benefit from the
redistribution and those who through tax payments
are made worse off by it. All three incentives are
important with respect to the financing of income
support programs through a progressive income tax.
On the side of income support payments, which is the
concern of this section, discussion may be confined
to the effect on work incentives. Thus, in this section we are solely concerned with the effects of the
income support payments on the work incentives of
recipients under the various income support programs.
A complete analysis would attempt to measure not
only the direction but also the precise magnitude of
the reductions in initial earned income attributable
to the receipt of income support payments and would
accordingly recompute in the second instance the
correspondingly higher levels of program cost. In
this model we make an initial assumption about the
direction of work incentive effects attributable to
income support payments and a first crude attempt at
measuring the magnitude of the effects by designing
a points scale--incorporating what are considered
to be the two most important variables in the labor
supply function--by which each income support program

may be evaluated. A points score for each program
will thus be part of the output vector for each program; in the section on the financing of the various
programs we add to the initial work incentive points
score an additional dimension reflecting the progressivity of tax financing and aggregate the effects of
income support payments on recipients and the effects
of tax financing on tax contributors into a composite
points score for the total work incentive implications
of the income support program seen as a general redistributive process.

The Conventional Static Theory. The view that a
guaranteed minimum income will diminish the work incentives of recipients has been a perennial comfort
to opponents of welfare policy and a source of concern to its supporters. A. C. Pigou expressed concern over those welfare measures

> . . . which differentiate in favour of
> idleness and thriftlessness by making the
> help that is given larger, the smaller is
> the provision the recipients have made
> for themselves. Some resort to this type
> of transference is involved in all Poor
> Law Systems that fix a state of minimum
> fortune below which they will not allow
> any citizen to fall. For, in so far as
> they raise to the level the real income
> of all citizens whose provision for them-
> selves falls below it, they implicitly
> promise that any reduction in private
> provision shall be made good by an equi-
> valent addition to State provision. It
> is plain that the expectation of these
> differential transferences will greatly
> weaken the motive of many poor persons
> to make provisions for themselves.[13]

It is assumed throughout this development of the
work incentive criterion that leisure is not an inferior good. Under the NIT approach there are two
aspects of the work incentive problem. First, a
NIT provides a guaranteed minimum income even if an
individual chooses not to work at all. For an indi-

vidual whose income from work is below or close to
that minimum level, both a substitution effect and
an income effect will operate in favor of leisure
against work. The substitution effect may be seen
as a reduction in the cost of leisure in terms of
work income foregone; the individual may therefore
prefer more leisure and less or perhaps no work.
The income effect may be seen as a lowering or abandonment of work effort by an individual in order to
maintain his income at its level prior to the introduction of the NIT scheme.

To summarize under this first head, it is clear
that any subsidy plan for supplementing low incomes
will tend to reduce labor supply, to the extent that
leisure is not an inferior good, by raising incomes
over what they would be in the absence of the subsidy. The predicted adverse effect on work is likely
to be greater the greater the subsidy, i.e., the
higher is the basic allowance.

The situation is aggravated by the second aspect
of the incentive problem. Beyond the absolute minimum income guarantee where there is no other source
of income further income guarantee payments are inversely related to work income, in that a dollar
earned effectively reduces the NIT payment by some
proportion of a dollar, dependent on the NIT rate.
The net effect is of a positive tax on earnings.
There is therefore a second substitution effect that
again may be seen as a reduction in the cost of
leisure in terms of work income foregone. In this
case, however, the income effect may be seen as partially offsetting the substitution effect against
work, in that the individual with some predetermined
income level in mind may work harder in order to
offset the reduction in income caused by the positive
tax rate. The resultant effect is indeterminate,
but it seems reasonable to infer that the higher the
NIT rate involved and, as a consequence, the higher
the effective marginal tax on earnings the greater
will be the substitution effect and, ceteris paribus,
the more likely it will be that the scheme will have
an adverse effect on work.

Under a universal demogrant where the demogrant
is completely excluded from income for tax purposes
the first effect is conceptually similar to that

described above for a NIT, i.e., positive income and
substitution effects in the direction of increased
leisure. The implications of this first effect must,
of course, be considered on a much wider scale since
the demogrant is payable to all rather than simply
to those below a stipulated income level. The second
aspect, where a second substitution effect operates
against work as a result of the inverse relationship
of NIT payments and work earnings, is avoided under
the universal demogrant. If, however, in an attempt
to recoup part or all of the high cost of a demogrant
from higher income groups the demogrant is gradually
phased into income for tax purposes, then, of course,
the second substitution against work will operate as
in the case of a NIT scheme. The important distinction between the NIT and UD approaches is that,
financing considerations apart, the absence of a positive tax on first work earnings for "poverty" income
groups in the case of a UD scheme would suggest a
smaller adverse effect on work on the part of those
low income groups than in the case of a NIT scheme.
In general the higher is the UD level the greater is
likely to be the adverse effect on work incentives.

   A CA scheme would operate exactly like a UD,
only in a categorical sense. Presuming that CA payments were made taxable (if earnings + CA payments
exceeded income tax exemption levels), the analysis
is exactly similar for families with children to
that presented above for a UD scheme in which UD payments were included in income for tax purposes. As
in the case of the UD one can infer that adverse effects on work incentives are likely to be greater
the higher the level of CA payments and, specific to
the CA alternative, the greater the number of children
up to the specified maximum number for which payment
is allowed. These various points are illustrated
diagrammatically in Figure 3.5.

   It may be inferred that, first, the higher is
Y_g, given the NIT rate, the greater the likelihood
of an adverse effect on work under the first head
discussed above; and, second, the greater the NIT
rate, i.e., the steeper the slope of DB, given Y_g,
the greater the likelihood of an adverse effect on
work under the second head. In general the higher
the basic allowance and the higher the NIT rate the

more serious the work incentive effects may be expected to be.

In the case illustrated in Figure 3.6 three UD
(or CA) schemes are shown, of progressively greater
generosity. Under a UD scheme, where Y_{g_1} is the
demogrant payment, the entire budget constraint rises
to $B_1Y_{n_1}$ (since the effective tax rate on earnings
is zero). The corresponding budget constraints under
the more generous UD levels are $B_2Y_{m_2}$ and $B_2Y_{m_3}$.
The diagram follows the logic of the argument above
and illustrates more severe work disincentive effects
the higher the demogrant payment, at equilibrium
points E_1, and E_2, and E_3, respectively.

FIGURE 3.5

The Work-Leisure Trade-Off
Under Negative Income Tax Programs

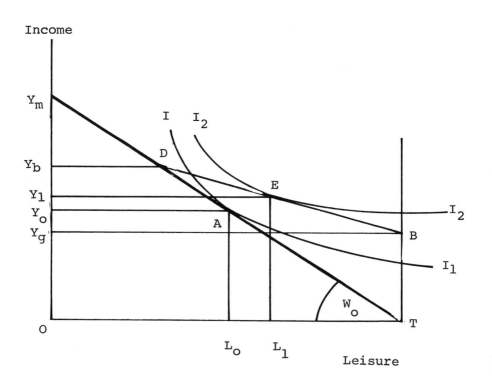

J. Conlisk[14] has questioned the static theory
on the grounds that work motivation is a function
of lagged income, that aspirations, tastes, commitments on asset purchases, and health care expenditures are all positively related to lagged income,
and that this positive motivation effect on work effort will tend to outweigh over time the negative
effect predicted by the static theory. This alternative view is interesting, but its conceptual and
theoretical development is as yet insufficient to
warrant the confident inclusion of these additional
factors in a labor supply function. Over time social
experimentation may reveal new insights into the undoubtedly complex labor supply function, particularly
in its dynamic aspects.

Empirical Work. Six studies or groups of studies
are presently available in the general field of
evaluating the effect of income support programs on
work effort. The first and second categories of
study investigate the incentive effect of existing
income support and maintenance plans in the United

FIGURE 3.6

The Work-Leisure Trade-Off Under
Universal Payment Programs

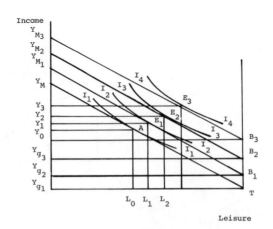

States. The first category investigates the response
of the aged to the OASDHI retirement test in the
United States;[15] and the second, the demand for public assistance in the United States.[16] The former
suffers from the fact that the aged are likely to
respond differently than the nonaged--the limited
degree to which the aged are full-time members of
the work force makes their work incentive response
of minimal interest in any event--and the latter from
their inability to separate in the results the response to implicit 100 percent effective marginal
tax rates on earnings that, by definition, eliminate
all monetary gains from work.

More interesting are the various attempts to
investigate the response to a negative income tax.
Three simulation studies have been completed[17] and
one actual social experiment conducted for which
both preliminary and midexperiment results are available.[18] The labor supply response coefficients in
the negative rate study by L. Galloway were estimated
from the response of the aged to OASDHI payments and
may thus be considered of limited usefulness; further,
they appear to depend significantly on the region of
the country used for investigation.[19] The study by
Jane H. Leuthold utilized information on a cross-
section sample of low-income workers and, on the basis of certain assumptions about the structure of
worker preferences, drew conclusions about the relation of work effort and income. The findings of the
study were that the average change in work effort
over the entire population would be likely to be
small but in a slightly positive direction, although
workers with low wages and/or large families might
be expected to reduce work effort substantially.
These rather puzzling conclusions may be a consequence
of the particular preference function that is used
in the model or may be related to data limitations.

The C. Green and A. Tella study utilized U.S.
Current Population Survey data for 1965 and 1966--
both high employment years--to investigate the differences in labor supply of families with and without
nonemployment income. The analysis concluded that
persons who receive nonemployment income work less
on the average (i.e., are less likely to be full-
time, full-year workers) than persons without nonem-

ployment income. Specifically, the study indicated
that the substitution effect of a NIT is likely to
be stronger than the income effect, i.e., that the
impact on work effort of a NIT scheme may be more
dependent on the NIT rate than on the magnitude of
the basic income guarantee, that a NIT plan with a
25 percent rate that adds from $600 to $1,000 to
the income of full-time, full-year workers in the
$2,000-3,000 bracket would produce, excluding possi-
ble dynamic motivational effects of the sort considered by Conlisk, about an 11.5 percent reduction in
annual hours of work, and, finally, that the reduction in hours would be slightly larger for NIT rates
higher than 25 percent. The study concluded with an
estimate of the significant cost in national product
foregone as a consequence of the predicted diminution
in work effort.

The preliminary results of the New Jersey experiment were based on returns from 509 out of the
1,359 participating families from August 1968 to
October 1969, in Trenton, Paterson, and Passaic; the
results are based on the experiences of 364 families
receiving various levels of support payments and a
control group of 145 families not receiving payments.
From this limited sample the conclusion arrived at
was that "there is no evidence that work effort de-
clined among those receiving income support payments.
. . . On the contrary, there is an indication that
the work effort of participants receiving payments
increased relative to the work effort of those not
receiving payments."[20] The adjusted preliminary results maintained the optimistic view: " . . . to
the extent that differences appear between control
and experimental families they are generally in
favor of greater work effort for experimentals.
Hence, anyone who seeks to support an argument of
drastic disincentive effects cannot expect to find
even weak support in the data so far."[21] The mid-
experiment report, reflecting a more serious analysis of full sample data for the first year of the
experiment, revealed differential labor supply response of control and experimental families: " . . .
the results indicate a continuation of the earlier
findings on earnings change, i.e., no significant
difference between control and experimental families.

There are significant differences, however, in two
alternative indicators of labor supply: (1) persons
employed per family, and (2) hours worked per family.
These differences indicate fewer workers or hours
for the experimental families as static labor-supply
theory would predict. There is also a differential
in average hourly earnings that reconciles the different indications given by earnings and hours."[22]
A preliminary explanation for these unanticipated
results is that "the experimental treatment provides
the security to enable earners to get better jobs";[23]
what is interesting in terms of estimating the long-
run costs of income support schemes is the first
confirmation of the behavioral response predicted by
static theory to the diminished price of leisure at
the margin--in terms of both income and substitution
effects--implied by income support payments.

The Work Incentive Criterion Adopted in the Model.
The criterion adopted makes no attempt to incorporate
the dynamic aspects of work motivation suggested by
Conlisk and focuses in a static sense on the two
variables in the labor supply function that would
appear to be most directly affected by income support payments--the size of the basic allowance (NIT
basic allowance, level of UD per person, and level
of CA per child) and the amount by which disposable
income rises when earnings rise by one dollar. The
former is defined as G, the latter as $w = \$1(1-r)$,
where r is the NIT rate. We exclude from consideration in the computation of w increased positive tax
liability for recipients of income support payments.
Only the NIT approach has within itself an implicit
tax on earnings, unrelated to standard positive tax
liability, and the NIT rates employed in the model--
25 percent, 50 percent, and 75 percent--are far
higher than the first marginal positive tax rates
to which recipients would be subject in Canada.
Since these first positive tax rates would be added
to the NIT rates in a model that set out the total
effective marginal tax rate or rates on earnings,
and would operate in isolation in the case of the UD
and CA programs, it seems a reasonable first approximation to exclude them from consideration as a common factor in the first run of the model.

The range of G reflects the range of basic allowance levels employed in the various programs tested.
The range of w is $0 \leq w \leq 1$; if $r = 0$, as in the UD
and CA programs, $w = 1$, and if $r = 100$ percent, as
in the case of traditional welfare programs in the
United States and Canada, $w = 0$. It is assumed, on
the basis of the theoretical and empirical evidence
cited above, that labor supply is negatively related
to G and positively related to w, i.e., the higher
the basic allowance the lower the labor supply; and
the higher the proportion of an earned dollar that
can be retained by the worker the greater the labor
supply.

Two ten-point scales were prepared as follows:

G-scale: Using weighted average G for each income support program (the level used in, for instance,
a particular NIT program would be the average basic
allowance payable, determined by weighting each family
level by the number of recipient units in that category), the following cardinal ranking scale was con-
structed: a score of 10 points indicating minimal
adverse effect on labor supply, a score of 1 point
indicating maximum adverse effect, and the scores
from 10 through 1 indicating progressively more adverse effect on labor supply.

Points Score	G (dollars)
10	$0 \leq G < 1{,}000$
9	$1{,}000 \leq G < 2{,}000$
8	$2{,}000 \leq G < 3{,}000$
7	$3{,}000 \leq G < 4{,}000$
6	$4{,}000 \leq G < 5{,}000$
5	$5{,}000 \leq G < 6{,}000$
4	$6{,}000 \leq G < 7{,}000$
3	$7{,}000 \leq G < 8{,}000$
2	$8{,}000 \leq G < 9{,}000$
1	$9{,}000 \leq G$

w-scale: For values of w in the range
$1 \geq w > .9$, a score of 10 points was awarded, and so
on until a score of 1 point was given for values of
w in the range $.1 \geq w \geq 0$. The scores and corresponding ranges of w emerged as follows:

Points Score	w
10	$1 \geq w > 0.9$
9	$0.9 \geq w > 0.8$
8	$0.8 \geq w > 0.7$
7	$0.7 \geq w > 0.6$
6	$0.6 \geq w > 0.5$
5	$0.5 \geq w > 0.4$
4	$0.4 \geq w > 0.3$
3	$0.3 \geq w > 0.2$
2	$0.2 \geq w > 0.1$
1	$0.1 \geq w \geq 0$

The final indicator employed was a points score derived by adding the points score obtained on both scales expressed as a percentage of the possible maximum. It seemed appropriate to weight the w points score more heavily than the G score, but such a procedure biased the results heavily against NIT schemes, and such a result seemed at variance with available empirical evidence; both scores were thus weighted identically.

Spending Effects of Income Support Programs. It was argued earlier that the effect of income support programs on saving and investment by recipients of support payments might be neglected and that the aggregate allocative implications of income support payments with respect to the behavior of recipients could be confined to labor supply. The question is, however, frequently raised whether the receipt of income support payments is likely to result in modifications in the spending pattern of recipients-- particularly in the direction of "wasteful" dissipation of the support payments. An examination of this question falls far short of a detailed demand prediction on the basis of marginal propensities to consume, which are assumed constant, given relative prices, over the period of the analysis, or an examination of changes in marginal propensities to consume in response to changes in relative prices over time.

The first results from the New Jersey experiment[18] suggested that income support payments of the NIT form, which are received in the form of a mailed check

much like a standard salary or wage check, are likely
to be spent as one would expect an increase in work
earnings to be spent and would seem to have no peculiar qualities that lead to their being dissipated
in idle living.

Whether or not a particular form of income support is regarded as different from an increase in
earned income may be considered to depend on the manner in which, and the circumstances under which, the
support payments are made. Accordingly, a categori-
zation of a particular income support program as
likely to result in the dissipation of the payment
because of the nature of the income support process
will be postponed until and subsumed under the discussion of the stigmatization-alienation indicator,
on the ground that a payment to which social stigma
is attached is likely to be distinguished from other
increments in income and, possibly, used somewhat
differently.

The Family Stability Indicator

Concern in the definition of this indicator
focuses on the extent to which an income support program provides an implicit monetary incentive for one
spouse in a two-parent family to establish a separate household, and the criterion may be expressed as
the difference between the total disposable income
received by a family unit (e.g., a man, wife, and
two children) that remains intact and the total disposable income received by the members living separately (e.g., a separated husband constituting one
unit, the wife and two children constituting the
other unit). Although the problem is generally
couched in terms of the incentive for a spouse to
abandon the household, the problem is, in fact,
broader in scale, encompassing such cases as an
elderly person living in a family unit faced under
the program with the possibility of an individual's
payment if he or she chooses to live separately and
the teenage child, perhaps attending a university,
who may choose to move out and attain individual's
status under the scheme. We will deal here only
with the problem of the incentive for a spouse to
desert at least de jure if not de facto and will

simply note that the method of dealing with the cases of the adolescent and elderly person has implications for the cost of a particular scheme,* as well as for other less clearly defined objectives, such as the degree to which family stability in general is held to be more or less desirable.

It is worth noting that we are not concerned here with the intuitively appealing notion that family stability is directly related to income but with the possibility that increments in income given in particular ways may reverse this relation, i.e., may increase family instability.

There are several characteristics of income support programs that may provide an incentive to family disintegration. First, the program may have attached to it a particular eligibility criterion that effectively denies payments until one or the other spouse has departed--this remains the case with AFDC administration in several states in the United States, which bars a household from eligibility as long as it contains an employable adult male. Such a provision may be called a disintegrative eligibility criterion and receives priority weighting in the design of the family stability criterion below.

Second, the program may provide an upper limit on the number of eligible recipients in the family unit and/or may provide for a diminishing scale of payments as the number of members in the family unit increases. If, for instance, provision is made under a NIT program for, say, $500 for the first two members of a family unit, and $300 for subsequent mem-

---

*The problem of encouragement to an elderly relative to move out might be dealt with by treating the elderly quite separately under the scheme, providing the same payment--like existing Old Age Security in Canada--whether or not the recipient lives alone or in a family unit; and the adolescent problem might be dealt with most cheaply simply by disqualifying all those below twenty-five years of age attending school or university, or most expensively by allowing all those adolescents who wish to adopt separate individual status to do so.

bers up to a maximum of five, there is, in fact,
both an upper limit effect and a diminishing scale
effect. Even if there had been no reduced scale for
third and subsequent members the upper limit effect
would provide a strong incentive to disintegration.
Imagine, for instance, a family of eight, two parents
and six children, who would obtain $1,900 under the
proposal, or $2,500 without the diminishing scale.
If the husband and wife were to separate, each taking
three children, their total combined resources under
the separate arrangement would be $4,000 without the
diminishing scale. If one now envisages the above
situation without an upper limit on the number of
eligible recipients, but the diminishing scale indicated, the incentive to separate is still strong.
From a family income of $2,800 under the above rates
without an upper limit, the separation of husband
and wife, again with each taking three of the children, would provide a combined income of $3,200. In
the example illustrated the incentive to separate
attributable to the upper limit is clearly greater
than that attributable to the diminishing scale, but
the relative contribution could clearly be reversed
by sharpening the rate of reduction in payment in
the diminishing scale; it follows that not merely
the existence of a diminishing scale is relevant but
also the rate of reduction of that scale. The influence of the upper limit will also be greater the
more parsimonious the upper limit provision. Finally,
we may note that given an upper limit and/or a diminishing scale, the monetary incentive to separate
will be greater the greater the generosity of the
program, i.e., the greater the weighted basic allowance provided by the program.

The formal definition of the family stability
indicator incorporates five of the variables indicated above: the disintegrative eligibility criterion, the existence of an upper limit, the existence
of a diminishing scale, the rate of reduction of the
diminishing scale, and the generosity of the program;
only the parsimony of the upper limit provision is
omitted, this issue being resolved in the model by
assigning identical upper limit provisions to comparable income support programs.

The disintegrative eligibility criterion is incorporated as a multiplier, having a value of zero if the criterion exists in the program in question, and 1 in the absence of such a criterion. In the first case, the final indicator value emerges as zero; in the second case the indicator score in terms of the remaining four components remains unaffected. The other components in the indicator were: first, the existence of an upper limit on payments--a maximum score of 10 was assigned if no such limit existed, a score of 5 assigned if such a limit existed; second, the existence of a diminishing scale of payments--a maximum score of 10 being assigned if there were no diminishing scale and a score of 5 assigned if such a scale existed; third, the rate of diminution of the diminishing scale defined as the amount of the first payment less the amount of the last payment divided by the number of payment intervals-- a points score from 10 to 1 being assigned according to the following scale:

Points Score	Rate of Diminution (dollars)
10	$0 \leq RD < 100$
9	$100 \leq RD < 200$
8	$200 \leq RD < 300$
7	$300 \leq RD < 400$
6	$400 \leq RD < 500$
5	$500 \leq RD < 600$
4	$600 \leq RD < 700$
3	$700 \leq RD < 800$
2	$800 \leq RD < 900$
1	$900 \leq RD$

fourth, the size of the weighted average allowance payable under the program, scores of 10 through 1 being assigned in exactly the same manner as in the G-scale under the work incentive criterion.

The final family stability indicator is defined by adding the scores under each of the last four variables and expressing the result as a percentage of the possible maximum, the whole being multiplied by 1 or zero according to the absence or presence of a disintegrative eligibility criterion.

The Stigmatization-Alienation Criterion

<u>The Stigmatization Criterion</u>. This criterion re-
flects the conventional view that income support payments should not be provided in a manner that, in
some defined sense, "stigmatizes" the recipients.
Historically, the notion of stigma has played an important role in welfare policy. Until this century
in both Europe and North America the official policy
in welfare administration was deliberately to create
a sense of shame and moral inferiority among those
falling on relief, the object of such a policy being
to encourage recipients to depart from the relief
rolls and become self-supporting and to discourage
potential applicants. Particularly since World War
II this view has been greatly modified, and there
would appear to be some consensus that, at the very
least, recipients are no less entitled to dignity and
social acceptance than the balance of the population.
Such dignity is usually taken to imply that the behavior and circumstances of recipients should not be
subject to more detailed examination and monitoring
than those of others. This new norm has been recently articulated by a prominent U.S. authority on
welfare reform:

> Much of the dissatisfaction with our current
> welfare system stems directly from discretion
> at the lower levels of authority. The in-
> equities resulting from uneven and sometimes
> capricious use of this discretion are bad
> enough, but it can also be argued with some
> merit that the experience of face-to-face
> dealing with one who has the authority to
> withdraw or grant a principal means of sup-
> port itself encourages and even promotes
> the very habits and attitudes of dependency
> our society is at some pains to eliminate.[24]

What will be attempted here is an operational
definition of stigma, a ranking of income support
alternatives on the basis of theory and such empirical evidence as is available, and a qualifying cavil
on the dynamic implications of stigma.

The major authorities on stigma define it essentially in terms of societal disapproval.[25] Erving Goffman contends that "the central feature of the stigmatized individual's situation in life" occurs when "those who have dealings with him fail to accord him the respect and regard which the uncontaminated aspects of his social identity have led him to anticipate extending, and have led him to anticipate receiving. . . ."[26] A society that holds welfare recipients in disrepute will, presumably, either be parsimonious with such payments or introduce some administrative procedure that stigmatizes recipients, or both. The administrative procedure and the degree of parsimony of a particular scheme must then both be reflected in our stigma criterion.

Dealing first with the administrative procedure, there can be little doubt that a traditional welfare payment given after what is generally referred to as a "means test" or a detailed, personalized examination of available resources of all kinds, generally accompanied by a monitoring of behavior in both an economic and social sense throughout the period of dependency, is stigmatizing. It is explicitly intended to be of such a nature. In the light of changing attitudes on the way in which welfare recipients should be treated, several more reasonable variations on the means test theme have been developed. The next category of administrative procedure may be described as a "needs test," through which resources and budgetary requirements are established as a basis for payment but in which general rules are provided for the payment of certain levels of transfer, and in which arbitrariness and the room for welfare administrator discretion have been carefully circumscribed. The eligibility criterion under which the Canada Assistance Plan--a major federal-provincial shared cost program consolidating previous welfare programs--is administered is of this nature and is, in fact, specifically referred to as a "needs test." Even this more reasonable variation has been subject to considerable attack on the ground that the recipients are subject to a more detailed examination of circumstances than others in the population, and the notion of a simple "income test" has become very fashionable.

The case for an income test is quite convincing.
Since those who pay positive income tax are obliged
to submit to an income test to determine their income tax obligation, it is held to be reasonable to
require welfare recipients to submit to an exactly
similar income declaration, on the basis of which
their payment--conveniently viewed as a negative
tax--will be automatically made. It is, however,
worth pointing out that it would be hasty to dismiss
any notion of stigma from the comfortable symmetry of
the positive tax-negative tax argument. The fact remains that every week or month, whatever the payment
period, a welfare recipient is obliged by an income
declaration to declare himself as having been poor
(or likely to be poor, if an ex-ante eligibility procedure is used), that an explicit test of any kind,
even one as simple as an income test, nevertheless
implies the drawing of a line that demarcates the
poor from the nonpoor, and that such a line might
remain in societal terms as the line dividing those
who are to be respected from those who are to be held
in some form of disrepute. Such a view supports the
case for the complete elimination of testing of any
kind in welfare programs and brings us to the case
for universalism as against selectivity in welfare
administration.
Historically, it is interesting to reflect that
in the United Kingdom the reaction to the old means
test led to the establishment of untested universality in one step in many of the basic income support
programs introduced in this century, the needs test
and income test evolutionary process having been
telescoped in the reaction to "Poor Law" administration. In the current debate in North America on
welfare reform, the "elimination of stigma" argument
for universalism is making heavy weather against the
other objective of effectiveness in reducing the
poverty gap, this latter objective leading directly
to selectivity and, at a minimum, income testing.
Economic effectiveness considerations aside, however,
it seems reasonable to conclude that, in terms of
stigma, a scheme that is completely untested is by
definition nonstigmatizing and is therefore superior
to a scheme that is income-tested; this latter form
may be considered superior to a scheme that is sub-

ject to a needs test, and the needs-tested scheme
considered superior to a scheme tested in the old
means test fashion.

The second device used by society to indicate
its approval or disapproval of welfare recipients is
the level of payment used. It seems reasonable to
postulate that the more generous a particular scheme,
ceteris paribus, the less serious perceived stigma
would be, and a useful way of incorporating parsimony
into the consideration of any particular scheme would
be to include in the overall evaluative criterion a
measure of adequacy--aggregative adequacy as defined
above being the most obvious choice. It is important
to include the adequacy of any scheme for more than
the simple reason that recipients will feel more or
less stigmatized according to the degree of parsimony. The inclusion of adequacy is one way of considering various schemes according to our strict
model criterion of stigma per unit of effectiveness.
It is not, of course, possible to do this completely,
other than for very similar schemes such as various
NIT formulations, because several of the effectiveness indicators differ widely as between the various
schemes; but the inclusion of even one effectiveness
indicator modifies slightly the reliance placed on a
simple stigma per dollar of transfer criterion implicit in the use only of the administrative procedure as the sole criterion. The usefulness of stigma
per dollar of transfer is very limited. We might,
for instance, conclude that no stigma whatever could
be attached to a universal CA scheme but that a degree
of stigma could be attached to, say, a NIT scheme
for families with children, if only in the sense set
out above for income-tested schemes. Prima facie, the
CA scheme would receive a higher ranking. If, however, the CA scheme, because of low performance on,
say, the vertical efficiency criterion or the aggregative adequacy criterion, required the retention of
more of the pre-existing means-tested or needs-tested
welfare system than did the NIT approach, then the
total stigma effect of a welfare system that contained the unstigmatized universal scheme might well
be less than that of the total welfare system that
contained the slightly stigmatized NIT scheme.

With regard to the formal incorporation of the
degree of parsimony in the evaluative criterion, we
shall assume that the greater the aggregative adequacy of a particular scheme--i.e., the greater the
percentage closing of the poverty gap--the lower the
degree of stigma. We have drawn attention to two
variables in the stigma function, the administrative
procedure used to determine eligibility and the aggregative adequacy of the scheme, assuming that stigma
is positively related to the form of testing as set
out above and is negatively related to the aggregative
adequacy of the scheme. Admittedly this is primitive social technology, but it seems to offer an interesting first basis for computing the stigmatization effect on an ex-ante basis; the validity of the
criterion might be validated or invalidated by social
experimentation.

Much of the discussion and criticism of stigma
is based on conjecture, albeit intuitively appealing
conjecture. It is therefore most interesting to be
able to refer to a useful survey done in Wisconsin
on the attitudes of welfare recipients to the AFDC
system in that state.[27] Relating the definition of
stigma to feelings of embarrassment and discomfort on
the part of welfare recipients in the presence of
people not on welfare and to a sense of the community
attitude toward welfare recipients, J. F. Handler and
E. J. Hollingsworth found that more than one-half the
respondents in their sample of 766 welfare families
expressed some feelings of stigma--inasmuch as they
were either "sometimes" or "often" embarrassed or
felt that the community was "hostile" to welfare recipients. If one adds to this group those who felt
the community to be "indifferent" to welfare recipients, a total of 61 percent of the sample expressed
some feelings of stigma. This rather large percentage is all the more interesting in that around 85 percent of the sample reported "satisfaction" with AFDC
administration in Wisconsin, and the Wisconsin system emerged as one involving minimal caseworker in-
tervention. The results may be held to confirm that
stigma is associated with means-tested welfare
schemes, and, although no results on stigma have yet
been published from the New Jersey experiment, the
author's conversations with the administrators of the

experiment in the summer of 1969 suggested no significant stigma effect to be associated with NIT welfare payments, thus suggesting confirmation of the directional disparities in stigma proposed above.

To make possible the comparison of all combinations of test and adequacy, we resort, as in the case of the work incentive criterion, to a cardinal points scale in the bifurcated evaluation criterion. The stigmatization indicator is defined as a product of two measures suitably scaled to give a maximum value of 100 percent. The administrative test is defined by a points scale ranging from 100 percent for completely untested schemes such as universal CA and UD, 75 percent for income-tested schemes such as GNIT, CNIT, and FISP 1 and FISP 2, 50 percent for needs-tested schemes such as the Canada Assistance Plan, and 25 percent for schemes tested in a comprehensive, personalized way, such as AFDC in some U.S. states and traditional welfare payments in Canada.*

The second variable used is the aggregative adequacy percentage score attained by each scheme (under disposable income definition 1), and the final indicator measures the average percentage score under the two constituent variables.

We end this section on a rather sour cavil on the dynamics of stigma. The Handler-Hollingsworth study offered one rather interesting vindication of traditional welfare philosophy, at least in an efficiency sense. They found a rather sharp relationship between feelings of stigma and departure from welfare rolls. Those who indicated feelings of stigma tended to leave the welfare rolls more by their own efforts than those who did not express feelings of stigma. The implications for the cost of the scheme over time are clear. A stigmatized scheme clearly contains an incentive for recipients to leave by their own efforts and a disincentive to potential applicants for assistance. Jay Forrester has drawn attention to the dynamic implications of a (relatively

---

*In practice we tested no schemes that received either a 50 percent or 25 percent rating but have defined the indicator in a sufficiently general way to be applicable to such schemes.

unstigmatized) NIT scheme in attracting increasing
numbers to the welfare rolls and discouraging departure from these rolls, using his analysis to justify an emphasis on job-creating policies rather than
redistributive schemes.[28] What we are trying to say
is not that stigma is desirable but that people can
be made to act in socially respectable ways by feelings of shame and that the removal of stigma from a
transfer scheme may be considered likely to make that
scheme more costly over time than one in which stigmatization is retained. The moral of the story is
presumably that ethics must prevail over economic efficiency in determining that stigma is a bad thing
but that the economic implications of eliminating
stigma should not be ignored in the setting up, for
instance, of associated manpower policies alongside
an unstigmatized transfer scheme.

The Inclusion of Alienation and the Definition of a
Composite Criterion. It may reasonably be contended
that in a broad social sense the major objective of
a reformed income support system ought to be the
"social integration" of the poor into the community
at large, i.e., the alleviation or elimination of
"alienation" defined as a sense of apartness or social
isolation on the part of payment recipients. We are
viewing alienation therefore as a sociopsychological
phenomenon, closely related to stigmatization, but
far from trivial since the "alienation effect" may be
considered to complement the "stigmatization effect"
and therefore to be worth considering in its own
right, albeit on the same scale of evaluation as that
used to measure stigma. We are primarily interested
in the alienation effect of various income support
schemes, i.e., the extent to which recipients feel
more or less alienated under the relevant options.
Only indirectly are we interested in the behavioral
implications of alienation, since options that, say,
are less alienating than the present welfare system
may be expected to lead to behavioral patterns more
in accordance with societal norms. It is perhaps
worth noting that the view that alienation is a bad
thing implies that the norms of the majority are desirable and that it is desirable to make the poor
feel and behave like everyone else. There is clearly

a debate here, and it may suffice at this point to state as our premise that societal cohesion, or homogeneity in the sense of community or common purpose, is more desirable than separateness or heterogeneity in the sense of a disintegrated society in which little sympathy or sense of community exists between its component parts.

The concept of alienation has deep roots in sociological tradition and has recently enjoyed a new vogue. There have been several attempts to rationalize the broadly ranging discussion of the concept and to come up with an operational definition.[29] The M. Seeman article is particularly useful in classifying the many uses of the concept into five basic aspects--powerlessness, normlessness, meaninglessness, social isolation, and self-estrangement--and in devising operational rules to measure these concepts. The D.G. Dean article elaborates a measure of alienation that combines the first, second, and fourth of the Seeman group, whereas the G. Nettler article focuses exclusively on the fourth aspect. There would appear to be little value here in attempting to examine the definitional debate, and we will simply say, with Nettler, that a sense of apartness or social isolation is the aspect of alienation most relevant to the discussion of income support options. The inclusion of some measure of "powerlessness," or the absence of ability on the part of the poor to influence decisions affecting them, might prove interesting in a discussion of different administrative mechanisms that might offer various degrees and forms of participation to the poor; but this is clearly a considerable conceptual step from the apartness definition we have selected as most appropriate to the immediate discussion.

Having limited the definition of alienation to a sense of apartness from the community, we shall use the same evaluation scale as was developed to measure stigmatization, renaming the composite effect the "stigmatization-alienation effect." This implies that, as for stigma, an income support program is more alienating the more detailed its form of eligibility testing, given its weighted adequacy, and the lower its weighted adequacy, given its form of eligibility testing. The usefulness of including a

measure of the degree of parsimony seems just as
relevant for the alienation effect as for the stigmatization effect. Ceteris paribus, a recipient may
be expected to feel less isolated from the rest of
society if his income allows him to function at normal consumption levels.

The Political Acceptability Criterion

Political acceptability is defined from the
point of view of the electorate, i.e., as a measure
of the nature and extent of support for a particular
income support program, and a first crude measure of
ex-ante political acceptability is defined as one of
the output variables generated for the comparative
evaluation of alternative income support programs.
As in the case of the work incentive indicator and
the stigmatization-alienation indicator, the validity
of the conclusions suggested by the political acceptability indicator may be tested by social experimentation.
It is interesting that in the United States at
present the principal and rising source of opposition
to new programs that benefit solely and specifically
the poor comes not from high income groups but from
the great range of families in perhaps the next two-
fifths in terms of income, who find themselves in a
position of financial stringency often despite regular employment, who feel caught by a variety of
forces over which they have no control--such as inflation and rising prices--and who have come to resent programs in which they are represented only as
contributors and not as recipients. The problem
would seem to lie in the sharply defined break-even
or cut-off point clearly defined in selective income
support programs of the NIT variety, whether general
or limited to families with children. Such programs
neglect the problems of the so-called near-poor--
unless they have a high break-even point, which in
turn implies a high cost, the second factor in political acceptability to be examined below. In this
sense it may be provisionally inferred that universal
programs such as CA and UD might create less political resentment, even if the payments under such programs are made taxable, since the break-even point

would be more indirectly defined as the point where
increased positive income tax liability equalled the
amount of the demogrant payment; all income groups
would receive payments under a universal program
even if the final distribution of net benefits were
to be similar to that for a selective program. A
sharply defined break-even point may be considered to
be divisive in the sense that it draws an arbitrary
line between the poor and the near-poor and focuses
attention on the differences between these groups
rather than on the needs and discontents held in
common. This problem is enormously aggravated if
the sharp contributor-recipient line coincides with
racial and regional lines, as it does in the United
States. The problem is fortunately not as acute for
Canada, but it might be reasonable to postulate that
the income-group dividing line problem will be more
serious if such a line implies that beneficiaries
under a scheme are defined as regionally, racially,
or ethnically distinct.

This argument may be considered to be qualified
by the view that selective programs are likely to be
more politically popular because they are more "efficient," i.e., do not give payments to those who do
not need them. It has been argued above that this
is probably an academic view, couched largely in
terms of distributive effectiveness, and misses the
essential point that the problem of redistribution
is concerned with more than simply a poverty stratum
of income and that a universal program by dint of
its broader focus may serve to generate a sense of
participation and therefore acceptability. The tre-
mendous popularity of universal, untaxed, family allowances in Canada is a case in point.[30]

We conclude provisionally, therefore, that, for
a given cost, a universal program such as CA or UD
may be considered more politically acceptable in a
broad sense than a selective program of the NIT
variety, and assign, on a simple percentage scale,
100 percent to CA and UD programs and 50 percent to
NIT programs.

The second factor to be briefly considered in
this rough attempt to define an evaluatory criterion
is cost. We pointed out that a NIT scheme with a
high break-even point would seem likely to be more

politically acceptable than a low break-even point
NIT scheme because the difficulties of the near-poor
would be recognized by the higher break-even point.
The problem here, of course, is that, ceteris paribus,
a higher break-even point implies a higher cost. For
any income support scheme of the kind considered in
this model, a higher cost implies a greater degree
of redistribution and greater increased taxes (negative net benefits) on all net contributors to the
scheme. It may then be reasonably inferred that the
broad political acceptability of income support
schemes in countries such as the United States and
Canada, where net recipients under an income support
scheme will be in a minority, will be inversely related to the cost of the scheme. The actual cost of
the various schemes under appraisal has been defined
as a model output. Using cost in terms of the first
definition of disposable income (the narrowest definition of the poverty gap), we define programs in
terms of cost in the following way:

Cost Designation	Cost (C) (billion dollars)
Low cost	$C \leq 1$
Moderate cost	$1 < C \leq 2$
High cost	$2 < C \leq 3$
Very high cost	$3 < C$

A program defined as low-cost is then assigned
100 percent on a percentage scale; a moderate-cost
program, 75 percent; a high-cost program, 50 percent;
and a very high-cost program, 25 percent.

The total political acceptability score for any
program is then obtained by averaging the percentage
score under the two variables. Again this is primitive social technology, focusing in a crude manner
on only two variables in what is undoubtedly a complex
political acceptability function, but it is superior,
in the absence of experimental evidence, to simply
neglecting the whole question.

In the section on the financing of the various
income support programs, the political acceptability
indicator will be extended to include the acceptabil-

ity of the actual mode of financing employed. A
high-cost program financed, say, by a sales tax of
proportional incidence or a moderately progressive
income tax would clearly be more acceptable than one
financed by a sharply progressive income tax, and
this latter distinction will be included in the definition of the composite general political acceptability indicator--i.e., the indicator incorporating
both the transfer and tax effects of income support
programs.

     Income support programs might also be appraised
in terms of their political acceptability to the
level or levels of government responsible for such
programs. This is particularly important in a federal state such as Canada where income support is
provided by the three levels of government, and jur-
isdictional boundaries are unclear. There has been
considerable debate in Canada over the interpretation
of the constitution provided in the British North
America Act, which made no direct mention of income
support measures as such but did assign hospitals,
charities, and eleemosynary institutions to the provinces (Section 92 [7]). The federal government has,
in fact, been responsible for the bulk of what we
have chosen to call "income support" measures, leaving the provinces to deal with a range of what may
be called in contrast social services, including
specific income assistance by cash payments to the
needy. The province of Quebec has taken the position
that the provincial governments ought to have sole
jurisdiction over all income support and social security measures, and the province of Ontario has suggested that it might move toward the adoption of a
NIT program for the province; the federal government,
on the other hand, has recently strongly defended
its role in income support measures.[31]

     The model recognizes the redistributive impli-
cations of multiple jurisdiction and overlapping income support programs in the set of multilevel programs that include provincial and provincial-munici-
pal supplementation of federal programs. In terms
of political acceptability in the second sense, no
attempt is made to define an evaluatory criterion.
It may be stated, however, that the simple unitary
state model of income support--i.e., with the entire

responsibility resting with the federal government--
would be unacceptable to the governments of the two
largest provinces in Canada (Ontario and Quebec);
that a system based on the "derivation principle"--
i.e., where the federal government simply acts as a
tax collection agency, passing on the tax revenue
collected to the provincial governments for disburse-
ment as they see fit--would be unacceptable to a
federal government committed to the concept of national minimum standards in income support. Between
these poles lie options such as the multilevel options run in the model, where there is superimposition of provincial and/or municipal income support
programs on a basic federal program and a variety of
shared roles in which the federal government makes
room for provincial and/or municipal roles in income
support through various forms of tax sharing, federal
abandonment of certain tax fields in favor of the
other levels of government, and grant schemes of a
conditional and/or unconditional nature. It must be
apparent that the multilevel programs run in the
model are considered in the nature of the debate on
income support jurisdiction in Canada to be superior
in terms of political acceptability--i.e., to be acceptable to all levels of government--to the simple
unitary state options.

The Administrative Efficiency Criterion

Administrative efficiency may be conveniently
viewed in two senses with respect to income support
programs: first, in the usual sense of minimum administrative costs for both government and recipients
for a given level of effectiveness; and, second, in
the sense of the responsiveness of the alternative
income support programs to changes in need on the
part of recipients.
Prima facie, it would appear that a universal
approach--such as under a UD, where payment is made
to all individuals and families, or a CA, where payments are made to all families with dependent children on the basis of verification of the existence
of such dependents--would require lower administrative costs from the point of view of government per
unit of benefit than a selective scheme such as NIT,

which requires a rather elaborate machinery for the
determination of eligibility, prevention of cheating, etc. The catch lies in determining what exactly
is meant by a unit of benefit. It is rather simple
to come at cost effectiveness from the budget constraint side and to estimate administrative costs
per dollar of costs. In this event, i.e., for a
given budget sum, it is apparent that a universal
scheme would be more cost effective than a selective
scheme. However, we have determined to come at cost
effectiveness from the side of an effectiveness constraint, and in this case the cost of a universal
scheme such as CA--which attained the same level of,
say, aggregative adequacy as defined above as a NIT
scheme, even one limited to families with children--
would considerably exceed the corresponding NIT
cost; and the administrative costs per unit of adequacy might also exceed the corresponding NIT costs,
particularly if one includes the financing implications of raising a greater sum through taxation.
The rather different initial program specifications
(basic allowance and NIT rate under a NIT scheme and
payment levels under UD and CA) and the consequent
different levels of attainment of output indicators
such as aggregative adequacy therefore suggest that
the notion of administrative costs per unit of effectiveness is not particularly useful in broad comparisons of schemes as different as NIT, UD, and CA
--though it would be useful in comparisons of an in-
trasystem nature, i.e., as between several NIT
schemes.

     If any criterion is to be defined here at all,
one is left with the rather less satisfying notion
of administrative costs as a proportion of total
program costs; and in this very limited sense we
specify the criterion that a universal program such
as UD or CA, which requires no income or needs
eligibility test, is superior to a selective program
such as NIT, which does require the administration
of an eligibility test and other means to prevent
cheating, etc., and that a NIT program is superior
to a conventional welfare program such as AFDC in
the United States or Canada Assistance Plan (CAP)
payments in Canada, where a more detailed examination of personal needs is required. On a simple per-

centage scale we accordingly assign a score of 100 percent to UD and CA programs, 75 percent to NIT programs, and 50 percent to conventional welfare programs. Confirmation of the ranking of NIT programs as superior to the traditional welfare approach is suggested by the preliminary results from the New Jersey experiment, in which the administrative costs of the NIT programs used were between $72 and $96 per family per year, as against $300 to $400 per family per year for the existing welfare system.[18]

In terms of responsiveness to changes in need on the part of the recipient, the matter is rather more simple. In this sense, a program such as AFDC or CAP, although less than optimal from many other points of view, will offer the most immediate adjustment to changing circumstances and needs for a particular family. The incredibly detailed list of provisions for assisting families according to a wide variety of needs in the Wisconsin administration of AFDC has, for instance, been well documented.[32] The adjustment is not automatic--it will usually require a caseworker's authorization--but it is more immediate, thorough, and flexible in terms of peculiar circumstances than any alternative. A program such as NIT offers an automatic adjustment on a weekly, monthly, or annual basis, depending on the administrative period selected, according to changing income, but does not have the detailed flexibility of the conventional welfare approach. Clearly, for any group of NIT programs the one with the shortest basic administrative period would be superior in terms of responsiveness to changing recipient's circumstances. Any NIT program, even one with a basic administrative period of one year, would be superior to a universal program such as UD or CA, which does not take into account changes in income but only changing needs in terms of eligible additions to the recipient group. Accordingly, we may again resort to a simple percentage scale, where a score of 100 percent is assigned to programs like AFDC and CAP, a score of 75 percent to NIT programs (we may assume that the various NIT programs run in the model all have a basic administrative period of one month, and that, accordingly, it is not necessary to distinguish between NIT programs), and a score of 50 percent to UD and CA programs that make adjustments only according to the number of members in the recipient unit.

The final score on the composite administrative efficiency criterion reflects performance on the two components defined above and is obtained by averaging the two percentage scores.

A Partial Direct Indicator Attributable to
Tax Financing, and the General Direct and
Indirect Indicators Attributable to the
Complete (Support Payments plus Tax
Financing) Redistributive Process

The tax financing side of the model is concerned solely with the personal income tax. The exclusion of alternative tax sources, such as the corporation income tax or sales or excise taxation, is based largely on the difficulty of estimating with reasonable precision the incidence, or distribution of burden, of these taxes.*

We have already introduced the tax side into the model by applying existing rates and deductions to recipients of income support payments in order to arrive at a picture of after-tax adequacy of the various income support options. We now extend the tax side of the model to include the alternative rate schedule changes required to finance the various income support options, the latter being considered either as supplements to or replacements for the existing income support system. This procedure has been carried out for Canada on several occasions by calculating the proportional income tax rate necessary to finance a particular income support scheme;[32] we concern ourselves solely with alternative progressive rate schedules.

———————————

*In assuming new tax financing we clearly imply that the income support programs are not financed by the normal growth of tax revenue at existing tax rates. We further imply that deficit financing is not employed and that other government expenditures are not reduced to make room for the income support programs.

For each income support alternative the model
generates four cost levels corresponding to the four
definitions of disposable income. For cost defined
under the first definition of disposable income we
then explore various changes in the progressive rate
structure of the personal income tax, each change
designed to produce a revenue yield equal to the cost
requirement. This rather simple exploration of alternative equal-yield rate schedules applied to the
same aggregative income data used as the basic input
for consideration of the income support alternatives
continues the macrosimulation approach of the model
and falls short, in both complexity and accuracy, of
the detailed microsimulation approaches of, among
others, J. A. Pechman and J. Bossons.[33]

Given the cost of an income support scheme, we
postulated two hypothetical rate schedules, the
second more progressive than the first, to finance
that cost. Under both hypothetical tax schemes the
cost of the scheme was assumed to be financed entirely
by the top ten income groups in the available data,
i.e., those earning more than $4,500 per annum. The
increased tax share of a family in the lowest relevant income group is given a weight of 1 in both financing schemes, rising by steps of 0.25 in the first
scheme to a maximum weight of 3.25 for the top income group and by steps of 0.5 in the second scheme
to a maximum weight of 5.50. After the operation of
each financing scheme, the model generates a final
disposable income distribution for all income groups
resulting from the use of a specific support payment-
tax financing combination. From this distribution
we calculated a concentration ratio that, when compared with the concentration ratio calculated after
the introduction of the income support program in
question, demonstrates the additional redistributive
effect consequent on the progressive tax schedule
used to finance the program--listed in the output
vector for each program as the sole example of a partial direct indicator attributable simply to the tax
financing aspect of the program--and, when compared
with the original concentration ratio, demonstrates
the aggregative redistributive effect as a consequence of a specific support payment-tax financing
combination--listed in the output vector for each

program as the sole example of a general direct indicator attributable to the complete redistributive
process implied by each support payment-tax financing
combination.

We also derive supplementary information on the
effect of the tax financing employed on work incentives and combine a measure of this effect with the
work incentive indicator defined previously to provide a composite work incentive indicator covering
the general (income support payments plus tax financing) effects of the alternative income support programs. This composite work incentive indicator is
the first of two proposed general indirect indicators.

Conventional static theory on the effect of
taxation on work incentives postulates two effects--
a substitution effect that induces greater leisure
by reducing the relative gain from work and an income
effect that induces more work in order to restore
income to its pretax level.[34] The net effect depends
on the relative preference for work or leisure and
on the degree to which work motivation is based on
financial reward. Empirical work in the area suggests the predominance of nonmonetary over monetary
factors in work motivation and an insignificant reduction in work effort as a consequence of income
taxation.[35]

We simply postulate here that the greater the
degree of progressivity of the tax procedure employed
the more likely are adverse effects on work effort
of those taxed to finance the income support program.
We do not employ one of the conventional measures of
progressivity that refer only to the relation between
the percentage of income taken in successive income
brackets by a particular rate schedule[36] but take as
a measure of the degree of progressivity a measure
for which the model has conveniently generated all
the required information--the ratio between the concentration ratios before and after a particular tax
financing scheme.[37] The usefulness of this measure
is that it takes into account not only the rate
schedule employed but also the tax yield required.
Without such an overall measure of progressivity we
would have had to deal separately with the degree of
rate schedule progressivity and the tax yield required. If the ratio between before and after con-

centration ratios exceeds unity, the effect of the
tax financing procedure employed is progressive; if
that ratio equals unity the effect is neutral or proportional; if it is less than unity, the effect is
regressive. We therefore postulate that the higher
the ratio between the final concentration ratio,
taken after both income support payment and tax financing, and the intermediate concentration ratio,
taken after the income support program solely, the
more likely are adverse effects on work effort among
taxpayers and we take the additional change in the
concentration ratio attributable to the tax scheme
alone (for the two distinct tax schemes and for each
definition of disposable income) as the additional
variable to be included in the computation of a final
work incentive indicator. As in the case of the two
variables defined in the computation of the first work
incentive indicator, we use a cardinal points scale
from 1 to 10 and assign points in relation to changes
in the concentration ratio in the following fashion:

Points Score	Percent Change in Con-centration Ratio (ΔC)
10	$1 \leq C < 2$
9	$2 \leq C < 5$
8	$5 \leq C < 7$
7	$7 \leq C < 10$
6	$10 \leq C < 12$
5	$12 \leq C < 15$
4	$15 \leq C < 17$
3	$17 \leq C < 20$
2	$20 \leq C < 25$
1	$25 \leq C$

The points score obtained for each program (for
disposable income definition 1) was added to the
points score obtained under the previous work incentive criterion and the whole expressed as a percentage
of the maximum, a separate final work incentive indicator being calculated for the two tax financing
schemes.

We also modify the political acceptability criterion defined previously to incorporate the specific
mode of tax financing employed and postulate simply

that the greater the degree of progressivity as defined above the more likely is a substantial degree of political opposition to the scheme, or, in effect, the lower the degree of political acceptability. The mobilization of political opposition to the introduction of more progressive rate schedules may be illustrated by the reaction to the proposals contained in the 1969 White Paper on Tax Reform in Canada.[38]

In the computation of the composite political acceptability, which is given for each income support program as the second general indirect indicator, we employ the same scale used in the computation of the composite work incentive indicator, take the points score obtained in relation to the additional change in the concentration ratio (for the first definition of disposable income) expressed as a percentage, and average for each program the percentage score obtained on the three dimensions of political acceptability--the type of scheme, its aggregate cost, and its mode of tax financing; a separate composite political acceptability indicator is computed for the two tax financing schemes.

In the initial discussion of the work incentive indicator it was pointed out that the allocative implications of each income support program included the effects of the program on saving and investment, and, consequently, on the rate of economic growth. We neglected the implications of income support payments on the saving and investment of payment recipients but now must reconsider the implications of tax financing of income support programs for saving and investment of those taxed to finance these programs; i.e., we must consider the effect on the rate of economic growth resulting from tax-induced changes both in the proportion of national product saved and invested and in the composition of investment. Such a component in the output vector of a redistributive model is of great importance in a dynamic sense. A tax policy that redistributes income statically but impairs capital formation and reduces the rate of economic growth will in the long run leave everyone-- recipients and contributors in the static redistributive process--with lower real incomes than would have been the case in the absence of the initial

redistribution. The initial redistribution might
thus be considered to provide for initially higher
consumption for the recipients as aggregate saving
falls but, ultimately, to lower consumption levels
for all the community as the effects of the lower
capital stock begin to appear. In sum, focusing on
those who initially benefit under a tax-financed income support scheme, if redistribution lowers the
rate of economic growth the absolute share of income
going to the group initially favored will, after a
time, be less than it would have been with a higher
rate of growth--even though the relative share of
the initially favored group in a smaller national
product has increased.

Turning first to the effect of the tax financing
procedures on the proportion of national product
saved, it may be noted that a pure redistributive
process of the sort postulated in the model is neutral
with regard to the government deficit and surplus and
that no change occurs in public saving throughout
the process. The effect on aggregate saving is thus
a question of the effect on private saving alone.
An income support scheme financed by a progressive
income tax redistributes income from those with a
relatively high average propensity to save to those
with a relatively low average propensity to save,
and may therefore be considered likely to reduce aggregate private saving, even if the proportion of
after-tax income saved by those taxed to finance the
scheme does not fall. The literature on savings incentives suggests that it is unlikely that those
taxed to finance the scheme will choose to increase
the proportion of income saved in order to bring
saving back to its pretax income level.

The financial reward for saving competes with
the desirability of present consumption. The effect
of taxation on this relationship may again be divided
into the substitution and income effects, although
the nature of these effects is more complex than in
the case of work incentives. In the simplest case
saving may be considered to be undertaken simply for
the purpose of future consumption; a tax therefore
affects consumer choice between present and future
consumption. A general income tax may be regarded
as a tax on wages income plus interest from savings.

By failing to exempt interest from savings the tax,
in effect, raises the price of future consumption
(saving) relative to present consumption. The substitution effect will be greater the sharper the
progressivity of the rate schedule.[39]

Since the tax reduces the individual's real income the income effect may simply be considered to
reduce both present and future consumption and to be
neutral in regard to the propensities to consume and
save.[40] On the other hand, it might be reasonable
to widen the income effect to include the possibility
of an individual who has some predetermined notion
of a desirable level of future consumption. Since
that level would be reduced by the tax he might postpone present consumption (increase saving) in order
to maintain the desired level of future consumption.
The inclusion of the possibility of saving for accumulation does not substantially modify the analysis, though R. A. Musgrave points out that the substitution effect will be reinforced.[41] The net effect depends on saving motivation. Although the
static theory offers no firm conclusion on the effects of progressive income taxation on saving incentives, it seems reasonable to postulate that the
higher the cost of a particular scheme and the
sharper the progression of the rate schedule used to
raise that cost the more likely it is that the negative substitution effect will prevail over the positive income effect and, as a consequence, that there
will be a net saving disincentive that complements
the negative effect on the ability to save outlined
above.

Turning from the effect of the tax financing
provisions on the proportion of national product
saved (and, by definition, invested) to the effect
on the composition of investment, a substitution
effect and an income effect can again be distinguished. The imposition of even a proportional income tax without complete loss offset provision reduces the margin between prospective return and the
risk involved in equity investment. Whether or not
this will lead to a switch to low-risk bonds in the
asset portfolio depends on whether the ratio of
probability-weighted returns differs in the after-
tax situation. An income tax that does not affect

the security and liquidity of bonds may be considered
likely to have such a substitution effect, the more
so if tax rates are progressive. The income effect
again may simply be seen as reducing investment in
both equities and bonds or may be extended to include
the possibility of the investor who has a predetermined notion of a desirable level of income from assets and who thus is encouraged to switch a greater
proportion of his portfolio to equities in an attempt
to maintain post-tax income from assets at the desired level. The net effect will depend on the complex issue of investment motivation but, again, may
be considered more likely to be negative, i.e., to
lead to a reduction in equity investment through the
predominance of the negative substitution effect over
the positive income effect, the higher the tax bill
to be raised to finance a particular income support
scheme and the more progressive the rate schedule
used to raise that given sum.

With regard therefore to the effect of the tax
side of the model on the aggregate of saving and investment, on the composition of investment portfolios,
and ultimately on the rate of growth of national
product, we can return to the comprehensive measure
of progressivity used in the previous section on
work incentives and postulate that adverse effects
on economic growth are more likely the greater the
ratio of the before-tax to after-tax concentration
ratios. This amounts to saying that the greater the
total amount of redistribution attempted, and the
sharper the progressivity of an income tax rate
schedule used to finance that redistribution, the
more explicit is the trade-off between redistribution
and growth and the more serious is the dynamic effect
described above.

We do not attempt to define a new indicator describing the effects of each income support program
on the rate of economic growth but argue instead
that the composite work incentives indicator defined
above may be seen as a useful first surrogate for
such a measure. The first two components of that indicator incorporated the effect of income support payments on the work incentives of recipients and may
thus be seen as referring to the national output
foregone, both in the short run and, assuming that

the income support program is permanent in nature,
in the long run. The third component refers to the
work incentives of those taxed to finance the income
support programs and, in terms of the argument above,
may be extended to refer also to their saving and
investment incentives. We therefore take the score
on the composite work incentives indicator as a first
indicator of the effect of each income support program on the rate of economic growth, the measure, of
course, being separately defined for each tax financing scheme.

THE SET OF INCOME SUPPORT
ALTERNATIVES EXAMINED

General NIT Schemes

1. General NIT scheme with upper limit of five members.
   Basic allowance payments for different family
   sizes:

Family size	1	2	3	4	5	6
Payment (in dollars)	900	1,500	1,800	2,100	2,400	2,400

   NIT rate: 25 percent

2. General NIT scheme without upper limit.
   Basic allowance payments for different family
   sizes:

Family size	1	2	3	4	5	6
Payment (in dollars)	900	1,500	1,800	2,100	2,400	2,700

   NIT rate: 25 percent

3. General NIT scheme with upper limit of five members.
   Basic allowance payments for different family
   sizes:

Family size	1	2	3	4	5	6
Payment (in dollars)	900	1,500	1,800	2,100	2,400	2,400

NIT rate: 50 percent

4. General NIT scheme without upper limit.
Basic allowance payments for different family sizes:

Family size	1	2	3	4	5	6
Payment (in dollars)	900	1,500	1,800	2,100	2,400	2,700

NIT rate: 50 percent

5. General NIT scheme with upper limit of five members.
Basic allowance payments for different family sizes:

Family size	1	2	3	4	5	6
Payment (in dollars)	900	1,500	1,800	2,100	2,400	2,400

NIT rate: 75 percent

6. General NIT scheme without upper limit.
Basic allowance payments for different family sizes:

Family size	1	2	3	4	5	6
Payment (in dollars)	900	1,500	1,800	2,100	2,400	2,700

NIT rate: 75 percent

7. General NIT scheme with upper limit of five members.
Basic allowance payments for different family sizes:

Family size	1	2	3	4	5	6
Payment (in dollars)	1,800	3,000	3,600	4,200	4,800	4,800

NIT rate: 25 percent

8. General NIT scheme without upper limit.
   Basic allowance payments for different family sizes:

Family size	1	2	3	4	5	6
Payments (in dollars)	1,800	3,000	3,600	4,200	4,800	5,400

NIT rate: 25 percent

9. General NIT scheme with upper limit of five members.
   Basic allowance payments for different family sizes:

Family size	1	2	3	4	5	6
Payment (in dollars)	1,800	3,000	3,600	4,200	4,800	4,800

NIT rate: 50 percent

10. General NIT scheme without upper limit.
    Basic allowance payments for different family sizes:

Family size	1	2	3	4	5	6
Payment (in dollars)	1,800	3,000	3,600	4,200	4,800	5,400

NIT rate: 50 percent

11. General NIT scheme with upper limit of five members.
    Basic allowance payments for different family sizes:

Family size	1	2	3	4	5	6
Payment (in dollars)	1,800	3,000	3,600	4,200	4,800	4,800

NIT rate: 75 percent

12. General NIT scheme without upper limit.
Basic allowance payments for different family sizes:

Family size	1	2	3	4	5	6
Payment (in dollars)	1,800	3,000	3,600	4,200	4,800	5,400

NIT rate: 75 percent

13. General NIT scheme without upper limit. Senate committee proposal 1.*
Basic allowance payments for different family sizes:

Family size	1	2	3	4	5	6
Payment (in dollars)	1,500	2,500	3,000	3,500	4,000	4,700

NIT rate: 70 percent

14. General NIT scheme without upper limit. Senate committee proposal 2.
Basic allowance payments for different family sizes:

---

*The data available did not disaggregate families of six members and over. The Senate committee proposal, which continued a diminishing scale of payments up to a family size of ten members, was dealt with by assuming, first, that the average basic allowance to families of six members and over was $4,700, and, second, that this allowance was $5,000. The cost differences and output indicator differences are noted in the results.

Family size	1	2	3	4	5	6
Payment (in dollars)	1,500	2,500	3,000	3,500	4,000	5,000

NIT rate: 70 percent

15. General NIT scheme with separate treatment of the elderly.
    Basic allowance payments for families excluding the elderly:

Family size	1	2	3	4	5	6
Payment (in dollars)	900	1,500	1,800	2,100	2,400	2,400

NIT rate: 50 percent

Basic allowance payments for the elderly:

Family size	1	2	3	4	5	6
Payment (in dollars)	1,800	2,200	2,600	3,200	3,600	3,600

NIT rate: 75 percent

NIT Schemes Limited to Families with at Least One Child

1. NIT scheme limited to families with at least one child.
   Basic allowance for families with one child = $1,000.
   Incremental payment for subsequent children up to maximum of three = $300.
   NIT rate: 50 percent

2. NIT scheme limited to families with at least one child.
   Basic allowance for families with one child = $1,000.
   Incremental payment for subsequent children with no upper limit = $300.
   NIT rate: 50 percent

3.   NIT scheme limited to families with at least one
     child.
     Basic allowance for families with one child =
     $1,000.
     Incremental payment for subsequent children up
     to maximum of three = $600.
     NIT rate: 50 percent

4.   NIT scheme limited to families with at least one
     child.
     Basic allowance for families with one child =
     $1,000.
     Incremental payment for subsequent children with
     no upper limit = $600.
     NIT rate: 50 percent

5.   NIT scheme limited to families with at least one
     child.
     Basic allowance for families with one child =
     $2,000.
     Incremental payment for subsequent children up
     to maximum of three = $300.
     NIT rate: 50 percent

6.   NIT scheme limited to families with at least one
     child.
     Basic allowance for families with one child =
     $2,000.
     Incremental payment for subsequent children with
     no upper limit = $300.
     NIT rate: 50 percent

7.   NIT scheme limited to families with at least one
     child.
     Basic allowance for families with one child =
     $2,000.
     Incremental payment for subsequent children up
     to maximum of three = $600.
     NIT rate: 50 percent

8.   NIT scheme limited to families with at least one
     child.
     Basic allowance for families with one child =
     $2,000.
     Incremental payment for subsequent children with

no upper limit = $600.
NIT rate: 50 percent

Universal Demogrant Schemes

1. Universal demogrant with upper limit of five members.
   Basic allowance payments for different family
   sizes:

Family size	1	2	3	4	5	6
Payment (in dollars)	400	700	900	1,100	1,300	1,300

   NIT rate: 0 percent

2. Universal demogrant without upper limit.
   Basic allowance payments for different family
   sizes:

Family size	1	2	3	4	5	6
Payment (in dollars)	400	700	900	1,100	1,300	1,500

   NIT rate: 0 percent

3. Universal demogrant with upper limit of five members.
   Basic allowance payments for different family
   sizes:

Family size	1	2	3	4	5	6
Payment (in dollars)	600	900	1,100	1,400	1,700	1,700

   NIT rate: 0 percent

4. Universal demogrant without upper limit.
   Basic allowance payments for different family
   sizes:

Family size	1	2	3	4	5	6
Payment (in dollars)	600	900	1,100	1,400	1,700	2,000

   NIT rate: 0 percent

5. Universal demogrant with upper limit of five members.
   Basic allowance payments for different family sizes:

Family size	1	2	3	4	5	6
Payment (in dollars)	900	1,500	1,800	2,100	2,400	2,400

NIT rate: 0 percent

6. Universal demogrant without upper limit.
   Basic allowance payments for different family sizes:

Family size	1	2	3	4	5	6
Payment (in dollars)	900	1,500	1,800	2,100	2,400	2,700

NIT rate: 0 percent

7. Universal demogrant with upper limit of five members.
   Basic allowance payments for different family sizes:

Family size	1	2	3	4	5	6
Payment (in dollars)	1,200	1,800	2,100	2,400	2,700	2,700

NIT rate: 0 percent

8. Universal demogrant without upper limit.
   Basic allowance payments for different family sizes:

Family size	1	2	3	4	5	6
Payment (in dollars)	1,200	1,800	2,100	2,400	2,700	3,000

NIT rate: 0 percent

9. Universal demogrant with upper limit of five members.
   Basic allowance payments for different family sizes:

Family size	1	2	3	4	5	6
Payment (in dollars)	1,800	3,000	3,600	4,200	4,800	4,800

   NIT rate: 0 percent

10. Universal demogrant without upper limit.
    Basic allowance payments for different family sizes:

Family size	1	2	3	4	5	6
Payment (in dollars)	1,800	3,000	3,600	4,200	4,800	5,400

    NIT rate: 0 percent

Universal Children's Allowances Schemes*

1. Universal children's allowances scheme with upper limit of three children.
   Payment rate = $300 per child per annum
   NIT rate: 0 percent

2. Universal children's allowances scheme without upper limit.
   Payment rate = $300 per child per annum
   NIT rate: 0 percent

3. Universal children's allowances scheme with upper limit of three children.

_____

*Under all the universal children's allowances options examined the allowances were made taxable and the $300 income tax exemption for each child disallowed in the computation of taxable income.

Payment rate = $600 per child per annum
NIT rate: 0 percent

4. Universal children's allowances scheme without
    upper limit.
    Payment rate = $600 per child per annum
    NIT rate: 0 percent

5. Universal children's allowances scheme with upper
    limit of three children.
    Payment rate = $1,200 per child per annum
    NIT rate: 0 percent

6. Universal children's allowances scheme without
    upper limit.
    Payment rate = $1,200 per child per annum
    NIT rate: 0 percent

Family Income Security
Plan Proposals*

1. White Paper proposal (FISP 1).
    Selective children's allowances scheme for chil-
    dren under sixteen years.
    Basic payment per child = $192 per annum up to
    an income maximum of $4,500 per annum, diminish-
    ing to zero at an income of $10,000 per annum.

2. Legislative proposal (Bill C-264) (FISP 2).
    Selective children's allowances scheme. Separate
    treatment of children under twelve years and
    children between twelve and seventeen years.

    Income level up to which maximum payments made
    for one child = $4,500, rising by a further $500
    for each subsequent child.
    Maximum payment per child per annum for children
    under twelve = $180.
    Maximum payment per child per annum for children
    between twelve and seventeen = $240.

_____

*Both proposals under this head were run, first,
with payments taxable and, second, with payments nontaxable.

Multilevel Schemes

1. General federal NIT scheme supplemented by pro-
    vincial and municipal NIT schemes.

    Federal scheme:
    General NIT scheme with upper limit of five mem-
    bers.
    Basic allowance payments for different family
    sizes:

Family size	1	2	3	4	5	6
Payment (in dollars)	900	1,500	1,800	2,100	2,400	2,400

    NIT rate: 50 percent

    Provincial supplement in rich province only.
    General NIT supplement.
    Basic supplements for different family sizes:

Family size	1	2	3	4	5	6
Payment (in dollars)		200	200	100	100	100	100

    NIT rate: 50 percent

    Municipal supplement in municipality in rich prov-
    ince.
    General NIT supplement.
    Basic supplements for different family sizes:

Family size	1	2	3	4	5	6
Payment (in dollars)		100	100	100	100	100	100

    NIT rate: 50 percent

2. Federal FISP 2 scheme supplemented by provincial
    and municipal NIT schemes.

    Federal scheme:
    Selective children's allowances scheme (FISP 2).

    Provincial supplement in rich province only.
    General NIT scheme.
    Basic allowance payments for different family
    sizes:

Family size	1	2	3	4	5	6
Payment (in dollars)	500	700	900	1,100	1,300	1,300

NIT rate: 50 percent

Municipal supplement in municipality in rich province.
General NIT supplement.
Basic supplements for different family sizes:

Family size	1	2	3	4	5	6
Payment (in dollars)	200	100	100	100	100	100

NIT rate: 50 percent

RESULTS AND CONCLUSIONS

Introduction

The vector of output indicators derived for each income support program is displayed in Table 3.4. Columns 1 through 8 indicate cost in billions of dollars for the four distinct definitions of disposable income used: i.e., gross income minus taxes; gross income minus taxes and children's allowances; gross income minus taxes, children's allowances, and old age pensions; and, finally, gross income minus taxes and all government transfers (including insurance transfers). Cost in the first case may thus be seen as a measure of the cost of adding the program in question to all existing income support programs, and total income support cost would then be the cost figure generated in the model for the new program plus the costs of existing programs. The costs of existing programs in terms of the 1967 data were found to be $0.648 billion for children's allowances and youth allowances, $1.2 billion for old age pensions, and $0.755 billion for other transfers (mainly unemployment insurance). Cost in the second case is the cost of replacing existing children's and youth allowances; the net addition to income support costs of

adopting the new program in question as a replacement
for existing children's and youth allowances is thus
given by the second cost figure minus the cost of
the existing programs ($0.648 billion). The third
cost figure similarly indicates the cost of replacing
existing children's and youth allowances and old age
pensions, and the net addition to income support
costs is given by deducting the cost of existing programs ($1.848 billion) from the new cost in column 5.
Finally, the fourth cost measure indicates the cost
of replacing all existing government transfers.
This is perhaps the least likely eventuality but is
added to complete the logic of the reporting system.
The net addition to income support costs is given by
deducting the costs of all existing transfers ($2.1
billion) from the cost figure in column 7. In the
case of several of the more modest programs examined
the latter figure is negative, as might be expected.
The usefulness of listing (in columns 2, 4, 6, and
8) the new cost net of tax at existing rates is simply
to indicate the implications for income support programs of positive income tax rates that extend to
the lower income groups. Clearly, the cost of new
programs for a given desired achievement of the various effectiveness indicators will be higher the
greater the extent to which new income support gains
are eroded by increased positive income tax liability.
    Columns 9 through 12 indicate for the four defi-
nitions of disposable income the vertical efficiency
of each scheme, or the proportion of the total cost
of the scheme distributed to those whose initial disposable income places them below the prescribed poverty lines. Expressed as a percentage, the shortfall
of vertical efficiency from 100 percent measures the
extent to which the scheme in question makes payments
to those not defined as statistically poor.
    Columns 13 through 20 indicate for the four defi-
nitions of disposable income two related measures of
the extent to which the poverty gap (defined for each
definition of disposable income) is filled by the
various schemes. The first measure, aggregative adequacy, measures the simple percentage of the gap
filled; the second, weighted adequacy, is expressed
as a percentage and, in accordance with the weights
defined previously, indicates the extent to which the

various schemes direct payments to those whose initial
incomes are lowest.

The number of families (in hundreds) crossing the
prescribed poverty lines for each family size is set
out in columns 21 through 24. It is perhaps worth
reiterating that this politically popular statistic
is of dubious usefulness, since it weights a one-
dollar increase in income that results in a crossing
at 100 percent and a $1,000 increase in income that
does not result in a crossing at zero. The popularity
of this statistic demonstrates the fallacy of mis-
placed exactness.

Columns 25 through 28 specify for each definition of disposable income the percentage change in the
concentration ratio--the degree of relative inequality of income distribution, defined in detail pre-
viously--consequent on the introduction of the various income support schemes. This measure may be regarded as the most direct indicator of the progressivity of the various schemes.

The percentage change in the high/low ratio--
the ratio of the highest and lowest income quintiles
--is then displayed in columns 29 through 32 for the
four definitions of disposable income. The high/low
ratio escapes the generality of the concentration
ratio and focuses on the implications of the income
support schemes for the highest and lowest income
groups.

Columns 33 through 37 set out for each of the
schemes five indicators that make no claim to in-
ductive stringency and aspire only to conceptual
clarification and to stress the importance of income
support program outputs that are not amenable to
rigorous quantification. The work incentive indicator is defined as a points score between 100 and 1
and is calculated in terms of two elements in the labo:
supply function--the generosity of the weighted mean
basic allowance and the proportion of a dollar of
earned income that may be retained under the various
programs. The family stability indicator is defined
as a points score between 100 and zero* and reflects

---

*The lowest score of zero reflects the zero score
given to any scheme with a disintegrative eligibility

five income support variables considered relevant--
the presence of a disintegrative eligibility criterion, the presence of an upper limit on eligibility,
a diminishing scale of payments, the generosity of
the basic allowance, and the rate of diminution of
the diminishing scale. The stigmatization-alienation
indicator, measured on a points scale from 100 to 1,
is calculated in terms of the presence of an eligibility criterion or test and the aggregative adequacy
of the program. The political acceptability indicator,
measured on a points scale from 100 to 1, reflects
the nature of each income support program (universal
or selective) and its cost. Finally, the administrative efficiency indicator, again measured on a points
scale from 100 to 1, reflects postulated administrative costs per unit of program cost and the responsiveness of program payments to changes in recipients'
need.

Columns 38 through 57 set out the tax financing
implications of the various programs. It is assumed
in every case that the program is paid for entirely
through increased income tax rates and through the
two hypothetical tax schedules described in the previous section. For each program the percentage increase in the income concentration ratio attributable
to new tax financing is set out (ΔC_1), followed by
an overall redistributive measure, the percentage
increase in the concentration ratio attributable to
the income support program and its associated tax
financing (ΔC_2). The last measure is an attempt to
indicate the general budgetary implications of the
tax/transfer process. For each tax scheme the work
incentive indicator and the political acceptability
indicator are also recalculated to include the effects of tax financing. The variable included to
measure the effects of tax financing is the percentage change in the concentration ratio (disposable
income definition 1) attributable to the tax financing

---

criterion. None of the schemes examined has this
iniquitous aspect, but the criterion was defined with
sufficient generality to include schemes that do,
such as the AFDC (Aid for Families with Dependent
Children) schemes in some states in the United States.

TABLE 3.4

Output Indicators for All Schemes

Scheme	Indicator							
	1	2	3	4	5	6	7	8
	Cost (billions of dollars)							
	D.I.1.		D.I.2.		D.I.3.		D.I.4.	
	Before Tax	After Tax	Before Tax	After Tax	Before Tax	After Tax	Before Tax	After Tax
GNIT 1	2.99	2.52	3.11	2.61	3.35	2.80	3.52	2.94
GNIT 2	3.00	2.53	3.12	2.62	3.37	2.82	3.53	2.95
GNIT 3	0.88	0.84	0.96	0.91	1.28	1.17	1.50	1.36
GNIT 4	0.88	0.84	0.97	0.91	1.29	1.18	1.51	1.36
GNIT 5	0.49	0.48	0.53	0.53	0.79	0.75	1.02	0.95
GNIT 6	0.49	0.49	0.54	0.54	0.80	0.75	1.02	0.95
GNIT 7	12.46	9.62	12.62	9.74	12.90	9.95	13.08	10.08
GNIT 8	12.49	9.65	12.66	9.76	12.93	9.97	13.12	10.11
GNIT 9	5.98	4.89	6.22	5.08	6.71	5.46	7.04	5.71
GNIT 10	6.00	4.92	6.25	5.10	6.74	5.48	7.07	5.73
GNIT 11	2.96	2.57	3.18	2.75	3.78	3.22	4.18	3.54
GNIT 12	2.97	2.58	3.20	2.76	3.80	3.24	4.20	3.56
GNIT 13 (Senate 1)	2.02	1.81	2.19	1.94	2.71	2.36	3.05	2.64
GNIT 14 (Senate 2)	2.03	1.81	2.20	1.95	2.72	2.37	3.06	2.64
GNIT 15 (special provision for elderly)	1.71	1.49	1.79	1.55	2.05	1.76	2.28	1.96

			Indicator				
9	10	11	12	13	14	15	16
Vertical Efficiency (in percent)				Aggregative Adequacy (in percent)			
D.I.1.	D.I.2.	D.I.3.	D.I.4.	D.I.1.	D.I.2.	D.I.3.	D.I.4.
62	66	69	73	63.0	62.0	55.1	52.4
62	66	69	73	63.2	62.2	55.3	52.6
100	100	100	100	34.5	34.4	34.6	35.1
100	100	100	100	34.7	34.6	34.7	35.3
100	100	100	100	19.9	20.1	22.0	24.6
100	100	100	100	20.1	20.3	22.1	24.7
38	42	44	48	96.1	95.9	95.1	92.7
38	42	44	48	96.2	96.1	95.2	92.9
62	66	69	73	95.3	95.1	91.8	89.5
62	66	69	73	95.5	95.3	91.9	89.8
91	93	95	96	90.7	90.1	85.6	83.5
91	93	95	96	91.1	90.4	85.9	83.8
97	98	99	100	72.0	71.4	68.5	67.4
97	98	99	100	72.2	71.6	68.6	67.5
80	81	86	88	49.0	47.8	45.8	45.5

(continued)

Scheme	Indicator							
	17	18	19	20	21	22	23	24
	Weighted Adequacy (in percent)				Number of Families Crossing the Poverty Line (hundreds)			
	D.I.1.	D.I.2.	D.I.3.	D.I.4.	D.I.1.	D.I.2.	D.I.3.	D.I.4.
GNIT 1	72.5	71.6	69.9	70.0	4,857	5,669	4,524	5,725
GNIT 2	72.9	71.9	70.1	70.2	4,891	5,669	4,524	5,725
GNIT 3	52.1	51.7	56.5	56.4	0	0	0	0
GNIT 4	52.3	52.0	56.7	56.7	0	0	0	0
GNIT 5	36.6	36.8	39.0	41.7	0	0	0	0
GNIT 6	36.9	37.1	39.2	41.9	0	0	0	0
GNIT 7[*]	96.5	96.6	97.1	96.6	16,247	17,624	13,029	13,327
GNIT 8	96.6	96.6	97.1	96.7	16,273	17,639	13,044	13,347
GNIT 9	96.2	96.3	96.0	95.6	15,343	16,497	11,427	12,596
GNIT 10	96.3	96.3	96.0	95.7	15,415	16,551	11,481	12,596
GNIT 11	94.4	94.3	93.9	93.6	7,591	8,510	6,704	7,703
GNIT 12	94.6	94.4	94.0	93.8	7,668	8,567	6,761	7,786
GNIT 13 (Senate 1)	84.7	84.6	83.7	83.2	837	1,862	1,476	2,444
GNIT 14 (Senate 2)	84.6	84.7	83.7	83.3	871	1,896	1,510	2,483
GNIT 15 (special provision for elderly)	61.8	61.1	64.4	65.9	3,444	3,445	0	1,015

			Indicator				
25	26	27	28	29	30	31	32
Percentage Change in Concentration Ratio				Percentage Change in High/Low Ratio			
D.I.1.	D.I.2.	D.I.3.	D.I.4.	D.I.1.	D.I.2.	D.I.3.	D.I.4.
17	18	20	21	24	23	41	41
17	18	20	21	24	23	41	41
9	9	12	14	11	15	31	41
9	9	12	14	11	15	31	43
5	6	8	10	6	11	18	29
5	6	8	10	6	11	18	29
38	39	42	44	30	34	44	59
38	39	42	44	30	34	44	59
34	36	40	43	30	34	52	66
34	36	40	43	30	34	52	66
24	26	31	35	31	37	55	72
24	26	31	35	31	37	55	72
18	19	24	27	24	30	40	53
18	19	24	27	24	30	40	53
14	15	17	19	21	27	42	42

(continued)

217

	Indicator				
	33	34	35	36	37
	Work Incentive Score, High = 100 Low = 1	Family Stability Score, High = 100 Low = 1	Stigma Alienation Score, High = 100 Low = 1	Political Acceptabil- ity Score, High = 100 Low = 1	Administra- tive Effi- ciency Score, High = 100 Low = 1
Scheme					
GNIT 1	85	67	69	50	75
GNIT 2	85	75	69	50	75
GNIT 3	75	67	55	75	75
GNIT 4	75	75	55	75	75
GNIT 5	60	67	47	75	75
GNIT 6	60	75	48	75	75
GNIT 7	75	49	86	37.5	75
GNIT 8	75	60	86	37.5	75
GNIT 9	65	49	85	37.5	75
GNIT 10	65	60	85	37.5	75
GNIT 11	50	49	83	50	75
GNIT 12	50	60	83	50	75
GNIT 13 (Senate 1)	60	65	74	50	75
GNIT 14 (Senate 2)	60	65	74	50	75
GNIT 15 (special provision for elderly)	75	61	62	62.5	75

Indicator									
38	39	40	41	42	43	44	45	46	47
			Scheme 1					Work Incentive Score After Tax 1	Political Acceptability Score After Tax 1
D.I.1.		D.I.2.		D.I.3.		D.I.4.			
Δc_1	Δc_2	Δc_1	Δc_2	Δc_1	Δc_2	Δc_1	Δc_2		
5	23	5	24	5	25	5	27	83	65
5	23	5	24	5	26	5	27	83	65
1	10	1	11	2	14	2	16	83	87.5
1	10	1	11	2	14	2	16	83	87.5
1	6	1	7	1	9	1	11	73	87.5
1	6	1	7	1	9	1	11	73	87.5
22	68	24	73	22	73	22	76	57	23.7
22	68	24	73	22	73	22	76	57	23.7
11	49	12	53	12	57	12	61	63	48.7
11	49	12	53	12	57	12	61	48	48.7
5	31	6	33	6	40	7	44	60	65
5	31	6	33	6	40	7	44	60	65
3	22	4	24	4	29	5	33	70	70
3	22	4	24	4	29	5	33	70	70
3	17	3	18	3	20	3	23	80	76.2

(continued)

	Indicator									56	57
	48	49	50	51	52	53	54	55		Work In-centive Score After Tax 2	Political Accept-ability Score Af-ter Tax 2
	Scheme 2										
	D.I.1.		D.I.2.		D.I.3.		D.I.4.				
	Δc_1	Δc_2	Δc_1	Δc_2	Δc_1	Δc_2	Δc_1	Δc_2			
Scheme											
GNIT 1	5	24	6	25	6	27	6	28		83	65
GNIT 2	6	24	6	25	6	27	6	28		83	65
GNIT 3	2	10	2	11	2	14	2	16		83	82.5
GNIT 4	2	10	2	11	2	14	2	16		83	82.5
GNIT 5	1	6	1	7	1	9	1	12		73	87.5
GNIT 6	1	6	1	7	1	9	1	12		73	87.5
GNIT 7	27	75	30	81	27	80	27	83		53	23.7
GNIT 8	27	75	30	81	27	80	27	83		53	23.7
GNIT 9	13	52	15	56	14	60	15	65		60	43.7
GNIT 10	13	52	15	56	14	60	15	65		48	43.7
GNIT 11	6	32	7	35	8	42	8	46		60	65
GNIT 12	6	32	7	35	8	42	8	46		60	65
GNIT 13 (Senate 1)	4	22	4	25	5	30	6	34		70	70
GNIT 14 (Senate 2)	4	22	4	25	5	30	6	34		70	70
GNIT 15 (special provision for elderly)	3	18	3	19	3	21	4	24		80	76.2

	Indicator							
	1	2	3	4	5	6	7	8
	Cost							
	(billions of dollars)							
	D.I.1.		D.I.2.		D.I.3.		D.I.4.	
	Before	After	Before	After	Before	After	Before	After
Scheme	Tax	Tax	Tax	Tax	Tax	Tax	Tax	Tax
CNIT 1	0.21	0.21	0.25	0.25	0.25	0.25	0.34	0.33
CNIT 2	0.36	0.35	0.43	0.41	0.43	0.41	0.52	0.49
CNIT 3	0.61	0.56	0.72	0.65	0.72	0.65	0.84	0.75
CNIT 4	1.31	1.13	1.47	1.26	1.47	1.26	1.61	1.37
CNIT 5	0.83	0.75	0.96	0.85	0.96	0.85	1.09	0.96
CNIT 6	1.18	1.03	1.32	1.14	1.32	1.15	1.46	1.26
CNIT 7	1.76	1.50	1.96	1.65	1.96	1.65	2.13	1.78
CNIT 8	2.72	2.23	2.94	2.40	2.94	2.40	3.11	2.53
UD 1	5.25	4.02	5.25	4.03	5.25	4.03	5.25	4.02
UD 2	5.26	4.03	5.26	4.04	5.26	4.04	5.26	4.04
UD 3	6.86	5.24	6.86	5.24	6.86	5.24	6.86	5.24
UD 4	6.88	5.25	6.88	5.26	6.88	5.26	6.88	5.26
UD 5	10.38	7.85	10.38	7.85	10.38	7.85	10.38	7.85
UD 6	10.40	7.87	10.40	7.87	10.40	7.87	10.40	7.87
UD 7	12.20	9.20	12.20	9.20	12.20	9.20	12.20	9.20
UD 8	12.22	9.21	12.22	9.21	12.22	9.21	12.22	9.21
UD 9	20.76	15.31	20.76	15.31	20.76	15.31	20.76	15.31
UD 10	20.80	15.33	20.80	15.33	20.80	15.33	20.80	15.33

(continued)

	9	10	11	12	13	14	15	16
	Indicator							
	Vertical Efficiency (in percent)				Aggregative Adequacy (in percent)			
	D.I.1.	D.I.2.	D.I.3.	D.I.4.	D.I.1.	D.I.2.	D.I.3.	D.I.4.
Scheme								
CNIT 1	100	100	100	100	8.6	9.5	7.4	8.5
CNIT 2	100	100	100	100	14.5	15.6	12.1	12.7
CNIT 3	99	99	99	100	22.9	24.6	19.1	19.3
CNIT 4	78	84	84	92	34.2	36.9	28.7	28.3
CNIT 5	95	97	97	98	29.3	30.9	24.2	24.0
CNIT 6	85	90	90	95	35.9	37.6	29.4	28.7
CNIT 7	75	79	80	84	42.6	44.8	35.4	34.5
CNIT 8	64	71	71	78	46.5	49.7	39.3	39.1
UD 1	27	31	32	36	46.9	46.2	38.5	35.6
UD 2	28	31	32	36	47.1	46.3	38.6	35.7
UD 3	28	31	33	36	58.7	57.9	48.6	45.1
UD 4	28	31	33	36	58.8	58.1	48.7	45.2
UD 5	28	31	33	36	77.1	76.3	66.6	62.1
UD 6	28	31	33	36	77.3	76.5	66.8	62.2
UD 7	28	31	33	36	84.1	83.2	75.4	71.3
UD 8	28	31	33	36	84.2	83.3	75.5	71.4
UD 9	28	31	33	36	96.4	96.3	96.7	94.8
UD 10	28	31	33	36	96.5	96.4	96.8	95.0

				Indicator			
17	18	19	20	21	22	23	24
	Weighted Adequacy (in percent)			Number of Families Crossing the Poverty Line (hundreds)			
D.I.1.	D.I.2.	D.I.3.	D.I.4.	D.I.1.	D.I.2.	D.I.3.	D.I.4.
16.9	17.8	12.0	13.5	0	0	0	0
24.0	25.3	16.4	18.5	0	0	0	0
31.5	34.4	23.6	25.7	0	0	0	883
38.1	42.2	28.9	31.6	2,467	2,869	2,869	2,414
36.3	39.2	28.3	29.7	799	903	517	1,796
40.5	44.1	31.6	32.6	2,128	1,839	1,438	2,701
45.3	48.9	35.3	36.3	3,117	3,936	3,180	4,428
47.7	51.4	37.0	38.3	4,813	6,088	5,332	6,011
53.5	53.7	47.6	44.7	3,552	4,364	4,524	5,725
53.7	54.0	47.8	44.8	3,586	4,364	4,524	5,748
64.4	64.2	58.6	54.7	5,759	6,295	5,859	6,436
64.7	64.4	58.7	54.9	5,759	6,329	5,893	6,436
81.7	81.0	76.9	75.2	8,931	9,830	7,777	8,654
81.9	81.2	77.0	75.3	8,931	9,850	7,797	8,654
86.7	86.3	84.9	81.9	12,472	13,061	9,855	9,346
86.9	86.6	85.1	82.0	12,495	13,061	9,855	9,380
96.7	96.7	97.7	97.3	16,575	17,872	16,182	14,705
96.7	96.8	97.7	97.4	16,585	17,883	16,193	14,728

(continued)

223

TABLE 3.4, continued

	Indicator							
	25	26	27	28	29	30	31	32
	Percentage Change in Concentration Ratio				Percentage Change in High/Low Ratio			
	D.I.1.	D.I.2.	D.I.3.	D.I.4.	D.I.1.	D.I.2.	D.I.3.	D.I.4.
Scheme								
CNIT 1	2	2	2	3	1	6	18	21
CNIT 2	3	4	3	4	1	6	18	21
CNIT 3	4	5	5	6	11	15	18	29
CNIT 4	6	7	7	8	11	16	18	29
CNIT 5	6	7	6	7	11	17	19	32
CNIT 6	7	8	7	8	11	17	19	32
CNIT 7	9	10	9	10	11	16	21	31
CNIT 8	9	11	10	11	6	10	14	24
UD 1	10	10	11	11	10	14	22	31
UD 2	10	10	11	11	10	14	22	34
UD 3	13	14	14	15	11	16	27	37
UD 4	13	14	14	15	11	16	27	37
UD 5	20	21	22	22	16	17	43	40
UD 6	20	21	22	23	16	17	43	40
UD 7	25	26	27	28	21	22	49	48
UD 8	25	26	27	28	21	22	49	48
UD 9	36	38	39	41	25	30	45	60
UD 10	36	37	39	41	25	30	45	60

		Indicator		
33	34	35	36	37
Work Incentive Score, High = 100 Low = 1	Family Stability Score, High = 100 Low = 1	Stigma Alienation Score, High = 100 Low = 1	Political Acceptability Score, High = 100 Low = 1	Administrative Efficiency Score, High = 100 Low = 1
80	71	42	75	75
80	88	45	75	75
80	71	49	75	75
80	88	55	62.5	75
80	71	52	75	75
80	88	55	62.5	75
80	71	59	62.5	75
80	88	61	50	75
100	66	73	62.5	75
100	80	74	62.5	75
95	61	79	62.5	75
95	78	79	62.5	75
95	61	89	62.5	75
95	75	89	62.5	75
90	58	92	62.5	75
90	73	92	62.5	75
85	48	98	62.5	75
85	60	98	62.5	75

(continued)

	Indicator									
	38	39	40	41	42	43	44	45	46	47
	Scheme 1								Work Incentive Score After Tax 1	Political Acceptability Score After Tax 1
	D.I.1.		D.I.2.		D.I.3.		D.I.4.			
	Δc_1	Δc_2	Δc_1	Δc_2	Δc_1	Δc_2	Δc_1	Δc_2		
Scheme										
CNIT 1	0	2	0	3	0	3	0	3	87	87.5
CNIT 2	0	3	1	4	0	4	0	4	87	87.5
CNIT 3	1	5	1	6	1	6	1	6	87	87.5
CNIT 4	1	8	2	9	1	8	1	9	87	81.2
CNIT 5	1	7	1	8	1	7	1	8	87	87.5
CNIT 6	1	8	2	10	1	9	1	10	87	81.2
CNIT 7	2	11	2	12	2	11	2	12	87	76.2
CNIT 8	3	12	3	14	2	13	2	14	83	70
UD 1	6	17	7	17	5	16	5	16	93	71.2
UD 2	6	17	7	17	5	16	5	16	93	71.2
UD 3	9	23	9	25	7	23	7	23	87	66.2
UD 4	9	23	9	25	8	23	7	23	87	66.2
UD 5	16	39	17	41	14	38	13	38	77	51.2
UD 6	16	39	17	41	14	38	13	38	77	51.2
UD 7	21	51	22	53	18	50	17	50	67	41.2
UD 8	21	51	22	53	18	50	17	50	67	41.2
UD 9	32	79	35	86	30	81	31	85	60	36.2
UD 10	32	79	35	86	30	81	31	84	60	36.2

				Indicator					
48	49	50	51	52	53	54	55	56	57
				Scheme 2				Work Incentive Score After Tax 2	Political Acceptability Score After Tax 2
D.I.1.		D.I.2.		D.I.3.		D.I.4.			
Δc_1	Δc_2	Δc_1	Δc_2	Δc_1	Δc_2	Δc_1	Δc_2		
0	2	0	3	0	3	0	3	87	87.5
1	4	1	4	1	4	1	5	87	87.5
1	5	1	6	1	6	1	7	87	87.5
2	8	2	9	2	9	2	10	87	76.2
1	7	1	8	1	7	1	8	87	87.5
2	9	2	10	2	9	2	10	87	76.2
3	11	3	13	2	12	2	13	83	76.2
3	13	4	15	3	14	3	15	83	70
8	18	8	19	6	18	6	18	90	66.2
8	18	8	19	7	18	6	18	90	66.2
11	26	11	27	9	25	9	25	83	61.2
11	26	11	27	9	25	9	25	83	61.2
19	43	20	45	17	42	16	42	73	46.2
19	43	20	45	17	42	16	42	73	46.2
25	57	27	60	23	56	22	56	67	36.2
25	57	27	60	23	56	22	56	67	36.2
40	90	44	98	38	92	38	95	60	36.2
39	89	43	97	37	91	38	95	60	36.2

(continued)

	Indicator							
	1	2	3	4	5	6	7	8
	Cost (billions of dollars)							
	D.I.1.		D.I.2.		D.I.3.		D.I.4.	
Scheme	Before Tax	After Tax	Before Tax	After Tax	Before Tax	After Tax	Before Tax	After Tax
CA 1	2.00	1.54	2.00	1.54	2.00	1.54	2.00	1.54
CA 2	2.60	2.00	2.60	2.00	2.60	2.00	2.60	2.00
CA 3	4.00	3.04	4.00	3.04	4.00	3.04	4.00	3.04
CA 4	5.20	3.93	5.20	3.93	5.20	3.93	5.20	3.93
CA 5	8.00	5.94	8.00	5.94	8.00	5.94	8.00	5.94
CA 6	10.42	7.64	10.42	7.64	10.42	7.64	10.42	7.64
FISP 1 (untaxed)	1.13	1.13	1.17	1.17	1.17	1.17	1.18	1.18
FISP 1 (taxed)	1.13	0.92	1.17	0.95	1.17	0.95	1.18	0.96
FISP 2 (untaxed)	1.25	1.25	1.28	1.28	1.28	1.28	1.30	1.30
FISP 2 (taxed)	1.25	1.02	1.28	1.04	1.28	1.04	1.30	1.05

			Indicator				
9	10	11	12	13	14	15	16
	Vertical Efficiency (in percent)				Aggregative Adequacy (in percent)		
D.I.1.	D.I.2.	D.I.3.	D.I.4.	D.I.1.	D.I.2.	D.I.3.	D.I.4.
26	32	32	36	17.9	18.6	14.6	13.3
28	35	35	40	23.8	25.0	19.5	18.0
26	32	32	36	30.8	32.3	25.5	23.7
28	35	35	40	36.6	39.1	30.8	29.5
26	32	32	36	45.4	48.0	38.2	37.2
28	35	35	40	47.2	50.5	40.1	39.9
41	48	48	54	18.0	18.7	18.7	13.4
41	48	48	54	16.5	16.8	16.8	12.1
40	48	48	54	18.9	19.9	19.9	14.3
40	48	48	54	17.6	18.0	18.0	12.8

(continued)

Scheme	Indicator							
	17	18	19	20	21	22	23	24
	Weighted Adequacy (in percent)				Number of Families Crossing the Poverty Line (hundreds)			
	D.I.1.	D.I.2.	D.I.3.	D.I.4.	D.I.1.	D.I.2.	D.I.3.	D.I.4.
CA 1	19.4	20.6	14.9	15.1	1,502	1,866	1,453	2,701
CA 2	24.9	26.8	19.0	19.4	2,747	2,577	2,164	2,730
CA 3	32.9	36.0	24.7	24.3	3,151	3,959	3,203	4,457
CA 4	37.7	41.3	28.3	28.5	4,075	5,513	4,757	5,107
CA 5	45.6	49.2	34.6	36.5	5,518	6,672	6,333	7,073
CA 6	47.2	51.3	36.0	38.2	5,973	7,295	6,956	7,935
FISP 1 (untaxed)	18.8	20.2	20.2	13.9	2,151	1,453	1,453	2,701
FISP 1 (taxed)	18.1	19.4	19.4	13.0	1,116	1,453	1,453	2,701
FISP 2 (untaxed)	19.9	21.0	21.0	14.4	2,151	2,141	2,141	2,701
FISP 2 (taxed)	18.8	20.2	20.2	13.5	1,139	1,453	1,453	2,701

				Indicator			
25	26	27	28	29	30	31	32
Percentage Change in Concentration Ratio				Percentage Change in High/Low Ratio			
D.I.1.	D.I.2.	D.I.3.	D.I.4.	D.I.1.	D.I.2.	D.I.3.	D.I.4.
2	2	2	2	-7	-8	7	11
2	2	3	3	-10	-6	4	8
2	3	3	4	-6	-7	1	5
2	3	4	4	-8	-6	-4	3
2	3	4	5	-8	-7	-5	5
1	2	3	4	-15	-12	-10	0
3	3	3	3	-5	-1	-1	9
3	3	3	3	-4	0	0	10
3	3	3	4	-6	-3	-3	7
3	3	3	3	-5	-1	-1	8

(continued)

	Indicator				
	33	34	35	36	37
	Work Incentive Score, High = 100 Low = 1	Family Stability Score, High = 100 Low = 1	Stigma Alienation Score, High = 100 Low = 1	Political Acceptibil- ity Score, High = 100 Low = 1	Administra- tive Effi- ciency Score, High = 100 Low = 1
Scheme					
CA 1	100	83	59	87.5	75
CA 2	100	100	62	75	75
CA 3	100	83	65	62.5	75
CA 4	100	100	68	62.5	75
CA 5	100	83	73	62.5	75
CA 6	100	100	74	62.5	75
FISP 1 (untaxed)	100	88	59	62.5	75
FISP 1 (taxed)	100	88	58	62.5	75
FISP 2 (untaxed)	100	88	59	62.5	75
FISP 2 (taxed)	100	88	59	62.5	75

					Indicator			46	47
38	39	40	41	42	43	44	45	Work Incentive Score After Tax 1	Political Acceptability Score After Tax 1
				Scheme 1					
D.I.1.		D.I.2.		D.I.3.		D.I.4.			
Δc_1	Δc_2	Δc_1	Δc_2	Δc_1	Δc_2	Δc_1	Δc_2		
2	3	2	4	1	3	1	3	100	88.7
2	4	2	5	2	4	2	5	100	82.5
3	6	4	7	3	6	2	6	97	76.2
4	6	4	8	3	7	3	7	97	76.2
5	8	6	9	4	8	4	9	93	71.2
4	4	4	6	2	5	2	7	97	76.2
1	4	1	5	1	5	1	4	100	81.2
1	4	1	4	1	4	1	4	100	81.2
2	5	2	5	2	5	1	5	100	76.2
1	4	1	5	1	5	1	4	100	81.2

(continued)

Scheme	Indicator								56	57
	48	49	50	51	52	53	54	55	Work In-centive Score After Tax 2	Political Accept-ability Score After Tax 2
	Scheme 2									
	D.I.1.		D.I.2.		D.I.3.		D.I.4.			
	Δc_1	Δc_2	Δc_1	Δc_2	Δc_1	Δc_2	Δc_1	Δc_2		
CA 1	2	4	2	4	2	4	2	4	100	88.7
CA 2	3	5	3	6	2	5	2	5	97	82.5
CA 3	4	7	5	8	4	7	3	7	97	76.2
CA 4	5	8	5	9	4	8	4	8	93	71.2
CA 5	7	9	7	11	6	10	5	11	90	66.2
CA 6	5	6	6	8	4	7	4	8	93	71.2
FISP 1 (untaxed)	2	4	2	5	2	5	1	5	100	76.2
FISP 1 (taxed)	1	4	1	4	1	4	1	4	100	81.2
FISP 2 (untaxed)	2	5	2	5	2	5	1	5	100	76.2
FISP 2 (taxed)	2	4	2	5	2	5	1	4	100	76.2

234

scheme used. It will be noted that we have not recalculated the absolute redistributive indicators
after tax financing. To be completely accurate this
should be done, but we have chosen to demonstrate
the implications of tax financing through the change
in one relative indicator, in the belief that the
tax financing weights chosen would make the additional
tax burden on incomes below the poverty lines small
enough to make the neglect of that burden on the absolute indicators a reasonable approximation.

In sum, Table 3.4 provides a comprehensive output vector of performance indicators for the various
income support programs as an information input to
program selection.

The results may now be evaluated, first in general interpretive terms, and second, in more precise
cost-effectiveness terms.

General Interpretation

A total of fifteen general NIT programs are
displayed. The first twelve of these represent essentially two basic programs, the second considerably
more generous than the first, evaluated according to
the sensitivity of the performance indicators to the
imposition of an upper limit on eligibility and varying NIT rates. The general conclusion that emerges
is that general NIT programs are only marginally sensitive to the imposition of an upper limit but are
highly sensitive to changing NIT rates. With the
exception of the family stability indicator, which
explicitly incorporates the upper-limit question,
the complete range of output indicators is remarkably similar between schemes 1 and 2, schemes 3 and
4, 5, and 6, etc. On the other hand, all indicators
except the administrative efficiency indicator vary
sharply with the NIT rate. In general, the lower
the NIT rate the higher are cost, aggregative and
weighted adequacy, and the number of fortunates
crossing the poverty line. Equally the change in
the two relative indicators, the concentration ratio
and the high/low ratio, is negatively correlated
with the NIT rate. On the other hand, vertical efficiency is positively correlated with the NIT rate,

the degree of spillover being greater the more costly
the scheme. The work incentive indicator is higher
the lower the NIT rate and the lower the weighted
mean basic allowance; generous, high NIT rate schemes
thus receive a relatively low score on this indicator.
The family stability indicator falls short of maximum
score in every case since every NIT scheme examined
has a diminishing scale of payments. The indicator
is also lower if there is an upper limit and is negatively correlated with the generosity of the scheme
(measured by the weighted mean basic allowance) and
the rate of diminution of the diminishing scale.
The stigmatization-alienation indicator variations
for the general NIT schemes reflect differential aggregative adequacy, all such schemes receiving the
same score on the nature of the eligibility criterion.
Since each GNIT program receives the same score on
the first component of political acceptability, the
differential scores for the different programs reflect differential program cost, attributable, in
turn, to differential NIT rates and the size of the
basic allowance. The administrative efficiency
score is constant across the range of programs, each
GNIT program receiving the middle ranking (75 percent)
on both components of the overall criterion.

     In terms of tax financing the percentage change
in the concentration ratio attributable to such financing is a direct function of cost (and thus NIT
rates and the size of basic allowances) and the alternative weighting systems used in the two financing
schemes. The general work incentive indicator for
each program reflects the addition to the partial
work incentive indicator of a variable measuring the
change in the concentration ratio attributable to
tax financing, and thus tends to be lower the lower
the partial score (reflecting the size of the basic
allowance and the NIT rate) and the sharper the
progressivity of the tax scheme required to finance
the program. Similarly, the general political acceptability indicator reflects the addition to the
partial criterion of a variable reflecting the change
in the concentration ratio attributable to tax financing, and is lower the higher the required cost
and the sharper the progressivity of the tax scheme
employed in financing the program.

The scheme proposed by the Senate Committee on Poverty is displayed in options 13 and 14. Since the performance indicators are relatively insensitive to the assumption made as to average payment to families of six members and over, we describe option 13 as a reasonable approximation of the proposal. Viewed, as it is intended, as a replacement for existing old age pensions and family and youth allowances, the relevant definition of eligible disposable income is definition 3, i.e., gross income minus taxes, old age pensions, and family and youth allowances. The gross cost of the proposal is thus given by $2.71 billion, or $2.36 billion after taxes. The net cost of the proposal, given complete elimination of existing old age pensions and family and youth allowances, would thus be $2.71 billion minus $1.85 billion (the cost of existing old age pensions and family and youth allowances in the year in question), or $0.86 billion, if payments under the new scheme were not taxed, and $2.36 billion minus $1.85 billion, or $0.51 billion, if payments under the new scheme were to be taxable.

Although the actual costing procedure used is not detailed in the Senate Committee report, it is possible to infer that the procedure differed from that used in our model, being indirect in the sense that the program was applied to gross incomes (including taxes and all government transfers) providing an additional cost figure of $1.185 billion. From this figure it was then necessary to deduct, not the gross total of existing old age pensions and family and youth allowances, but simply that portion of those latter transfers that accrued to families whose income would have been above the specified poverty lines even if the old age pensions and family and youth allowances schemes were eliminated. The committee calculated that "saving" under those two schemes as $0.788 billion; the additional net cost resulting from the substitution of the general NIT scheme for old age pensions and family and youth allowances thus works out to $0.397 billion. Onto this figure the committee chose to add the cost of eliminating tax paid by those families below the poverty line ($0.088 billion) and a cost attributable to the assumption by the federal government of that

portion of social assistance payments presently paid
by the provinces ($0.17 billion), giving a total
additional cost attributable to the introduction of
the new system of $0.655.*

Since the committee did not wish to have income
support payments taxed, the relevant comparison is
thus between the committee figure of $0.655 billion
and our figure of $0.86 plus the two figures added
to cost by the committee, attributable to the abolition of taxes below the poverty line ($0.088 billion)
and the assumption by the federal government of provincial social assistance costs ($0.17 billion), or
$1.145 billion. The disparity between the two fig-
ures is $0.49 billion.

We initially attributed the disparity to the
different modes of costing, but checked this by running the scheme on gross income (including taxes and
all government transfers) and arrived at a cost figure in this case of $1.887 billion, as against the
committee's estimate on an inferred identical income
base of $1.185 billion. If the appropriate addi-
tions to and subtractions from this figure are made,
the additional cost of introducing the Senate scheme
works out to $1.384; the disparity in this case be-
tween our figure on the Senate Committee income base
and the Senate Committee figure is $0.729, somewhat
larger than the disparity between the Senate figure
and our cost estimate using the third definition of
disposable income. We believe the direct method of
costing employed in the first instance--i.e., applying the scheme directly to income net of taxes, old
age pensions, and family and youth allowances and
then deducting from this figure the total cost of
existing old age pensions and family and youth allow-
ances--to be the more accurate and conclude that the
Senate Committee proposal is undercosted by $0.49
billion.

Its cost aside, the Senate proposal emerges as
a relatively effective redistributive proposal, being
virtually 100 percent vertically efficient and filling
70 percent of the unweighted poverty gap and 84 percent of the weighted poverty gap; 147,600 families

---

*Not $0.645 as the committee report suggests.

are estimated to cross the poverty line under the
scheme, and the changes in the concentration ratio
and high/low ratio are quite dramatic, 24 percent
and 40 percent, respectively. The relatively low
score on work incentives, which, however, improves
slighlty in the adjustment made for tax financing,
is accounted for by the very high NIT rate employed
(70 percent), and the relatively low score on family
stability is accounted for by the high mean basic
allowance and sharply diminishing scale of payments.
On the stigmatization-alienation criterion, the effect of an income test is offset by the high aggregative adequacy to give a relatively high score.
The score of 50 on political acceptability reflects
the basic NIT form of the program and its cost of
just over $2 billion, which places the program in
the high-cost category. The administrative efficiency
score is, of course, identical to that of the other
NIT programs.

Option 15 is an interesting variant in which
particularly generous provision is made for the elderly in an otherwise modest general NIT scheme.
The increased generosity is accompanied by an increase in the NIT rate for the elderly from 50 percent to 75 percent. This model offers an interesting
cost-effectiveness comparison with general NIT and
other programs, and its relative performance will be
demonstrated in the next section.

Eight NIT programs limited to families with
children are displayed after the general NIT programs.
All programs were run at a NIT rate of 50 percent,
the programs differing in terms of the presence of
an upper limit and the generosity of payments. In
this case cost and redistributive effectiveness
proved to be quite sharply sensitive to the imposition of an upper limit and, as in the case of the
general NIT schemes, highly correlated with payment
levels. The performance of these options will be
compared directly with that of the general NIT
schemes in the subsequent section on cost-effectiveness.

Sixteen universal options, i.e., options the
payment levels of which are not income-related, are
displayed next, ten of them of the universal demogrant
variety and six of the children's allowance variety.

The universal demogrant options were tested in
relation to the presence of an upper limit and the
generosity of payments. As in the case of the general NIT schemes, the UD schemes were remarkably insensitive to the presence of an upper limit, and performance differences were highly correlated with
generosity. Although the general redistributive
performance of the UD schemes is relatively substantial, it is worth noting that the schemes are all
very high cost in nature, despite substantial tax
recoupment (which does not imply erosion of redistributive effectiveness, since the larger part of
this increased income tax liability will be borne
by higher income groups). The relatively high partial work incentive scores for the UD programs reflects the zero NIT rate implicit in such programs;
the lower general work incentive scores in turn reflect the high cost of such programs and the relatively severe degree of tax financing required.
Performance under the family stability criterion
varies for the UD programs according to the presence
of an upper limit on eligibility, the presence and
rate of a diminishing scale of payments, and the
generosity of the basic payment level. The relatively high scores under the stigmatization-alienation
criterion reflect the untested nature of the programs
and the generosity of the basic payment levels. The
political acceptability score varies according to
program cost, each UD program receiving a score of
100 percent on the first component of the criterion.
The administrative efficiency score for each UD program is 75 percent, exactly the same as for the NIT
programs; the identical score conceals, however, the
differential scores on the component parts of the
criterion, each UD program receiving 100 percent for
the first (administrative cost) component but only
50 percent for the second (responsiveness) component.
The relative performance of the UD programs will be
detailed in the next section.

The CA options examined all emerge as considerably more costly than the existing CA program,
even the most parsimonious option suggested being
$0.9 billion more costly, after taxes, than the
existing program. As with the UD options, performance in the CA schemes is highly correlated with

generosity, though an interesting aberration is the
negative effect, the degree of negativity increasing
with the generosity of the program, on the high/low
ratio--but, unlike UD option performance and paral-
lel to that of the NIT programs limited to families
with children, CA option performance is relatively
sensitive to the presence of an upper limit. It is
interesting to note that the CA programs all receive
a perfect score in terms of work incentives and that
all the options without an upper limit receive a perfect score on the family stability indicator. Each
CA option receives a score of 100 percent on the
first component of the political acceptability indicator, and the varying scores for the different CA
programs reflect increasing program cost as the generosity of the basic payment level is increased.
Like the UD programs, each CA program receives a
score of 75 percent on the administrative efficiency
criterion.

The federal government's Family Income Security
Plan proposals are examined next, both the White
Paper proposal (FISP 1) and the legislative proposal
(FISP 2) being examined under conditions where payments are taxable and nontaxable. Both basic schemes
are very similar in cost and performance, and we
confine our comments to the FISP 2 version.

If we consider the federal proposal that FISP 2
payments should not be taxable and all existing family and youth allowances should be discontinued the
gross cost of the proposal emerges as $1.28 billion
(on the second definition of eligible disposable income, i.e., gross income minus taxes and existing
family and youth allowances). The net additional
cost of replacing existing schemes is thus $0.63 bil-
lion. A taxable scheme would cost somewhat less--
$0.39 billion--the difference between the two costs
being accounted for by income tax recoupment on FISP
2 payments. FISP 2 (untaxed) is less than 50 percent vertically efficient and fills less than 20 percent of both the weighted and unweighted poverty gap;
performance is slightly worse under the taxed variety.
An estimated 214,100 families will cross the poverty
line as a consequence of the scheme, and performance
under the relative indicators is comparatively poor,
the change in the concentration ratio being 3 percent

and the high/low ratio actually worsening by 3 percent. Performance under work incentives and family
stability is very good, and the relatively low score
under the stigmatization-alienation criterion is accounted for by both the selective nature of the
scheme and its low aggregative adequacy. The political acceptability score reflects the 50 percent
score on the first component of the criterion and
the moderate cost category of the program. The 75
percent score on the administrative efficiency criterion is derived, given the selective nature of the
program, from a 75 percent score on both components
of the criterion.

Tables 3.5a and 3.5b set out the results of the
two sets of multilevel schemes. In the first set
(Table 3.5a) modest NIT supplements are added in the
rich province and in the municipality in that rich
province, respectively, to a moderate cost federal
NIT program. In the second (Table 3.5b) the not unreasonable possibility is explored that a federal
FISP 2 program (untaxed) will be supplemented by
modest provincial and municipal NIT programs, both
NIT programs again being confined to the rich province.

In both tables the complete set of output indicators, excluding tax financing, is displayed for
ten different populations. In rows 1 through 4 we
set out the implications of the basic federal program
in each of the four subpopulations and in row 5 the
aggregative implications of that program for the
country as a whole. In row 6 and row 7 we demonstrate
the implications in the two components of the rich
province of adding a modest provincial NIT supplement and in row 8 present the aggregative implications of the general federal NIT program in all four
areas and the provincial supplement in the rich province. In row 9 we set out the implications for the
municipality in the rich province of supplementing
both the basic federal program and the provincial
NIT supplement by a further municipal NIT supplement.
In row 10 the final aggregation demonstrates the implications for all four component areas of the complete set of programs, i.e., the general federal
program, the provincial NIT supplement in the rich
province, and the municipal NIT supplement in the
municipality in the rich province.

Except in the case of vertical efficiency, where increased generosity is likely to be accompanied by diminished efficiency (increased spillover), performance increases across the board on the redistributive indicators as one moves from the first aggregation (row 5) to the second (row 8) and the third (row 10). It is also interesting to compare row 1, row 2, row 6, and row 9, these rows representing the final state of the four component areas under the final set of programs in each case, with rows 1 through 4, these latter rows representing the first state of all four areas under the basic federal scheme. Under both combinations, but particularly under the FISP 2 aggregation, the performance of the aggregative redistributive indicators in the rich province is highly sensitive, in a positive sense, to the modest cost increment required by the provincial and municipal supplements.

Cost-Effectiveness of the Income Support Programs for Selected Indicators

Figures 3.7 through 3.10 present cost-effectiveness information for the major programs examined in relation to four indicators: aggregative adequacy, weighted adequacy, the percentage change in the concentration ratio, and the percentage change in the high/low ratio. It had been expected in designing the options to be examined that the use of an upper limit on eligibility would offer a distinct option to a program without such a constraint. In fact, this proved to be the case only for the CA options and the CNIT options. For the remainder of the options studied, the results for a particular scheme with and without an upper limit proved to be so close as to be virtually indistinguishable. Despite this disappointment, there proved to be enough readings in each case, and sufficient consistency in the results, to justify the construction of cost-effectiveness curves.

In the case of all four indicators—ignoring for the moment the rather curious behavior of the high/low ratio at very high cost levels—the GNIT options, of which the Senate Committee proposal and

TABLE 3.5a

Output Indicators for First Multilevel Set of Schemes (Tax Financing Omitted)

	Indicator							
	1	2	3	4	5	6	7	8
				Cost (billions of dollars)				
	D.I.1.		D.I.2.		D.I.3.		D.I.4.	
Scheme	Before Tax	After Tax	Before Tax	After Tax	Before Tax	After Tax	Before Tax	After Tax
1. Federal NIT scheme, poor province (rural area)	0.40	0.38	0.43	0.41	0.58	0.53	0.67	0.60
2. Federal NIT scheme, poor province (municipality)	0.19	0.18	0.20	0.19	0.29	0.25	0.33	0.29
3. Federal NIT scheme, rich province (rural area)	0.20	0.19	0.22	0.20	0.29	0.63	0.34	0.30
4. Federal NIT scheme, rich province (municipality)	0.09	0.09	0.10	0.09	0.14	0.13	0.17	0.15
5. Aggregation in areas 1-4	0.88	0.84	0.96	0.91	1.28	1.17	1.50	1.35
6. Federal NIT scheme and provincial NIT supplement, rich province (rural area)	0.26	0.24	0.28	0.26	0.39	0.32	0.41	0.36
7. Federal NIT scheme and provincial NIT supplement, rich province (municipality)	0.12	0.11	0.14	0.13	0.18	0.16	0.21	0.18
8. Aggregation for four areas including provincial supplement	0.97	0.92	1.06	0.99	1.39	1.26	1.61	1.45
9. Federal and provincial NIT schemes and municipal NIT supplement, rich province (municipality)	0.15	0.13	0.17	0.15	0.21	0.18	0.24	0.21
10. Aggregation for four areas including provincial and municipal supplements	1.00	0.94	1.09	1.01	1.42	1.29	1.64	1.47

Indicator							
Vertical Efficiency (in percent)				Aggregative Adequacy (in percent)			
D.I.1.	D.I.2.	D.I.3.	D.I.4.	D.I.1.	D.I.2.	D.I.3.	D.I.4.
100	100	100	100	35.3	35.5	35.6	36.1
100	100	100	100	34.3	34.2	34.4	35.0
100	100	100	100	34.5	34.3	34.5	35.0
100	100	100	100	31.1	30.0	30.8	31.4
100	100	100	100	34.4	34.3	34.5	35.0
98	98	100	100	43.4	42.8	42.3	42.0
98	99	100	100	40.2	38.8	38.8	38.5
99	99	100	100	37.5	37.3	37.2	37.5
97	98	100	100	47.6	45.5	44.6	44.0
99	99	100	100	38.3	38.1	37.9	38.1

(continued)

	Indicator							
	17	18	19	20	21	22	23	24
	Weighted Adequacy (in percent)				Number of Families Crossing the Poverty Line (hundreds)			
	D.I.1.	D.I.2.	D.I.3.	D.I.4.	D.I.1.	D.I.2.	D.I.3.	D.I.4.
Scheme								
1. Federal NIT scheme, poor province (rural area)	52.8	52.7	56.9	56.8	0	0	0	0
2. Federal NIT scheme, poor province (municipality)	51.9	51.6	56.8	56.5	0	0	0	0
3. Federal NIT scheme, rich province (rural area)	52.1	51.7	56.4	56.6	0	0	0	0
4. Federal NIT scheme, rich province (municipality)	49.4	47.7	54.2	55.0	0	0	0	0
5. Aggregation in areas 1-4	52.1	50.5	54.8	56.2	0	0	0	0
6. Federal NIT scheme and provincial NIT supplement, rich province (rural area)	61.8	61.4	63.7	64.7	0	0	138	0
7. Federal NIT scheme and provincial NIT supplement, rich province (municipality)	59.4	57.8	61.4	62.9	0	0	0	0
8. Aggregation for four areas including provincial supplement	55.4	55.7	59.7	60.2	0	0	138	0
9. Federal and provincial NIT schemes and municipal NIT supplement, rich province (municipality)	65.7	64.1	65.0	66.8	0	0	98	67
10. Aggregation for four areas including provincial and municipal supplements	58.0	55.9	60.6	61.2	0	0	236	67

Indicator							
25	26	27	28	29	30	31	32
Percentage Change in Concentration Ratio				Percentage Change in High/Low Ratio			
D.I.1.	D.I.2.	D.I.3.	D.I.4.	D.I.1.	D.I.2.	D.I.3.	D.I.4.
17	19	25	29	40	41	44	80
8	9	12	14	11	15	23	43
9	10	12	14	11	15	31	39
3	4	5	6	3	1	1	2
9	9	12	14	11	15	30	41
11	12	15	17	15	18	40	45
4	5	6	7	3	3	1	2
10	11	13	15	12	17	34	44
5	6	7	8	3	5	1	2
10	11	14	16	12	17	35	45

(continued)

	Indicator				
	33	34	35	36	37
	Work Incentive Score, High = 100 Low = 1	Family Stability Score, High = 100 Low = 1	Stigma Alienation Score, High = 100 Low = 1	Political Acceptabil- ity Score, High = 100 Low = 1	Administra- tive Effi- ciency Score, High = 100 Low = 1
Scheme					
1. Federal NIT scheme, poor province (ru- ral area)	75	61	55	75	75
2. Federal NIT scheme, poor province (mu- nicipality)	75	61	55	75	75
3. Federal NIT scheme, rich province (ru- ral area)	75	61	55	75	75
4. Federal NIT scheme, rich province (mu- nicipality)	75	61	55	75	75
5. Aggregation in areas 1-4	75	61	55	75	75
6. Federal NIT scheme and provincial NIT supplement, rich province (rural area)	75	61	59	75	75
7. Federal NIT scheme and provincial NIT supplement, rich province (mu- nicipality)	75	61	58	75	75
8. Aggregation for four areas in- cluding provin- cial supplement	75	61	57	75	75
9. Federal and provincial NIT schemes and mu- nicipal NIT sup- plement, rich province (mu- nicipality)	70	58	61	75	75
10. Aggregation for four areas in- cluding provin- cial and mu- nicipal supple- ments	73	59	59	75	75

TABLE 3.5b

Output Indicators for Second Multilevel Set of Schemes (Tax Financing Omitted)

	Indicator							
	1	2	3	4	5	6	7	8
	Cost (billions of dollars)							
	D.I.1.		D.I.2.		D.I.3.		D.I.4.	
Scheme	Before Tax	After Tax	Before Tax	After Tax	Before Tax	After Tax	Before Tax	After Tax
1. Federal FISP 2 scheme, poor province (rural area)	0.26	0.26	0.26	0.26	0.26	0.26	0.26	0.26
2. Federal FISP 2 scheme, poor province (municipality)	0.28	0.28	0.28	0.28	0.28	0.28	0.29	0.29
3. Federal FISP 2 scheme, rich province (rural area)	0.28	0.28	0.29	0.29	0.29	0.29	0.29	0.29
4. Federal FISP 2 scheme, rich province (municipality)	0.43	0.43	0.45	0.45	0.45	0.45	0.45	0.45
5. Aggregation in areas 1-4	1.24	1.24	1.28	1.28	1.28	1.28	1.29	1.29
6. Federal FISP and provincial NIT supplement, rich province (rural area)	0.32	0.32	0.33	0.33	0.35	0.35	0.38	0.38
7. Federal FISP and provincial NIT supplement, rich province (municipality)	0.45	0.45	0.47	0.47	0.48	0.48	0.50	0.49
8. Aggregation for four areas including provincial supplement	1.31	1.31	1.35	1.34	1.38	1.37	1.43	1.42
9. Federal FISP and provincial NIT supplement and municipal supplement, rich province (municipality)	0.46	0.46	0.48	0.48	0.50	0.49	0.52	0.51
10. Aggregation for four areas including provincial and municipal supplements	1.32	1.31	1.36	1.35	1.40	1.39	1.45	1.44

(continued)

	Indicator							
	9	10	11	12	13	14	15	16
	Vertical Efficiency (in percent)				Aggregative Adequacy (in percent)			
	D.I.1.	D.I.2.	D.I.3.	D.I.4.	D.I.1.	D.I.2.	D.I.3.	D.I.4.
Scheme								
1. Federal FISP 2 scheme, poor province (rural area)	67	71	71	74	15.4	15.1	11.8	10.6
2. Federal FISP 2 scheme, poor province (municipality)	40	48	48	54	19.4	20.3	15.8	14.4
3. Federal FISP 2 scheme, rich province (rural area)	40	48	48	54	18.7	19.8	15.5	14.2
4. Federal FISP 2 scheme, rich province (municipality)	23	31	33	34	29.2	33.6	26.8	25.3
5. Aggregation in areas 1-4	40	47	47	51	18.6	19.5	15.3	14.1
6. Federal FISP and provincial NIT supplement, rich province (rural area)	48	55	58	65	26.5	27.7	24.1	24.5
7. Federal FISP and provincial NIT supplement, rich province (municipality)	26	34	38	39	36.0	39.9	33.9	33.8
8. Aggregation for four areas including provincial supplement	42	49	51	56	21.1	22.1	18.1	17.4
9. Federal FISP and provincial NIT supplement and municipal supplement, rich province (municipality)	28	36	40	42	39.7	43.2	38.0	37.6
10. Aggregation for four areas including provincial and municipal supplements	43	50	52	56	21.5	22.5	18.6	17.9

Indicator							
17	18	19	20	21	22	23	24
Weighted Adequacy (in percent)				Number of Families Crossing the Poverty Line (hundreds)			
D.I.1.	D.I.2.	D.I.3.	D.I.4.	D.I.1.	D.I.2.	D.I.3.	D.I.4.
16.9	18.8	12.6	11.8	197	236	236	303
20.1	20.9	14.9	15.3	478	478	478	518
18.7	20.3	14.5	14.1	480	488	626	603
24.0	28.1	18.4	19.9	787	938	943	648
19.9	22.0	15.1	15.3	1,942	2,140	2,283	2,072
34.3	35.9	33.0	37.4	480	488	626	603
38.0	42.4	36.2	41.6	787	938	943	648
27.3	29.5	24.2	26.5	1,942	2,140	2,283	2,072
44.4	48.1	41.0	45.8	787	938	943	648
28.9	28.4	25.4	25.9	1,942	2,140	2,283	2,072

(continued)

Scheme	Indicator							
	25	26	27	28	29	30	31	32
	Percentage Change in Concentration Ratio				Percentage Change in High/Low Ratio			
	D.I.1.	D.I.2.	D.I.3.	D.I.4.	D.I.1.	D.I.2.	D.I.3.	D.I.4.
1. Federal FISP 2 scheme, poor province (rural area)	1	2	2	3	17	5	-6	-6
2. Federal FISP 2 scheme, poor province (municipality)	3	3	3	4	-6	-3	1	12
3. Federal FISP 2 scheme, rich province (rural area)	3	3	3	4	-6	-3	7	5
4. Federal FISP 2 scheme, rich province (municipality)	5	5	5	5	6	7	6	5
5. Aggregation in areas 1-4	3	3	3	4	-6	-3	6	9
6. Federal FISP and provincial NIT supplement, rich province (rural area)	5	6	7	8	-6	-2	9	11
7. Federal FISP and provincial NIT supplement, rich province (municipality)	5	6	6	7	6	7	6	5
8. Aggregation for four areas including provincial supplement	4	5	5	6	-6	-2	6	12
9. Federal FISP and provincial NIT supplement and municipal supplement, rich province (municipality)	6	6	7	8	6	7	6	5
10. Aggregation for four areas including provincial and municipal supplements	4	5	5	6	-6	-2	6	12

Indicator				
33	34	35	36	37
Work Incentive Score, High = 100 Low = 1	Family Stability Score, High = 100 Low = 1	Stigma Alienation Score, High = 100 Low = 1	Political Acceptability Score, High = 100 Low = 1	Administrative Efficiency Score, High = 100 Low = 1
100	88	58	75	75
100	88	60	75	75
100	88	59	75	75
100	88	65	75	75
100	88	60	62.5	75
80	65	51	75	75
80	65	55	75	75
80	65	55	62.5	75
75	63	57	75	75
80	65	55	62.5	75

the GNIT (elderly) program are examples, emerge as
absolutely superior in cost-effectiveness terms to
the UD and CA options, i.e., regardless of the cost
level selected as the reference point, the associated
effectiveness attainment level is higher under the
GNIT options than under the UD or CA options; correspondingly, regardless of the effectiveness level
selected as a reference point, the corresponding
cost level under the GNIT options emerges as lower
than under the UD and CA options. The CNIT options
emerge in the designs examined as relatively low-
cost schemes, offering a limited basis for comparison
with the other options. Over the part of the charts
where comparison is reasonable, the CNIT options
emerge consistently as inferior to the GNIT schemes
but superior to both the UD and CA options. The
GNIT (elderly) program behaves generally as a standard GNIT program but is more cost-effective in relation to the effect on the high/low ratio than the
Senate proposal. For the two absolute indicators,
FISP 2 emerges as less effective for a given cost
than the GNIT and CNIT schemes but superior for that
cost to the UD and CA options--suggesting that the
introduction of the principle of selectivity into
family allowances in Canada makes such payments a
more effective instrument in the reduction of poverty
defined in absolute terms. Interestingly, FISP 2
falls between a UD and CA option for a comparable
cost in terms of its effect on the concentration
ratio and performs as the worst scheme of all, for
the cost level in question, in terms of its effect
on the high/low ratio.

Comparison between the two universal options
suggests that the UD options are absolutely superior
to the CA options, and the tendency to diminishing
returns (in terms of effectiveness increments for
identical cost increments) is very marked for the
CA options and sets in more rapidly than for any
other options.

The behavior of the high/low ratio is rather
strange, increments in cost beyond a certain point
for all schemes actually reversing the (negative)
effect of the income support schemes on the high/low
ratio. In the case of the CA and CNIT options this
aberrant effect occurs at cost levels of around $2

FIGURE 3.7

Cost-Effectiveness in Relation to Aggregative Adequacy

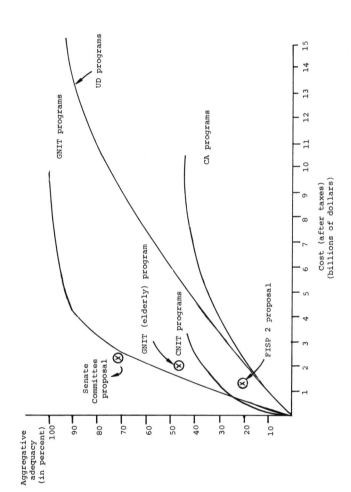

FIGURE 3.8

Cost-Effectiveness in Relation to Weighted Adequacy

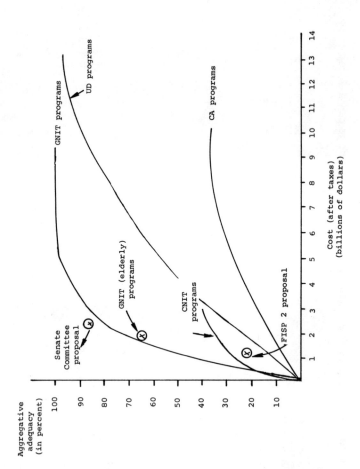

FIGURE 3.9

Cost-Effectiveness in Relation to
the Percentage Change in
the Concentration Ratio

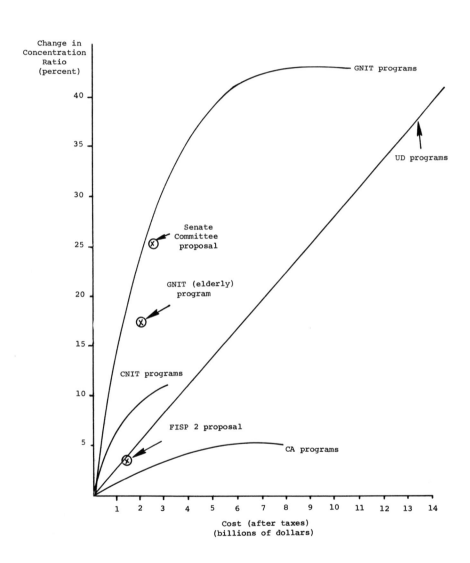

FIGURE 3.10

Cost-Effectiveness in Relation to
the Percentage Change in the High/Low Ratio

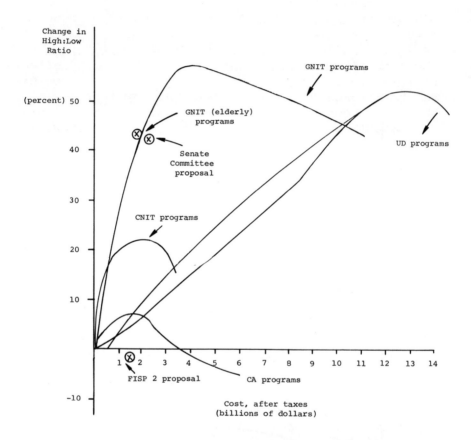

billion, and in the case of the GNIT schemes at cost
levels over $4 billion. We have investigated this
in some detail but have been unable to explain the
effect other than in terms of the diminished relative
emphasis on the lowest income groups as the cost
levels of the various schemes rise.

What may be alleged unequivocally from the cost-
effectiveness charts illustrated is that the selective
NIT approach, particularly in its general form but
also in its partial form limited to families with at
least one child, is superior either in terms of the
absolute alleviation of poverty or in terms of effect
on relative distributional indicators over the feasible cost range to the universal variants. It is also
apparent, however, that the effectiveness of the preferred GNIT variant is subject to sharply diminishing
returns and that increments in effectiveness, which
are very sharp up to cost levels of around $4 billion,
are negligible for cost increments beyond that point.
In this sense the Senate Committee proposal stands
as a particularly cost-effective scheme, even if its
cost is considerably higher than the committee main-
tains. About all that can be said about FISP 2 in
terms of its effect on the four redistributive indicators is that it is more cost-effective than universal CA variants; as a redistributive tool in general,
or as a means of diminishing absolute poverty in
particular, FISP 2 does not compare favorably with
NIT options.

The case for an income support option does not
lie, of course, simply in its short-run distributional
consequences but also in its effect on other indicators such as work incentives, family stability,
stigmatization, political acceptability, and administrative efficiency. In terms of these latter in-
dicators--with the exception of administrative ef-
ficiency--the universal schemes and the selective
FISP 2 option emerge much more strongly. The final
selection of an income support scheme will reflect
budget constraints associated with the trade-off of
cash transfer redistribution as one government expenditure option against other expenditure options and
on the weighting given by decision-makers to a set
of output indicators of the sort examined in this
study. The primary object of the exercise is to

provide more information for such decision-making.
As an exercise in program budgeting for income support options, the simulation employed above is limited
in its static nature to providing cost estimates and
distributive output indicators for one time period--
say, one year. The extrapolation of such information
over a longer time period has been approached only
in crude terms by defining a set of behavioral indicators on the basis of which the movement in cost and
distributive effectiveness over a longer period
might be inferred. The next stage in developing the
model illustrated is envisaged as the use of individual income data and the construction of a set of
rules for moving the population through time. In
this projected dynamic microsimulation, the first
stage ex-ante projections of the outcomes of income
support options obtained above might be refined into
a more sophisticated multiyear forecasting model.

The following shows the breakdown of the broad functional classification into functions, subfunctions, and programs, indicated by successively greater indentations. Pages 265 and 266 present a more detailed breakdown of the social measures function into subfunctions, programs, and program elements or activities, while pages 267 and 268 present a sample program and financial plan for the income maintenance subfunction.

FUNCTIONAL CLASSIFICATION

GENERAL GOVERNMENT SERVICES

Legislation and Administration

Legislative
Executive and Policy
Collection of Taxes and Duties
Internal Management Services
Contributions to Employee Pension and Medical
   Plans
Contingency Vote
National Capital Region
Bullion and Coinage
Other Legislation and Administration

GENERAL GOVERNMENT SERVICES (continued)

Protection of Persons and Property

Justice
Correctional Services
Police Protection
Consumer Services
Other Protection of Persons and Property

FOREIGN AFFAIRS

External Relations

Diplomatic Relations
Contributions to International Organizations

Assistance to Developing Countries

Other Foreign Affairs

DEFENSE

INTERGOVERNMENTAL FISCAL TRANSFER PAYMENTS

Statutory Subsidies to Provincial Governments
Revenue Equalization Payments
Other Fiscal Transfer Payments

ECONOMIC MEASURES

Primary Industry

Agriculture
Fisheries
Forestry
Minerals
Water Resources
Energy
Other Primary Industry

Secondary Industry

ECONOMIC MEASURES (continued)

   Transportation and Communications

      Air Transport
      Water Transport
      Rail Transport
      Road Transport
      Postal Services
      Telecommunications
      Other Transportation and Communications

   Service Industry

      Tourism
      Other Service Industry

   Foreign Trade

   Labor Force

      Working Conditions
      Training
      Immigration
      Other Labor Force

   General Research

      Social Science Research
      Physical Science Research
      Other General Research

   Housing and Urban Renewal

      Regional Development

   Other Economic Measures

SOCIAL MEASURES

   Health

      Public Health
      Medical Care
      Hospital Care
      Other Health

SOCIAL MEASURES (continued)

Income Maintenance

Payments to Aged
Payments to Families
Payments to Unemployed

Social Assistance

Canada Assistance Plan
Aid to Handicapped
Other Social Assistance

Veterans Benefits

Indians and Eskimos

Other Social Measures

EDUCATION, CULTURE, AND RECREATION

Aid to Education

Post-Secondary Education Transfer
Other Aid to Education

Culture and Recreation

Archives, Galleries, Museums, Libraries, and
  Theaters
Parks, Historic Sites, and Other Recreation Areas
Film, Radio, and Television
Other Culture and Recreation

PUBLIC DEBT

FINANCIAL TRANSACTIONS

SOCIAL MEASURES PROGRAMS

HEALTH

  Public Health

    General Health Grants (NHW)
    Grants to Health Organizations (NHW)
    Quarantine Services (NHW)
    Public Health Sanitarian Services (NHW)

  Medical Care

    Health Resources Fund (NHW)
    Medical Research Council (NRC)

  Hospital Care

    Hospital Insurance Grants (NHW)
    Hospital Construction Grants (NHW)

  Other Health

    Northern Health Services (NHW)
    NHW Department Administration
    Health and Medical Activities Administration (NHW)

INCOME MAINTENANCE

  Payments to Families

    Family Allowances (NHW)
    Youth Allowances (NHW)
    Family Assistance Payments (NHW)

  Payments to Unemployed

    Unemployment Insurance Administration
    Government's Contribution to UIC Fund
    Auto Workers, Transitional Assistance (LAB)

SOCIAL ASSISTANCE

  Canada Assistance Plan

SOCIAL ASSISTANCE (continued)

Aid to Handicapped

Rehabilitation Services (NHW)
Disabled Persons Allowances (NHW)
Blind Persons Allowances (NHW)
Vocational Rehabilitation, Disabled Persons (MI)

Other Social Assistance

Welfare Activities Administration (NHW)
Old Age Assistance (NHW)
Company of Young Canadians (SS)
Vanier Institute (FIN)
Mental Retardation Grants (NHW)
Special Assistance Bell Island (ADB)
Governments Annuities Act (LAB)
National Welfare Grants

VETERANS BENEFITS

Veterans Affairs Administration
Pensions (DVA)
Treatment Services (DVA)
Veterans' Land Act
Welfare Services (DVA)

INDIANS AND ESKIMOS

Indian Programs (LAND)
Indian Health Service (NHW)
Indian Integration (Citizenship Branch--SS)

Source: Planning-Programming-Budgeting Guide,
Government of Canada (Ottawa: Treasury Board, July
1968).

APPENDIX TABLE A.1

Program and Financial Plan (Hypothetical) for Income Maintenance

Financial Plan in Dollars

Code	Functional Category	FY 1968/69 (Active)	FY 1969/70 Current Estimate	FY 1970-71 Budget Estimate	FY 1971/72 Program Estimate	FY 1972/73 Program Estimate	FY 1973/74 Program Estimate	Total Costs 1968/74
1.	Social measures							
1.1	Health							
1.2	Income maintenance							
1.2.1	Payment to families							
1.2.1.1	Family allowances							
1.2.1.2	Youth allowances							
1.2.1.3	Family assistance payments							
1.2.2.	Payments to unemployed							
1.2.2.1	Unemployed insurance administration							
1.2.2.2	Government contribution to UIC							
1.2.2.3	Auto workers transitional assistance							

267

(continued)

APPENDIX TABLE A.1 (continued)

Program Plan in Selected Output Indicators

Code	Functional Category	FY 1968/69 Actual Output	FY 1969/70 Current Output	FY 1970/71 Budget Estimate	FY 1971/72 Program Estimate	FY 1972/73 Program Estimate	FY 1973/74 Program Estimate	Total Output 1968/74
1.	Social measures							
1.1	Health							
1.2	Income maintenance							
1.2.1	Payment to families							
1.2.1.1	Family allowances							
1.2.1.2	Youth allowances							
1.2.1.3	Family assistance payments							
1.2.2.	Payments to unemployed							
1.2.2.1	Unemployed insurance administration							
1.2.2.2	Government contribution to UIC							
1.2.2.3	Auto workers transitional assistance							

FY = Financial Year.

ILLUSTRATIVE VOLUME INDICATORS

Selected Program Elements	Volume of Services
Natural resource programs	
Forestry	Acres of forest lands maintained; acres planted
Agricultural extension services	Number of farmers assisted
Conservation	Number of acres with conservation practices
Reclamation	Irrigated acreage
City environmental programs	
Air pollution control	Number of violations corrected
Water supply system	Gallons of water consumed
Solid waste disposal	Tons of trash removed
Rodent control	Reduction in rat population
Mosquito control	Area sprayed and irrigated
Waste treatment works	Gallons of water treated
Public housing	Number of housing units

Selected Program Elements	Volume of Services
City environmental pro- **grams (continued)**	
Urban residential renewal	Number of housing units renovated; acreage renewed
Beautification	Trees planted; flower beds maintained
Recreational programs	
Parks	Number of persons using parks at peak time of day; number of parks; acreage maintained
Museums	Number of persons at- tending
Libraries	Number of library users; number of volumes on loan
Zoos	Number of persons at- tending
Recreation centers	Number of persons using or attending
Performing arts centers	Number of persons at- tending
Transportation programs	
Airports	Number of passengers em- barking; number of air- craft take-offs
Harbors and ship ter- minals	Dock area; number of berths
Highways	Miles of paved highways maintained
Mass transit facilities	Number of passengers per day
Parking facilities	Number of motor vehicles parked
Ship terminal ware- houses	Tons of freight stored
Public safety programs	
Parole activities	Number of persons pa- roled

Selected Program Elements	Volume of Services
Public safety programs (continued)	
Police surveillance	Number of surveillance hours
Traffic controls	Number of intersections controlled
Fire station activities	Number of alarms answered
Courts	Number of cases cleared
Jails and other detention institutions	Number of prisoners released; number housed
Street lighting	Number of street lights maintained; kilowatt hours
Child care and education programs	
Child care centers	Number of children in centers
Day care centers	Number of children in centers
Preprimary education	Number of children enrolled
Regular day programs-- elementary schools	Number of students enrolled
Regular day programs-- secondary schools	Number of students enrolled
Vocational schools	Number of students enrolled
Higher education (student teaching)	Number of students enrolled; number of degrees granted, total, or by field of specialization
Manpower training	Number of persons enrolled; number of persons employed at close of training
After-school-hour programs	Number of persons enrolled

Selected Program Elements	Volume of Services
Child care and education programs (continued)	
Summer school programs	Number of persons enrolled
Exceptional children programs	Number of children served
School lunch programs	Number of meals served
School health programs	Number of examinations; number of children screened, by types of screening
Job opportunity programs	
Neighborhood youth programs	Number of persons employed
Job counseling	Number of persons assisted
Employment services	Number of persons placed; number of persons interviewed
Sheltered workshops	Number of persons employed
Vocational rehabilitation	Number of persons receiving services; number of persons reemployed
Health programs	
General hospitals (inpatient care)	Average daily in-hospital patients; number of patients treated in outpatient departments
Mental hospitals (inpatient care)	Average daily patient loads
Institutions for the mentally retarded	Average daily patient loads
Mental health clinics	Number of patient-hours of care provided

Selected Program Elements	Volume of Services
Health programs (continued)	
Alcoholic clinics	Number of patients treated
Family planning clinics	Number of women counseled
Disease screening clinics	Number of persons screened
Immunization programs	Number of persons receiving services
Referral services	Number of families served
Home health services	Number of persons served; number of hours of care provided
Nursing homes	Average daily patient loads; number of institutions inspected; number of institutions participating in staff training sessions
Welfare programs	
Family counseling services	Number of families assisted; average daily caseload
Welfare payments	Number of persons and families receiving assistance, total and by type
Food distributions	Number of families receiving food surpluses
Foster home care	Number of families assisted; number of children or aged receiving care
Halfway houses	Number of persons assisted; number of persons restored to community

ILLUSTRATIVE QUALITY INDICATORS

Selected Program Elements	Quality of Service
Natural resource programs	
Forestry	Standing timber growth, by type of timber
Agricultural extension services	Farm output per acre, by crop
Conservation	Top soil depth, width, and quality; water levels
Reclamation	Farm output per acre in reclamation areas
City environmental programs	
Air pollution control	Current pollutant levels (carbon monoxide, sulfur dioxide, hydrocarbons, etc.)
Water supply system	Water rationing days; water quality indexes (dissolved oxygen, temperature, hardness, chloride, etc.)
Solid waste disposal	Periods elapsing between collections; proportion of wastes used as landfills
Rodent control	Rate bite cases reported
Mosquito control	Area cleared
Waste treatment works	Water quality levels attained (see water supply system)
Public housing	Physical condition of public housing (working condition of plumbing, lighting, heating or air-conditioning, and other equipment; noise)

Selected Program Elements	Quality of Service
City environmental pro-grams (continued)	
Urban residential re-newal	Number of families re-housed in satisfactory housing
Beautification	Measures of physical ap-pearance of selected sample areas
Recreational programs	
Parks	Lawn, trees, planted areas in satisfactory condition
Museums	Number of exhibits or paintings; scope of exhibit coverage; spe-cial shows
Libraries	Number of volumes re-quested not available; waiting lists of bor-rowers
Zoos	Number of species repre-sented
Recreation centers	Range of activities available for differ-ent age groups
Performing arts center	Number of performances of companies with na-tional reputations
Transportation programs	
Airports	Delay time; ground trans-port time
Harbors and ship ter-minals	Size of vessels accom-modated; tons of freight handled
Highways	Traffic delays; traffic accidents; vehicle ca-pacity per hour

Selected Program Elements	Quality of Service
Transportation programs (continued)	
Mass transit facilities	Extent of crowding at peak hours; frequency of service during off-peak hours
Parking facilities	Number of parked vehicle violations; number of parked vehicles towed from city streets
Ship terminal warehouses	Cubic area, by type
Public safety programs	
Parole activities	Number of persons restored to community; number of repeaters among parolees
Police surveillance	Age adjusted crime rates; number of offenders, by number of prior arrests
Traffic controls	Number of motor car accidents; number of traffic fatalities and injuries
Fire station activities	Time elapsing between calls and fire fighting; fire insurance premium rates
Courts	Length of court dockets; number of decisions sustained on appeal
Jails and other detention institutions	Number of repeaters; numbers rehabilitated and employed
Street lighting	Illumination indexes (kilowatts)
Child care and education programs	
Child care centers	Hours of education, health, and counseling services provided

Selected Program Elements	Quality of Service
Child care and education programs (continued)	
Day care centers	Hours of education, health, and counseling services provided
Preprimary education	Number of children by reading-readiness scores
Regular day programs-- elementary schools	Number of children with achievement scores at or above grade level
Regular day programs-- secondary schools	Number of graduates; number of school leavers; number admitted to colleges
Vocational schools	Number of persons receiving training who are employed
Higher education (student teaching)	Number of college graduates admitted to graduate or professional school; attrition rates; number of graduate students receiving fellowships
Manpower training	Number of persons receiving training who are employed
After-school hour programs	Changes in school achievement scores
Summer school programs	Changes in school achievement scores
Exceptional children programs	Number of children, by achievement or adjustment score level
School lunch programs	Number of children purchasing school lunches; nutritional status of children

Selected Program Elements	Quality of Service
Child care and education programs (continued)	
School health programs	Number of children with correctable deficiencies who have received treatment
Job opportunity programs	
Neighborhood youth programs	Number of persons employed by skill levels
Job counseling	Number of persons employed by skill levels; length of unemployment period
Employment services	Length of unemployment period
Sheltered workshops	Number of persons reemployed in community
Vocational rehabilitation	Earning levels of rehabilitated persons
Health programs	
General hospitals (inpatient care)	Number of appendectomy, hysterectomy cases reviewed by medical boards; waiting lists; special care units
Mental hospitals (inpatient care)	Number of therapy hours of care provided; length of stay
Institutions for the mentally retarded	Number of persons functioning in community; discharges
Mental health clinics	Number of persons functioning in community
Alcoholic clinics	Number of patients cured; number of nonrepeaters
Family planning clinics	Number of women planning families

Selected Program Elements	Quality of Service
Health programs (continued)	
Disease screening clinics	Number of positive cases receiving treatment
Immunization programs	Decline in rates of smallpox, tetanus, whooping cough, measles, polio
Referral services	Number of persons receiving appropriate types of care or services
Home health services	Range of services provided; hospitalizations avoided
Nursing homes	Hours of professional nursing time provided; accessibility of physician care
Welfare programs	
Family counseling services	Changes in separation and divorce rates
Welfare payments	Number of families moving across the poverty line; number at defined budget levels
Food distributions	Nutritional levels of assisted families
Foster home care	Number of cases of institutionalization avoided
Halfway houses	Number of persons restored to community

Source: PPB Note 7, The State-Local Finances Project (Washington, D.C.: The George Washington University, 1968).

C

The program used to generate the results described in the text was designed to enable many different income support programs to be studied. It was further designed to permit the superimposition of, and evaluation of the effects of, sets of multiple programs.

1. POPULATION INCOME DATA

In order to simulate the effect of a proposed scheme it was necessary to provide data describing the income statistics of the population under study. The program was designed about a set of data that divided the population into groups of families of sizes from one to six members. Each size group was subdivided into income classes, the following data being available for each class:

- Total income for class
- Total number of families
- Total family allowance payments for class (FAMALL)
- Total number of families receiving family allowance (NFA)
- Total old age pension for class (OAP)
- Total number of families receiving pension allowance (NFO)
- Total other government income for class (OGI)

No information was available as to the distribution of income sources among the families and the
following assumptions were made:

      a.   All families in an income class re-
ceived the average amount of "other government income."

      b.   A family could contain children or
pensioners but not both.

      c.   All families with children had the
same number of children (NKIDS). This was
derived from

$$NKIDS = \frac{FAMALL}{72*NFA} \quad \text{(rounded to nearest integer)}$$

      d.   All families with pensioners had
the same number of pensioners (NOAP), derived from

$$NOAP = \frac{OAP}{900*NFO} \quad \text{(rounded to nearest integer)}$$

      e.   The incomes of the three types of
family (with children, with pensioners, with
neither) were derived as follows:
Let

    NFA   = Number of families receiving
              family allowances.
    NFO   = Number of families receiving
              old age pensions.
    NREST = The remaining number of fam-
              ilies in the combination.
    XFA   = The family allowance paid to
              each of the NFA families.
    XOAP   = The pension paid to each of
              the NFO families.
    TOTINC = The total income of all fami-
              lies in the combination.
    XINC   = The total income of a family
              receiving all types of income.

Then the overall income of a family receiving family allowance (and hence from [b] receiving no old age pension) is XINC - XOAP.
Similarly, the overall income of a family
receiving old age pension is XINC - XFA.
And the remaining (NREST) families receive

XINC - XFA - XOAP.
Thus

$$TOTINC = NREST* (XINC - XOAP - XFAO)$$

$$- NFA* (XINC - XOAP) - NFO* (XINC - XFA)$$

and hence

$$XINC = \frac{TOTINC + XOAP* (NREST + NFA) \quad XFA* (NREST + NFO)}{NREST + NFA + NFO}$$

XINC is used as a basis in the program for income calculations.

2.   PAYMENT MODEL

Prior to discussing the payment model in detail, it is necessary to define some terms.

Reduced Income

The reduced income of a family is an income that is specified using data control cards. It is arrived at by deducting various types of income from the total income of a family. The types of income that may be deducted are family allowance, old age pension, and other government income. Reduced income may be considered either before or after scheme payments, the difference being the amount of the payment. As an example, using the notation in (e), above, and assuming that family allowance was not to be included in reduced income, the old reduced income (before the scheme) for a family with children would be

$$RIO = XINC - XOAP - XFA$$

The new reduced income (after a scheme giving a payment XPAY) would be

$$RIN = XINC + XPAY - XOAP - XFA$$

Disposable Income

The disposable income of a family is the reduced income less some multiple (XXTAX) of the taxes paid.

The multiple is set by data control cards and is usually 1 or 0. The disposable income may be either before a scheme (old disposable income) or after (new). Thus, if the taxes paid prior to and after the scheme were TAXO and TAXN, respectively:

$$DISPO = RIO - XXTAX*TAXO$$

$$DISPN = RIN - XXTAX*TAXN$$

NIT Repayment (NITPAY)

In a GNIT scheme each family receives a basic allowance (BASIC) and repays a fraction of it depending upon the NIT rate (SNR) and the disposable income. NITPAY cannot exceed the basic allowance and may not be negative. Thus

$$0 \leq (NITPAY = XNR*DISPO) \leq BASIC$$

A generalized expression was used to define the payments to be made under a specific scheme. For each combination of family size and income class let

NKIDS = Number of children in a family.
JKIDS = NKIDS up to a data-specified maximum.
NOAP   = Number of pensioners in a family.
BASIC = Basic allowance for this family size.
FISP   = A payment of the FISP type dependent upon family income and NKIDS.
XNR   = A NIT repayment factor for families with neither children nor pensioners.
XNRKID = A NIT rate for families with children.
XNROAP = A NIT rate for families with pensioners.

Then the payments made would be

a. No pensioners or children

$$PAY = BASIC - NITPAY$$

where

$$0 \leq (NITPAY = XNR*DISPO) \leq BASIC$$

b. Pensioners (and hence no children)

PAY = BASIC - NITPAY + K1OAP + K2OAP * NOAP

where

   $0 \leq$ (NITPAY = XNROAP * DISPO) $\leq$ BASIC

c. Children (and hence no pensioners)

PAY = BASIC - NITPAY + K1KID + K2KID*JKIDS + FSPMLT*FISP

where

   $0 \leq$ (NITPAY = XNRKID * DISPO) $\leq$ BASIC

FSPMLT is a multiplier (specified in the scheme definition data and usually 1 or 0).

3. TAXATION MODEL

Various tax options may be specified using control data:
     a. A basic exemption for each family
depending upon its size,
     b. An exemption for each child in the
family,
     c. An exemption for each pensioner in
the family.
The income from family allowance payments is
not included when deriving pre-scheme taxes.
All scheme payments are taxed with the exception
of FISP payments, which may be optionally taxed.

4. MULTIPLE SCHEMES

In order to simulate supplementary payment
schemes provided at a number of different levels,
e.g., federal, provincial, and municipal, the program
allows for the pooling of scheme costs and benefits.
Each level is treated entirely independently,
i.e., the income used in calculating payments for
scheme 2 does not include any income provided by
scheme 1.

Any number of schemes may be pooled together by a suitable combination of data control cards. The results for each scheme are printed normally, and a special control card calls in the routines to merge the schemes together.

The total payment in the combined scheme is the sum of the individual payments, and the post-scheme taxes are based upon the pre-scheme income and the combined payments.

The various efficiency statistics are the result of pooling the payments and treating the multiple scheme as a single scheme.

NOTES

CHAPTER 1

1.   A. Schick, "The Road to PPB: The Stages of Budget Reform," Public Administration Review, 27, no. 4 (December 1966), 243-358.

2.   C. L. Schultze, The Politics and Economics of Public Spending (Washington, D.C.: Brookings Institution, 1968).

3.   B. A. Gross, "The New Systems Budgeting," Public Administration Review, 29, no. 2 (March/April 1969), 113-37.

4.   The Royal Commission on Government Organisation, Government of Canada (Ottawa: Queen's Printer, 1962).

5.   C. J. Hitch and R. N. McKean, The Economics of Defense in the Nuclear Age (Cambridge, Mass.: Harvard University Press, 1965).

6.   A Williams, Output Budgeting and the Contribution of Micro-Economics to Efficiency in Government, CAS Occasional Papers no. 4 (London: H.M.S.O., 1967).

7.   Output Budgeting for the Department of Education and Science, Department of Education and Science, Education Planning Paper no. 1 (London: H.M.S.O., 1970).

8.   A Manual for Programme and Performance Budgeting, U.N. Department of Economic and Social Affairs (New York, 1965), where performance budgeting is defined in much the same way as in the text, but program budgeting, rather than being defined as a grander concept including the whole analytical support system, is simply viewed as the first, restruc-

turing stage in the development of performance budgeting.

9. The Analysis and Evaluation of Public Expenditure: The PPB System, U.S. Government, Joint Economic Committee, 3 vols. (Washington, D.C., 1969).

10. H. R. Balls, "Planning, Programming and
Budgeting in Canada," Public Administration, 48
(Autumn 1970), 289-305.

11. Command 2235 (London: H.M.S.O., 1964).

12. Command 4017 (London: H.M.S.O., 1969).

13. Command 4234 (London: H.M.S.O., 1969).

14. Sir Samuel Goldman, "The Presentation of
Public Expenditure Proposals to Parliament," Public
Administration, 48 (Autumn 1970), 247-61.

15. P. Huet, "The Rationalisation of Budget
Choices in France," Public Administration, 48 (Autumn
1970), 273-87.

16. Report of the Second Workshop on Problems
of Budget Reclassification and Management in the
ECAFE Region, United Nations (Bangkok, 1957).

17. B. Gross, "The New Systems Budgeting and
the Developing Nations," International Social Science
Journal, 21, no. 1 (1969), 23-44.

18. S. S. Viswanathan, "Performance Budgeting
in India: A Review of the Developments, Present
Status and Prospects," Indian Journal of Public Administration, 16, no. 2 (April-June 1970), 188-202.

19. E. S. Quade, Systems Analysis Techniques
for Planning-Programming-Budgeting (Santa Monica,
Calif.: The Rand Corporation, 1966).

20. R. D. Specht, "The Nature of Models," in
E. S. Quade and W. I. Boucher, eds., Systems Planning
and Policy Analysis (New York: Elsevier, 1968), pp.
211-27.

21. O. Lange, Wholes and Parts (New York: Pergamon Press, 1965) (trans. from Polish by Eugeniusz Lepa).

22. C. McMillan and R. Gonzalez, Systems Analysis (Homewood, Ill.: R. D. Irwin, 1968).

23. R. C. Meier, W. T. Newell, and H. L. Pazer, Simulation in Business and Economics (Englewood Cliffs, N.J.: Prentice-Hall, 1969).

24. J. M. Beshers, ed., Computer Methods with Analysis of Large Scale Social Systems (Cambridge, Mass.: M.I.T. Press, 1968).

25. Jay Forrester, Industrial Dynamics (Cambridge, Mass.: M.I.T. Press, 1961).

26. R. Judy, et al., "Systems Analysis of Alternative Designs of a Faculty," in Budgeting, Programme Analysis and Cost-Effectiveness in Educational Planning (Paris: O.E.C.D., 1969), pp. 252-86.

27. W. M. Jones, Fractional Debates and National Commitments: The Multi-Dimensional Scenario (Santa Monica, Calif.: The Rand Corporation, 1967).

28. O. Helmer, Social Technology (New York: Basic Books, 1966).

29. O. Helmer and N. C. Dalkey, "An Experimental Application of the Delphi Method to the Use of Experts," Management Sciences, 9, no. 2 (April 1963), 458-67.

30. H. W. Watts, Graduated Work Incentives: An Experiment in Negative Taxation (Madison: University of Wisconsin Institute for Research on Poverty, 1969).

31. R. Turvey, "On the Development of Cost Benefit Analysis," in M. G. Kendall, ed., Cost Benefit Analysis (London: The English Universities Press, 1971), pp. 5-14.

32.   J. String, Jr., <u>A Model for Resource Analysis of Space Programs</u> (Santa Monica, Calif.:   The Rand Corporation, 1967).

33.   G. H. Fisher, <u>Military Systems Cost Analysis</u> (Santa Monica, Calif.:   The Rand Corporation, 1962).

34.   <u>The Role and Nature of Cost Analysis in a PPB System</u>, PPB note 8, State-Local Finances Project (Washington, 1967).

35.   M. C. Heuston and G. Ogawa, "Observations on the Theoretical Basis of Cost-Effectiveness," <u>Operations Research</u>, 14, no. 2 (March/April, 1966), 242-66.

36.   G. H. Fisher, <u>A Discussion of Uncertainty in Cost Analysis</u> (Santa Monica, Calif.:   The Rand Corporation, 1962).

37.   R. L. Petruschell, "Cost Sensitivity Analysis: An Example," in E. S. Quade and W. I. Boucher, eds., <u>Systems Analysis and Policy Planning</u> (New York: Elsevier, 1968), pp. 138-52.

38.   B. M. Gross, <u>The State of the Nation</u> (London: Social Science Paperbacks, 1966).

39.   J. Robinson, <u>Economic Philosophy</u> (New York: Doubleday Anchor, 1965).

40.   University of Birmingham, Department of Scientific and Industrial Research, Road Research Laboratory, <u>The London-Birmingham Motorway</u>, Road Research Technical Paper no. 46 (London: H.M.S.O., 1964).

41.   <u>Report of the Commission on the Third London Airport</u>, Papers and Proceedings, vol. 7 (London: H.M.S.O., 1970); Final Report (London: H.M.S.O., 1971).

42.   C. D. Foster and M. Beasley, "Estimating the Social Benefit of Constructing an Underground

Railway in London," Journal of the Royal Statistical Society, ser. A, 126, pt. I (1963), 46-92.

43. O. Eckstein, Water Resource Development (Cambridge, Mass.: Harvard University Press, 1958).

44. The wide range of articles in this area is documented in W. D. Wood and H. F. Campbell, Cost-Benefit Analysis and the Economics of Investment in Human Resources (Kingston: Queen's University Industrial Relations Centre, 1970).

45. S. A. Marglin, "Objectives of Water Resource Development: A General Statement," in A. Maass, et al., Design of Water Resource Systems (London: Macmillan, 1962), pp. 17-87.

46. Toward a Social Report, U.S. Department of Health, Education and Welfare (Washington, D.C., 1969).

47. R. A. Bauer, ed., Social Indicators (Cambridge, Mass.: M.I.T. Press, 1965).

48. B. M. Gross, The State of the Nation (London: Social Science Paperbacks, 1966).

49. Annals of American Academy of Political and Social Science (June and September 1967), a symposium on social indicators edited by Bertram Gross.

50. Social Trends No. 1, 1970 (London: H.M.S.O., 1970); Social Trends No. 2, 1971 (London: H.M.S.O., 1971).

51. A recent discussion is in I. V. Sawhill, "The Role of Social Indicators and Social Reporting in Public Expenditure Decisions," in The Analysis and Evaluation of Public Expenditures: The PPB System, U.S. Joint Economic Committee (Washington, D.C., 1969).

52. R. McKean, Efficiency in Government Through Systems Analysis (New York: John Wiley and Sons, 1966).

53. R. A. Dahl and C. E. Lindblom, _Politics,_ _Economics and Welfare_ (New York: Harper and Row, 1953).

54. A. Maass, "System Design and the Political Process: A General Statement," in A. Maass, _et al.,_ _Design of Water Resource Systems_ (Cambridge, Mass.: Harvard University Press, 1962).

55. O. Eckstein, "A Survey of Public Expenditure Criteria," in J. Buchanan, ed., _Public Finances:_ _Needs, Sources and Utilization_ (Princeton, N.J.: Princeton University Press, 1961).

56. A. M. Freeman, "Project Design and Evalua- tion with Multiple Objectives," in _The Analysis and_ _Evaluation of Public Expenditures: The PPB System,_ U.S. Joint Economic Committee (Washington, D.C., 1969).

57. A. C. Pigou, _The Economics of Welfare_ (Lon- don: Macmillan, 1950).

58. E. J. Mishan, _Welfare Economics: An Assess-_ _ment_ (Amsterdam: North-Holland, 1969).

59. M. Woodhall and M. Blaug, "Productivity Trends in British University Education 1938-1962," _Minerva_ (Summer 1965).

60. S. Marglin, "The Social Rate of Discount and the Optimum Rate of Investment," _Quarterly Jour-_ _nal of Economics_ (February 1963).

61. R. Lind, "The Social Rate of Discount and the Optimum Rate of Investment: Further Comment," _Quarterly Journal of Economics_ (May 1964).

62. A. K. Sen, "Isolation, Assurance and the Social Rate of Discount," _Quarterly Journal of Eco-_ _nomics_ (February 1967).

63. M. S. Feldstein, "The Social Time Preference Discount Rate in Cost-Benefit Analysis," _Economic_ _Journal,_ 74 (June 1964), 360-79.

64. M. S. Feldstein, "The Derivation of Social Time Preference Rates," Kyklos, 18, no. 2 (1965), 277-87.

65. M. S. Feldstein, "Opportunity Cost Calculations in Cost-Benefit Analysis," Public Finance, 19, no. 2 (1964).

66. W. J. Baumol, "On the Social Rate of Discount," American Economic Review, 58, no. 3 (September 1968), 788-802.

67. S. A. Marglin, "The Social Rate of Discount and the Optimal Rate of Investment," Quarterly Journal of Economics, 73, no. 1 (February 1963), 95-112.

68. G. Tullock, "The Social Rate of Discount and the Optimal Rate of Investment: Comment," Quarterly Journal of Economics, 74, no. 2 (May 1964), 331-36.

69. The Choice of Discount Rates and the Investment of Opportunity Costs for Cost-Benefit Analysis, discussion paper, Government of Canada, Treasury Board, Systems Analysis Division.

70. S. Reutlinger, Techniques for Project Appraisal Under Uncertainty, World Bank Occasional Paper no. 10 (Washington: International Bank for Reconstruction and Development, 1970).

71. R. P. Mack, Planning on Uncertainty (New York: John Wiley and Sons, 1971).

72. D. R. Luce and H. Raiffa, Games and Decisions (New York: John Wiley and Sons, 1958).

73. M. K. Starr, Product Design and Decision Theory (Englewood Cliffs, N.J.: Prentice-Hall, 1963).

74. A. Madansky, "Uncertainty," in E. S. Quade and W. I. Boucher, eds., Systems Planning and Policy Analysis (New York: Elsevier, 1968), pp. 81-96.

75. R. Dorfman, "Operations Research," in R.E.S./A.E.A., Surveys of Economic Theory (London: Macmillan, 1966).

76. P. D. Henderson, "Political and Budgetary Constraints: Some Characteristics and Implications," in J. Margolis, ed., Public Economics, Proceedings of the 1966 Conference of the International Economic Association (London: Macmillan, 1969).

77. J. S. MacDonald, "Benefit-Cost Analysis of Social Welfare Programs," Industrial Relations Research Association Proceedings, Proceedings of the Seventeenth Meeting (December 1964), pp. 186-194.

78. The distinction is explored in B. Schwab, "Current Limitations and Possible Extensions of Some Common Criteria for Investment Evaluation," in M. Kendall, ed., Cost Benefit Analysis (London: The English Universities Press, 1971), pp. 305-13.

79. R. Turvey, "Present Value versus Internal Rate of Return--An Essay in the Theory of the Third Best," Economic Journal (March 1963), specifies this simple ranking procedure as that appropriate to the IR approach.

80. P. D. Henderson, "Notes on Public Investment Criteria in the United Kingdom," Bulletin of the Oxford University Institute of Economics and Statistics (1965), pp. 55-89.

81. M. S. Feldstein and J. S. Flemming, "The Problem of Time-Stream Evaluation: Present Value versus Internal Rate of Return Rules," Bulletin of the Oxford University Institute of Economics and Statistics (February 1964).

82. S. M. Greenhouse, "Today's PPBS: The Fatal Triumph of Financial Management over Economics," The Analysis and Evaluation of Public Expenditures: The PPB System, U.S. Joint Economic Committee (Washington, D.C., 1969).

83. Report of the Commission on the Third London Airport (London: H.M.S.O., 1971).

84. L. D. Attaway, "Criteria and the Measurement of Effectiveness," in E. S. Quade and W. I. Boucher,

eds., Systems Planning and Policy Analysis (New York: Elsevier, 1968), pp. 54-80.

CHAPTER 2

1. J. Tobin has labeled these approaches "structural" and "distributive," respectively: "The Case for an Income Guarantee," The Public Interest (Summer 1966), pp. 31-41.

2. Ibid.

3. E. E. Schwartz, "A Way to End the Means Test," Social Work (July 1964), pp. 3-12.

4. R. J. Lampman, "Approaches to the Reduction of Poverty," American Economic Review (May 1965), pp. 521-29; and "Negative Rates Income Taxation" and "Preliminary Report on a Plan for Negative Income Taxation," papers prepared for the Office of Economic Opportunity in Washington, D.C.

5. M. Friedman, Capitalism and Freedom (Chicago: University of Chicago Press, 1962), pp. 177-95.

6. R. J. Lampman, "Nixon's Family Assistance Plan," University of Wisconsin, Institute for Research on Poverty, Discussion Paper no. 57, 1969.

7. J. Cutt, A Guaranteed Income for Canadians (Toronto: Ontario Woodsworth Memorial Foundation, 1968).

8. Poverty in Canada, A Report of the Special Senate Committee (Ottawa: Information Canada, 1971).

9. The proposal was originally made in a pamphlet, "Something to Look Forward To," in 1943, and is written up in revised and updated form in Lady Rhys-Williams, Taxation and Incentive (New York: Oxford University Press, 1953).

10. J. E. Meade, Planning and the Price Mechanism (London: Allan and Unwin, 1948).

11. *The Reform of Income Tax and Social Security Payments* (London: Liberal Party Yellow Book, March 1950).

12. D. B. Smith, "A Simplified Approach to Social Welfare," *Canadian Tax Journal* (May-June 1965).

13. R. W. Crowley and D. A. Dodge, "Cost of the Guaranteed Annual Income," *Canadian Tax Journal* (November-December 1969), pp. 395-408.

14. James Vadakin, *Children, Poverty, and Family Allowances* (New York: Basic Books, 1968), p. 6.

15. W. I. Gillespie, *The Incidence of Taxes and Public Expenditure in the Canadian Economy*, Studies of the Royal Commission on Taxation no. 2 (Ottawa: Queen's Printer, 1966).

16. *Income Security for Canadians*, Government of Canada, Department of National Health and Welfare (Ottawa, 1970).

17. The House of Commons of Canada, Bill C-264, an act to provide for the payment of benefits in respect of children, First Reading, September 13, 1971.

18. The term has been recently used by Olaf Helmer in *Social Technology* (New York: Basic Books, 1966).

19. See the detailed discussion of modeling and simulation in G. H. Orcutt, "Simulation of Economic Systems," *American Economic Review* (December 1960), pp. 893-907.

20. The terms are again those of Olaf Helmer; see, with N. Rescher, *On the Epistemology of the Inexact Sciences* (Santa Monica, Calif.: The Rand Corporation, 1960).

21. J. Cutt, "Income Support Alternatives for Families with Children--Alternatives for Canada," *International Social Security Review*, no. 1 (1970), pp. 100-112.

22. See H. W. Watts, "Graduated Work Incentives: An Experiment in Negative Taxation," _American Economic Review_ (May 1969), pp. 463-72.

23. S. Briar, "Why Children's Allowances," _Social Work_ (January 1969), p. 9.

24. _Preliminary Results of the New Jersey Graduated Work Incentive Experiment_ (Washington, D.C.: Office of Economic Opportunity, February 1970). H. W. Watts, "Mid-Experiment Report on Basic Labor-Supply Response," University of Wisconsin, Institute for Research on Poverty, Discussion Paper no. 98, 1971.

25. R. A. Levine, "Policy Analysis and Economic Opportunity Programs" (mimeo., U.S. Office of Economic Opportunity); J. W. Evans, "Evaluating Social Action Programs" (mimeo., U.S. Office of Economic Opportunity); W. Williams, "Developing an Agency Evaluation Strategy for Social Action Programs," (mimeo., U.S. Office of Economic Opportunity); G. G. Cain and R. G. Hollister, "The Methodology of Evaluating Social Action Programs," University of Wisconsin, Institute on Poverty, Discussion Paper, 1969.

26. See, for instance, _Cost-Benefit Analysis of Manpower Policies_, Proceedings of a North American Conference (Kingston: Queen's University Industrial Relations Centre, 1969); W. Lee Hansen and B. S. Weisbrod, _Benefits, Costs, and Finance of Public Higher Education_ (Chicago: Markham Publishing Company, 1969).

27. Westinghouse Learning Corporation, _The Impact of Head Start_, A Report to the Office of Economic Opportunity, published by U.S. Department of Commerce, June 1962, 2 vols.

28. See the detailed discussion of this problem in Evans, "Social Action Programs," pp. 2-5.

29. For a discussion of the origins of simulation, see G. Orcutt, "Simulation of Economic Systems," _American Economic Review_ (December 1960), pp. 893-907. A recent comprehensive review of the literature

is R. C. Meier, W. T. Newell, and H. L. Pazer, Simulation in Business and Economics (Englewood Cliffs, N.J.: Prentice-Hall, 1969).

30. G. H. Orcutt, "Microanalytic Analysis for Prediction of National Accounts," Arquivo Do Instituto Gulbenkian De Ciencia, 2, no. 1, 23-84.

31. J. S. Duesenberry, G. Fromm, L. R. Klein, and E. Kuh, The Brookings Quarterly Econometric Model of the United States (Chicago: Rand McNally, 1965). See also, G. Fromm and P. Taubman, Policy Simulations with an Econometric Model (Washington, D.C.: The Brookings Institution, 1968).

32. J. F. Helliwell, L. H. Officer, H. T. Shapiro, and I. A. Stewart, The Dynamics of RDX1 (Ottawa: Bank of Canada, 1969).

33. Jay Forrester, Industrial Dynamics (Cambridge: M.I.T. Press, 1961); Urban Dynamics (Cambridge: M.I.T. Press, 1969).

34. E. P. Holland and R. W. Gillespie, Experiments on a Simulated Underdeveloped Economy: Development Plans and Balance-of-Payments Policies (Cambridge, Mass.: M.I.T. Press, 1963).

35. J. A. Pechman, "A New Tax Model for Revenue Estimating," in A. T. Peacock and G. Hauser, Government Finance and Economic Development (Paris: O.E.C.D., 1965); and, "Simulation of the Carter Commission Tax Proposals for the United States," National Tax Journal (March 1969).

36. J. Bossons, A General Income Tax Analyser, Carter Commission Special Study Series (Ottawa: Queen's Printer, 1967).

37. Mimeographed details on the data base, simulation procedures, and results from the Unemployment Insurance Commission, Ottawa.

38. M. David and Jane Leuthold, "Formulas for Income Maintenance: Their Distributional Impact," National Tax Journal (March 1968).

39. N. McClung, "Evaluation of Income Transfer Programs," Working Paper, The Urban Institute, Washington, D.C., February 1970. This paper describes the basic model used by the President's Commission on Income Maintenance to arrive at estimates of costs and distributive effectiveness of various programs.

40. James Schulz, The Economic Status of the Retired Aged in 1980, U.S. Department of Health, Education and Welfare, Social Security Administration, Office of Research and Statistics, Research Report no. 24 (Washington, D.C., 1968).

41. James Schulz, "A Dynamic Social Security System for the U.S.--A Simulation Analysis Based upon the West German System," paper delivered to the Conference of the International Social Security Association, Vienna, September 1969.

42. R. L. Michielutte and J. T. Sprehe, "Problems and Prospects in Simulating Large-Scale Social Change" (mimeo., Institute for Social Research, Florida State University).

43. Mimeographed working papers from the Urban Institute, 2100 M Street, Washington, D.C., 20037.

44. G. Orcutt, M. Greenberger, J. Korbel, and A. M. Rivlin, Microanalysis of Socioeconomic Systems: A Simulation Study (New York: Harper & Row, 1961).

CHAPTER 3

1. Molly Orshansky, "Poverty Statistics--What They Say and What They Don't Say," in Hearings before the Sub-Committee on Economic Statistics of the Joint Economic Committee, Congress of the United States, 90th Congress, First Session, Appendix 1 to Hearings on May 17, 18, June 7, 8, 1967, p. 168.

2. Molly Orshansky, "Counting the Poor: Another Look at the Poverty Profile," Social Security Bulletin, 28 (January 1965), 3-27.

3. J. R. Podoluk, Incomes of Canadians (Ottawa: Dominion Bureau of Statistics, 1968), pp. 179-206.

4. This concept is defined in detail below. See discussion in Podoluk, Incomes of Canadians, pp. 271-74.

5. C. W. Meyer, A Base for the Negative Income Tax, Institute for Research on Poverty, University of Wisconsin, Discussion Paper 54, 1969.

6. Gail Oja, "Problems of Defining Low Economic Status for Poverty Studies," Canadian Statistical Review (September 1968), reprinted in pamphlet form by the Queen's Printer, Ottawa.

7. Compensation payments are being made in the extension of the New Jersey experiment to a rural situation in Iowa and North Carolina. See D. Lee Bawden, Income Maintenance and the Rural Poor (mimeo., Institute for Research on Poverty, University of Wisconsin).

8. For a detailed mathematical explanation of the calculation of the concentration ratio, see M. G. Kendall, Advanced Theory of Statistics, 1 (New York: Hafner, 1943), 42-44; for approximate means of calculation, see W. S. Woytinsky, Earnings and Social Security in the United States (Washington, D.C.: Social Science Research Council, 1943), Appendix; and J. L. Morgan, "The Anatomy of the Income Distribution," Review of Economics and Statistics (August 1962), pp. 270-83, Appendix. The approximate technique used by Morgan is followed in this work.

9. H. T. Oshima, "The International Comparison of Size Distribution of Family Income with Special Reference to Asia," Review of Economics and Statistics (1962), pp. 439-45. Oshima offers an interesting technique for comparing the distribution of income in different countries with the least possible degree of ambiguity, but since this is not the primary focus of this work the matter will not be further explored.

10. See the proposal for such a tax in H. Brazer, "The Federal Income Tax and the Poor: Where Do We Go from Here?" California Law Review (April 1969), pp. 422-49.

11. See the discussion of weighting in R. Musgrave, G. E. Peterson, and P. Heller, "Cost Effectiveness of Alternative Income Maintenance Schemes," a report to the Social Security Administration of the U.S. Department of Health, Education and Welfare, Washington, D.C.; and H. Watts, "An Economic Definition of Poverty," Discussion Paper, Institute for Research on Poverty, University of Wisconsin, 1968.

12. B. A. Weisbrod, "Collective Action and the Distribution of Income: A Conceptual Approach," Institute for Research on Poverty, University of Wisconsin, Reprint Series no. 34.

13. A. C. Pigou, The Economics of Welfare, 4th ed. (London: Macmillan, 1948), p. 728.

14. J. Conlisk, "Simple Dynamic Effects on Work-Leisure Choice: A Skeptical Comment on the Static Theory," Journal of Human Resources (Summer 1968), pp. 324-26.

15. L. Galloway, The Retirement Decision: An Exploratory Essay, U.S. Department of Health, Education and Welfare, Research Report no. 9 (Washington, D.C., 1965).

16. C. T. Brehm and T. R. Saving, "The Demand for General Assistance Payments," American Economic Review (December 1964), pp. 1002-1018.

17. L. Galloway, "Negative Income Tax Rates and the Elimination of Poverty," National Tax Journal (September 1967); Jane H. Leuthold, "An Empirical Study of Formula Income Transfers and the Work Decision of the Poor," Journal of Human Resources (Summer 1968), pp. 312-23; C. Green and A. Tella, The Effect of Nonemployment Income and Wage Rates on the Work Incentives of the Poor, special study prepared for the President's Commission on Income Maintenance, Washington, D.C., 1969.

18. _Preliminary Results of the New Jersey Graduated Work Incentive Experiment_, U.S. Office of Economic Opportunity (Washington, D.C., February 1970).
H. W. Watts, "Adjusted and Extended Preliminary Results from the Urban Graduated Work Incentive Experiment," Institute for Research on Poverty, University of Wisconsin, Discussion Paper no. 69, 1970.
H. W. Watts, "Mid-Experiment Report on Basic Labor-
Supply Response," Institute for Research on Poverty,
University of Wisconsin, Discussion Paper no. 98,
1971.

19. M. Taussig, "Negative Income Tax Rates and
the Elimination of Poverty: Comment," _National Tax
Journal_ (September 1967).

20. _Preliminary Results of the New Jersey Graduated Work Incentive Experiment_, p. 3.

21. "Adjusted and Extended Preliminary Results,"
p. 39.

22. "Mid-Experiment Report," p. i.

23. _Ibid._, p. 30.

24. Harold W. Watts, Testimony Before the Com-
mittee on Ways and Means, House of Representatives,
U.S. Congress, on H. R. 14173, "Family Assistance
Plan."

25. Erving Goffman, _Stigma_ (Englewood Cliffs,
N.J.: Prentice-Hall, 1963); E. M. Lemert, "Some Aspects of a General Theory of Sociopathic Behavior,"
in Proceedings of Meetings of the Pacific Sociological Society, State College of Washington, XVI, 1948;
D. Matza, "Poverty and Disrepute," in R. Martin and
R. Nesbit, eds., _Contemporary Social Problems_ (1966),
pp. 619-42.

26. Goffman, _Stigma_, pp. 8-9.

27. J. F. Handler and E. J. Hollingsworth, _The
Administration of Welfare Budgets: The Views of AFDC
Recipients_ and _Stigma, Privacy and Other Attitudes
of Welfare Recipients_, Institute for Research on Pov-

erty, University of Wisconsin, Discussion Papers nos.
39 and 49, 1969.

28. Jay Forrester, Urban Dynamics (Cambridge,
Mass.: M.I.T. Press, 1969).

29. See, as examples of the recent debate, G.
Nettler, "A Measure of Alienation," American Sociological Review (1957), pp. 670-77; M. Seeman, "On
the Meaning of Alienation," American Sociological Review (1959), pp. 783-91; D. G. Dean, "Alienation:
Its Meaning and Measurement," American Sociological
Review (1961), pp. 753-58; J. P. Clark, "Measuring
Alienation with a Social System," American Sociological Review (1959), pp. 849-52; L. I. Pearlin, "Alienation from Work: A Study of Nursing Personnel,"
American Sociological Review (1962), pp. 314-26.

30. R. H. Parkinson, "Ten Years of Family Allowances," Canadian Welfare (November 1, 1955), where
Gallup polls on family allowances suggest something
of the order of 90 percent acceptance as a "good
thing"--a remarkably high, indeed consensual, view
of an important policy matter.

31. Income Security and Social Services, Government of Canada (Ottawa: Queen's Printer, 1969).

32. D. B. Smith, "A Simplified Approach to Social
Welfare," Canadian Tax Journal (May-June 1965), pp.
260-65; R. W. Crowley and D. A. Dodge, "Cost of the
Guaranteed Annual Income," Canadian Tax Journal
(November-December 1969), pp. 395-408.

33. J. A. Pechman, "Individual Income Tax Provisions of the Revenue Act of 1964," Journal of Finance (May 1965); "A New Tax Model for Revenue Estimating," in A. T. Peacock and G. Hauser, Government Finance and Economic Development (Paris:
O.E.C.D., 1965); and, with B. A. Okner, "Simulation
of the Carter Commission Tax Proposals for the
United States," National Tax Journal (March 1969).
J. Bossons, A General Income Tax Analyser, Studies
of the Royal Commission on Taxation, no. 25 (Ottawa:
Queen's Printer, 1967).

34. R. Goode, "The Income Tax and the Supply of Labour," Journal of Political Economy, 58, no. 5 (October 1949), 428-37.

35. Royal Commission of the Taxation of Profits and Income, Second Report, Command 9105, Appendix 1, pp. 91-124; C. D. Long, The Labor Force Under Changing Income and Employment (Princeton, N.J., 1958), and Impact of the Federal Income Tax on Labor Force Participation, U.S. Committee on the Economic Report (Washington, D.C., 1955), pp. 153-66; G. F. Break, "Income Taxes and Incentives to Work: An Empirical Study," American Economic Review, 47 (September 1957), 529-49; C. A. Hall, Jr., Effects of Taxation: Executive Compensation and Retirement Plans (Boston: Harvard University, Bureau of Business Research, 1951); T. H. Saunders, The Effects of Taxation on Executives (Boston: Harvard University, Graduate School of Business Administration, 1951).

36. See, for a detailed discussion of various measures of rate schedule, R. A. Musgrave and Tun Thin, "Income Tax Progression, 1929-48," Journal of Political Economy (1948).

37. R. A. Musgrave, The Theory of Public Finance (New York: McGraw-Hill, 1959), pp. 223-25; J. Pechman and B. A. Okner, "Simulation of the Carter Commission Tax Proposals for the United States," National Tax Journal (March 1969), pp. 2-23.

38. Proposals for Tax Reform, Ministry of Finance (Ottawa: Queen's Printer, 1969). The White Paper abandoned the commitment of its precursor, "The Report of the Royal Commission on Taxation" (1966), to base widening as an alternative to rate increasing and proposed substantial rate increases across the middle-income groups. Opposition to the White Paper proposals was intense and well orchestrated, and the final manifestation of the proposals as legislation in 1971 returned to the Royal Commission view that tax rates should not be increased.

39. See Musgrave, The Theory of Public Finance, pp. 257-68, for a detailed discussion of the substitution effect under various forms of tax.

40. Ibid., p. 262.

41. Ibid., pp. 266-68.

ABOUT THE AUTHOR

JAMES CUTT has taught at the University of Toronto and is now Associate Professor of Economics at York University in Toronto. He studied Economics and Law at the University of Edinburgh and did post-graduate work at the University of Toronto. His major fields of interest are public finance, human resource economics, development economics, and quantitative methods. His work on alternative approaches to income transfer policy had its origins in a Canada Council Research Grant in 1969-70 and reflects in part an association with the Special Senate Committee on Poverty in the summer of 1969.